S0-BKC-260

THE
ROAD

SUMMIT BOOKS

New York London Toronto
Sydney Tokyo Singapore

TO
EXTREMA

BOB
REISS

SUMMIT BOOKS
Simon & Schuster Building
Rockefeller Center
1230 Avenue of the Americas
New York, New York 10020

Designed by Deirdre C. Amthor

Manufactured in the United States of America

10   9   8   7   6   5   4   3   2   1

Library of Congress Cataloging-in-Publication Data

Reiss, Bob.
    The road to extrema / Bob Reiss.
        p.   cm.
    1. Man—Influence on nature—Amazon River Region. 2. Man—
Influence on nature—New York (State) 3. Rain forest ecology—
Amazon River Region. 4. Deforestation—Amazon River Region.
5. Pollution—New York (State) I. Title.
    GF532.A4R45   1992
    333.75′0981′1—dc20   91-40644
    ISBN 0-671-68700-X   CIP

333.75
REI
6/92

To my Uncle Charlie, who taught a city kid
to love nature.

Acknowledgments

A very special thanks to Mark Bryant and *Outside* magazine, Randy Curtis, Lan Chile Airlines, CARECEN center for Central American refugees, Ted Conover, Doug Daly and the New York Botanical Garden, Fabio Filho, FUNAI, the Fund for Investigative Reporting, Lamond Godwin, Rose Gannon, Vim Groenevald, the Guardian Angels, Ann Hood, Darlene Huertas, Cizinio Karitiana, Dan Katz and the Rainforest Alliance, Dr. Sandy Kuehl and the staff of Cornell Hospital Emergency Room, Dr. Tom Lovejoy, Dr. Larry Lutwick, Dr. Michael Levy, Rosa Lemos, the New York Mets, New York University Medical Center, Esther Newberg, the people of Extrema and New California, the Ninth Precinct of the New York Police Department, Linda Turner, Robson Vitali, Rooster, and Varig Airlines.

And an extra thanks to friend, translator, and scholar Miguel Nenevé of the University of Rondônia whose research skills, courage, companionship, and advice were invaluable in completing this book.

Contents

Introduction

Cool Plexiglas brushed my forehead. Rain forest filled the horizon every direction I looked. Canopy so thick below it might have formed the surface of the planet, swelling or ebbing with the contours of the earth. I saw a miles-long line of concentric ridges. A bowl-shaped depression severed by a river's curve. Silty brown water smeared the jungle spectrum: turquoise, aqua, emerald, jade. Some Amazon Indians have a hundred words for "green."

"There is much malaria there, yes?" said the voice beside me, the Swiss engineer who worked for Nescafé. "We think there is excellent cocoa in the region. And why do *you* go to Pôrto Velho?"

I told him about the book I wanted to write. A series of personal stories linking people in the Amazon and people in New York. The Brazil sections: stories of Indians, gold miners, rubber tappers, dam builders, colonists, ranchers and scientists along a frontier stretch of highway. A new road cutting through the green immensity below.

"And the New York part?" he asked politely, sipping his fourth beer. "Are there really connections between these places?"

I told him I was fascinated by how people's lives affected each other, thousands of miles apart. And that I wanted to test scientists' claims that in medicines, climate, commerce, and finance, the fate of jungles affected life as far away as Geneva, Munich, Peking, New York. I'd already met bankers, cancer patients, advertising executives, even refugees and baseball players, in New York whose daily lives impacted or were affected by rain forests. I hoped their personal stories would give a reality to what was hidden in statistics and reports. I said the book I planned would alternate chapters—Brazil to New York, and back to Brazil. Sometimes the connections would be formed by hard evidence; other times they would be scientific predictions experts made.

The Amazon reached up and tossed us, spit lightning, bounced us in our seats. My red wine spilled and stabilized. We broke from the clouds. I wouldn't have been surprised to see dinosaurs below.

After a while the half moon rose and the lights of Pôrto Velho shone from the darkness as electric power blinked from miles ahead. I felt the kind of relief transatlantic passengers experience reaching landfall.

And here came the signs of people; square-cut fields hewn from the jungle. Geometry marking habitation where forest had been. And here was the highway I'd come four thousand miles to visit. Bright red globules, taillights, floating in a straight line below. I saw shantytowns and boulevards materializing from the jungle. Big buildings, offices or apartment houses. "Fasten your seat belts," said the pilot of the Varig 727, and gold miners, ranchers, and businessmen, flying into a city that most Brazilians had never heard of twenty years before, complied.

The engineer leaned over my shoulder. "Those aren't electric lights. They're fires," he said.

He was right. Hundreds of fires burned below, eerily illuminating shanties and roads. Stripping away the veneer of progress and giving a beleaguered quality to the city below.

I made out human forms as we drew closer. Walking or looking up. Fires were normal here for light, I supposed. Or food.

Fires seemed a fitting welcome. They were what had brought me here. Fires blazing in newspapers and on television. Fires burning into the last, biggest rainforest on earth.

"Pôrto Velho! Welcome!" the pilot said.

. . .

When does a trip begin? When you buy a ticket? When you begin to plan logistics? When the seed is planted in your head that traveling to a faraway place is possible?

In 1964 I went to the World's Fair, with my family in Flushing Meadow, New York. My favorite exhibit showed wonders of the future. We rode in a Ford convertible past motorized dioramas dramatizing advances to come. Electric houses. Monorails. But the scene that captivated me most was the rolling Amazon factory. The mechanized miracle to tame the jungles of the world. Built to scale, it rose higher than the diorama's treetops, rolling into virgin jungle on wheels the size of two story homes. Blue laser beams shot in a swath, from the factory, neatly severing trees that fell on an advancing conveyor belt. The belt swept them inside to be processed. The complex left neat piles of planks for construction behind. It also ground up tree stumps as it moved, bulldozed earth, and laid down a smooth black road of asphalt to allow humans to follow.

A miracle. Like space travel, a wonder to be admired. Nobody criticized Brazil in 1964 for wanting to develop its interior. That was the way countries advanced. Who ever thought the earth's forests could ever run out.

"The Amazon is our space program," one Brazilian told the *Washington Post*.

That was why I loved that rolling factory. It would enable people like me to reach places we'd only dreamed about. The magical rain forests I'd wanted to see since I was nine, sitting in a Queens, New York, living room on rainy Sundays, watching Tarzan movies. Or reading Mark Trail books about exotic animals. Or visiting the Bronx Zoo and seeing them, alive but behind bars. I wanted to visit the jungle, touch its wonders, marvel at a place wilder than Queens, New York.

Thirty years ago there was nothing odd about loving wild areas *and* wanting roads built to them. There was little sense that the vast jungles of the world couldn't accommodate human settlement.

But by 1984, when I started researching this book, roads were being blamed for destroying forests in Brazil, Peru, Indonesia, Madagascar, Zaire, and many countries straddling the equator.

"All deforestation begins with roads," conservationist Stewart Hudson told me at the National Wildlife Federation in Washington.

What had happened? What had changed? I wanted to spend time with the people moving to the forests, and the people who had always been there. To see the Amazon through their eyes. But now conservationists warned it was disappearing so fast I'd better hurry while there was still an Amazon to see.

For months I read books, histories, studies, reports. I interviewed conservationists and Brazilian diplomats, the ambassador in Washington, the consul general in New York. I woke up each morning at six and over coffee studied Portuguese with cassettes and books. I hired a tutor. I filled a file cabinet with newspaper and magazine clippings. I went to speeches at the Museum of Natural History in Manhattan and to an exhibit on tropical forests at the Smithsonian Institution in Washington, D.C. I taped National Geographic specials.

"I know every forest is unique," I wrote scientists and journalists in Brazil and the United States, "but I'm hoping to concentrate on one small area, get to know it, spend months there. I hope what I see will show processes affecting forests around the world. *Is* there a place like that in Brazil, in the Amazon? A small place where I can find a road, Indians, giant construction projects, a city, land wars, ranchers, colonists, wildlife?"

I was amazed. The answers came back uniform. The flowery letters in Portuguese, from Brazil, and the shorter, crisper replies from U.S. researchers recommended the same place, the same stretch of highway in the western Amazon, straddling the states of Rondônia and Acre (Ah-cray), linking their capitals, Pôrto Velho, and Rio Branco.

"Pôrto Velho is the past," Dr. Tom Lovejoy, Smithsonian Institution assistant secretary for external affairs, told me. "Rio Branco is the future." We'd been sitting on the floor in his Victorian parlor of an office in the Smithsonian Castle building. Files, articles, books, reports, and an ecology award lay in piles blanketing any other conceivable resting place: a loveseat, sitting chairs. And the bow-tied, slightly dandyish scientist-turned-biopolitician leaned a cardboard map of Brazil against the wall and traced routes with his finger.

The highway, BR-364, was the most controversial road in Latin America. Under a controversial development plan called the Polonoroeste project it had been paved as far as Pôrto Velho in the early 1980s, and immediately settlement had exploded out of control. The road of Brazil's dreams had become the road of environmentalists' nightmares. Rondônia, the size of West Germany, was twenty percent deforested within ten years.

Now the next leg of road, to Rio Branco, was scheduled to be paved by 1991. BR-364, the two-lane dirt highway with the technical name, had become a battle line between banks and developers on one side, and conservationists on the other. The backwater strip of jungle was suddenly one of those epitome places on the planet, symbol of the future. U.S. senators gave speeches about it. Murders along the road made international news. Satellites spinning over Rondônia sent back pictures of hundreds of fires consuming jungle along the path of BR-364.

I interviewed Brazilians about the road, politicians and scientists in Brasília, Belém, Manaus. "The road will go through!" said the Minister of Interior. To link us to the Pacific! To realize a hundred years of dreams! To sell our goods to Japan! And we can do it without destroying forest!

Environmentalists had other ideas.

"It will be a straw sucking up the Amazon," said Congressman James Scheuer of New York.

"It will mean the end of the western Amazon as we know it," Conservation International Vice President Mark Plotkin told me. "Roads are the cancer of the rainforest."

"It will tell us what will happen to the Amazon," said Tom Lovejoy, sitting in his Victorian-style office at dusk in a half-light emanating from a lampshade over a statuette.

.   .   .

The cabdriver's name was Paulo; a short, dark, mideastern-looking man who had moved to Pôrto Velho from Brazil's northeast, which was, more or less, in a condition of permanent drought. "Why did you come here?" I asked, testing my faltering Portuguese. He rubbed his thumb and forefinger together. "Money." Is there more money here, I asked. "Yes." Do you like living here? "No." Will you stay here? "Yes." Why? Paulo rubbed his fingers again. "Dineiro."

We rocketed into town along a paved four-lane road lit by electric lights, Paulo aggressively swerving to avoid holes half the size of his Volkswagen bug. Already the frontier worked its surprises on me. Like the airport terminal, new, with glass walls and souvenir shops selling T-shirts. One depicted a blue-and-red parrot with RONDÔNIA stenciled down the front in proud black. Another showed a gold miner surfacing in a river, his dredge behind him as he gave a thumb-up signal to signify a find. Souvenir shops? Airport cafes? I tried to put the images together with warnings I had heard.

"Watch out for the people in Rondônia and Acre. They're rough." That from a PR official at the foreign ministry in Brasília. "We've lost control on the frontier." That from the consul general in New York. "You'll get malaria for sure at the gold fields," from a scientist at the Brazilian Institute of the Amazon. "Carry vodka. You can drink it, disinfect cuts, and bathe with it if there's no water," from an old United Press International (UPI) hand. "Don't forget to take hypodermics. If you get sick, pharmacists give injections, and you want to make sure the needle is clean." "You'll never get to see the Indians. The government blocks access." "You don't speak good Portuguese? Ha ha ha ha! They don't even speak *regular* Portuguese! You won't be able to talk to anybody!" "The ranchers hate journalists. You could get shot."

The truth was, I was tired of reading reports and sitting in offices. Frustrated by distance, I wanted to be on the road. Politicians seemed the same in the United States and Brazil; men in offices citing statistics about places they'd never visited. Conservationists suspiciously kept revising their numbers on the extent of rainforest destruction. And at the point in my interviews where I asked people if they'd ever actually gone to this stretch of BR-364, they almost always said no.

Paulo tried to convince me to change hotels. Mine was too expensive, he said. And bad. But New Yorkers feel at home in taxicabs. I was under the illusion that I knew what I was doing. No thanks, I said. Take me there, please. He crouched further over the wheel and the door rattled as we hit another pothole. He muttered something I couldn't understand, probably "It's your funeral."

Notes from the taxicab, scribbled while riding. Dark. Few streetlights. Surprise! Nice home, southern California style, with gate, car, driveway. Trees line dark boulevards. Dusty feel. Stop lights. Jungle gone. Saturday night, midnight. People in shack cafes. Teenage couple on motorcycle. Like any town? Where's frontier? Tutti-frutti sign in candy colors. People eating pizza, eating ice cream. Plaza with couples on benches. Big church.

We turned into a thoroughfare that seemed more a border between order and anarchy. In the half light thrown up by headlights, dust, stars, and lit hotels, we joined a hellish traffic being thrown in and out of dirt pits lined up to form a road. Pinballs knocking back and forth, jockeying a continent.

Paulo left me under a neon sign saying PALACE. A five-story building with a parking lot outside filled with mud-smeared pickup trucks. A palace rising from a frontier street. Dogs snarled and fought between the pickups. The steady stream of cars, Volkswagen taxis, and Mercedes trucks lurched in and out of ruts through a red dust haze. Dimly I made out prostitutes in high heels leaning into windows of cars parked along a dark median strip. Across the two lanes on the far side was a bus station and a street lined with bars. The night echoed with a mix of Latin music on a hundred faraway radios. The lobby smelled of Lysol, vegetation, and plaster crumbling from heat.

If a frontier is a squall line between the wild and civilization, I felt like I'd reached the outer limit of the line.

The desk clerk told me it was better *not* to take a walk just now in this area. "Dangerous." A bellboy led me to a clean room upstairs with a single bed and a gigantic cockroach crawling down a wall.

I leaned out the window, the breath of the jungle moved across my face. But then it was obscured by the howls of dogs, the dust balling up from traffic, the gears of Mercedes trucks. A bus pulled out across the median strip. A chord of guitar music and a plaintive bit of song floated out in Portuguese.

It was 1989, my first trip to Pôrto Velho, and there was no wonder-of-the-future rolling factory laying highway in the western Amazon. There were a few million migrants cutting and burning their way out from urban bases like this, seeking a better life.

I put off the light and lay in bed listening to horns and traffic. There was the high-pitched whine of a mosquito in the room—a nuisance in New York, but here I started thinking about malaria.

The malaria capital of the world, a town called Ariquemmes, lay a short way back along BR-364.

Tomorrow I had an appointment to meet a potential translator, an English literature professor at the university, the school itself another surprise. Then I would leave Pôrto Velho along 364 and visit a dam in the jungle forty kilometers east, due to come on-line in two weeks. And after that I would double back through the city and head toward Rio Branco, spending a few months traveling the road.

The mosquito grew louder. The moonlight lay yellow on a dresser. In the Amazon, it's so hot, you don't get blankets even at a Palace unless you ask.

Kilometer 1

The Dam

Dawn in the Amazon. "What I expected to find were dead animals everywhere," Rosa Lemos said. "Animals in conflict. A mess."

She slung binoculars over her neck and smeared Avon Skin-So-Soft down her arms below her flower print blouse, to repel insects. Rosa was a slim, wry biologist in khaki slacks and canvas buckle-up shin protectors against snakes. She led her tracker into the jungle beneath a natural arch of crossed palm leaves fifteen feet up.

"Engineers see a dam site ten years before it's completed," Rosa said. "But ecologists come only after it's finished, to measure the result."

An unworldly intensity marked the forest, a tangible feeling of life. Not only in the heavy, wet air but the sense of activity when nothing was moving among the stationary trees. Strangler vines twisted around buttressed trunks as thick as redwoods. Logs crumbled underfoot. A giant morpho butterfly, the most vivid blue in the world, fluttered toward me on the trail and slipped sideways through sunlight slicing down from above.

We were in a nature reserve abutting the rising waters behind the brand-new Samuel (Sam-well) Dam. "The power company spent a lot of money rescuing animals from the new lake and moving them here. But nobody has measured the effect," Rosa said. "Can the forest sustain the influx?"

"Rescue workers banded the monkeys when they released them, but the monkeys tore off the bands," she continued. "They tattooed sloths on their legs, but sloths live at the top of the canopy. How do I see the tattoo?"

Rosa's cropped black hair and narrow face gave her a resemblance to actress Liza Minnelli. I followed her tracker, Chico, a quiet man who'd smoked hand-rolled cigarettes in the pickup on the ride out. The back of his shirt crawled with sweat bees, stingless creatures that eat salt.

In 1980 only two small dams operated in the Amazon. By the year 2010, seventy-three more are planned. Dams will launch Brazil into the twenty-first century, planners say. Dams will fuel the iron ore complexes in the jungle. Build cities in the frontier, light homes, factories, schools. Provide electricity for 150 million power-starved people along the coast. Dams will eliminate the need to burn costly oil or wood for energy.

Environmentalists predict that acidic water from decomposing trees will corrode turbines. That the dams will fill up with sediment and be useless after a short life. Thousands of plant and animal species will be killed by dams.

Proponents counter that the charges are only theories. That the price is small to pay. Brazil is already experiencing blackouts. Dams will only flood two-tenths of one percent of the Amazon, they say.

The Amazon River system is the biggest on earth. It has ten thousand tributaries, ten of them longer than the Mississippi. The main river flows four thousand miles from the Andes to the Atlantic, pumps 170 billion gallons an hour, sixty times the flow of the Nile, into the ocean as far as one hundred miles out.

The Amazon is wider than the English Channel in places, so wide it accommodates an island the size of Switzerland in its mouth.

With so much water at its disposal, Brazil chose hydroelectric power to achieve its development dreams.

During the 1980s, new dams came on-line. The Tucurui' Dam inundated twenty-five hundred square kilometers of rain forest in the state of Pará. Balbina Dam went into operation to provide power for Manaus, a city of one million in the jungle. Engineers planned dams for the Xingú River Basin, the Tocantins River, the Jamari and Madeira in Rondônia.

On paper the projects looked good, but they didn't always turn out that way. Balbina's lake was so shallow it didn't have enough force to run all the turbines at the same time. The reservoir was the same size as Tucurui's but provided seventy-five hundred megawatts less! "It's the worst disaster to ever happen in the Amazon," said Brazil's environmental secretary. There were charges of graft and inefficiency after millions of dollars of valuable timber was left in the reservoir to rot.

Samuel was proposed in the 1960s, but construction didn't begin until 1982. Contractors loaded earth-moving machinery on ships in São Paulo, twenty-five hundred miles away, and floated it up the Atlantic to Belém and down the Amazon and Madeira rivers to the site. Seven thousand workers arrived to complete the dam.

Now, when Rosa stopped on the trail, at first I thought she was resting. Ahead, a line of tiny green bits floated across the trail, half an inch off the ground. They were ants, thousands of leaf cutters, carrying fodder to their nests, thousands more going back for another load.

Rosa stared hard at the canopy, 120 feet up. Chico cocked his head. Look for a break in the pattern of light, they had told me. Or a branch moving while everything else is still.

But all I saw was a tangle of ferns, lianas, trunks, orchids. The forest filled with a low, insect buzzing. The scream of a bird beyond the trees.

Then through the canopy I saw the tiniest sway of a bower, heard the crashing of a heavy animal hitting a branch. Something black scrambled up there, on all fours, ten stories above the ground.

Suddenly they were overhead. Four spider monkeys, leaping between trees. Running down branches. Barking to each other in quick, hoarse bites.

They moved smoothly, long limbs suited for travel above the earth. They showed none of the depression of caged animals in zoos. Or the bursts of savage energy. Lords of the treetops, big enough to feel safe and make noise, they traveled with a casual freedom that filled me with awe.

And then they were gone. My heart pounded. Chico smiled. Rosa wrote in her book: "Two adult males. One female and one juvenile. Twenty meters away."

At that moment the long odds of her quest were revealed. Rosa

Lemos was the weak half of a lopsided alliance between development and research. On one side, a new $500 million dam. The World Bank. The National Power Company of Brazil. On the other, a thirty-two-year-old scientist with a waterproof pad, dreaming of influencing national policy, of saving animals in the path of new development.

Wildlife versus progress. All over the Amazon the debate was the same. Rosa's work was research of the most basic kind. How do you determine a population of wild animals? Count them. Slash a grid of trails through the jungle. Bring in researchers, Rosa being one. Walk the trails for three months each summer, counting the animals, seeing which live, what they eat, how they interact, how the dam changes them. Hope the results reflect a true situation. Hope somebody influential sees your work.

Other researchers, working on fish, climate, plants, crops, insects, water systems, and medicines, hoped the same thing.

Rosa showed a half smile. "I hope my work can be used in planning new dams," she said, "because we don't know yet how they will affect the Amazon, and seventy-three more are going to be built."

.   .   .

"Rescue" was what they called it when the waters began to rise, backing into the Jamari River floodplain, drowning trees. Workers and volunteers steered boats into half-submerged branches, shaking them, netting screeching primates as they leaped into the flood. Lassoing anteaters. Caging tapirs and snakes. All of Brazil thrilled to nightly television coverage of the operation.

Noahs of the jungle. Twenty-two-thousand creatures pulled from the rising waters of the 130,000-acre lake. Sixteen thousand sent to universities and laboratories. Three thousand taxidermized, including the ones who died during quarantine at the dam. A lucky three thousand actually released into the nature reserve abutting the lake.

Now the Samuel Dam was due to come on-line in two weeks. Power lines ran in wide swaths toward Pôrto Velho through the jungle. Workmen put finishing touches on the powerhouse and control room. Guards patrolled the nature reserve to keep out hunters. Inspectors drove the sixty miles of dike roads daily, checking for seepage or armadillos burrowing into the works. Public relations men brought out politicians, schoolchildren, ambassadors, and journalists. Ecologists and engineers argued about Samuel at symposiums. It was too shallow. It would power schools. It would kill animals. It would give jobs.

I knew statistics about the dam. The generating capacity, 280 megawatts. The average depth of the lake, six feet. The number of turbines, five.

But numbers didn't prepare me for the powerful impact. It was impossible to visit Samuel and come away unaffected. From the air the dam had seemed minuscule beside the massive lake behind. With a *Time* magazine reporter I flew over Samuel in a twin-engined Aztec. "It's like cancer," gasped the reporter. "Isn't it? Cancer?" I was too affected to speak. The lake had killed everything in its radius, but the dead trees still stood. I'd never flown over a volcano's aftermath, or earthquake's but the damage took our breath away. It was the black forest of fairy tales where nothing lived. Thousands of stripped trunks protruded from the water. Newly dead trees retained their branches. Older ones rose like twisted stakes. Trees submerged the longest had split apart, and floating logs nudged against a barrel and net barrier around the dam to protect it from debris.

The green forest around the lake made the destruction seem worse.

Later I had toured the lake by boat with Rosa. At treetop level we glided through dead canopy, ducking branches, nosing past rotting logs, all floating in a black opaque soup cloudy with acid from decomposing vegetation. The acid used up the oxygen in the water. No fish swam in Lake Samuel.

"It looks like winter," I said.

"Yeah, nuclear winter," a scientist said.

Dams bred malaria. Displaced Indians. Siphoned away public funds, environmentalists said.

But then I'd stood on the dam another day, a blue-skied afternoon with a cool breeze coming off the lake. Beside me, Electronorte's PR man, José Humberto, said the dead trees would be harvested by divers with underwater chainsaws. That the dam saved Pôrto Velho millions on oil fuel. That there were plans for a nature reserve, a marina, sports fishing. That scientists like Rosa Lemos had been brought here by Electronorte, supported by Electronorte. That everybody made mistakes. The important thing was that Electronorte had learned from theirs.

"Everyone else talks about the environment, but Electronorte is doing something about it," he said.

A fierce, unexpected pride pervaded me. Not just at the structure itself but the new road cut through the jungle—the beautiful median strip that led to the complex blooming with bougainvilleas, the town of 270 homes for workers; with schools, stores, cars. The restaurant where we'd eaten lunch; delicious steak, rice, beans, salad, and ice cream for a subsidized twenty-seven cents.

That men had actually come here. Created something so powerful. Close-up, Samuel was a colossus of sun-drenched concrete. The railings at the top vibrated from the flood rushing through. Water roiled from the chutes, churned yellow-green, sent up a rainbow spray blanketed by clouds of hovering dragonflies. It swept into rapids, smeared foam on sandy banks, curved out of sight around a bend. Huge winches sat on railroad tracks on the dam. Oil barrels lay in piles. Industrial hooks the size of Volkswagens hung suspended. It was beautiful, Samuel.

In the powerhouse we stood on rickety wooden scaffolding fifty feet up while masked welders crouched below in the glow of their torches. The weld-smoke mixed with concrete dust rising through sunlight shooting through portals in the dam. The turbine housing looked like missile silos. The elevator shafts dropped down sixty feet, black holes filled with electrical cables. New computers ringed the control room, along with windows looking out on the sparkling lake, ready to funnel electricity around a state as big as West Germany.

I remembered a conversation I'd had at the Pôrto Velho airport with the Nigerian ambassador to Brazil, Patrick Delle Cole. He had been touring the interior, visiting development projects. He came from a rain forest country too. "The need to conquer forest is basic in human nature," he said. "People in the West have sublimated that need for dominance. You see the forest, and you *have to go into it.*"

The sheer emotional draw of a dam! To be able to do it! Numbers, speeches, national aspirations faded. That was the primal challenge.

Back in the city, which was experiencing one of its regular power failures, Mayor Francisco Erse told me a more practical reason for construction: "Samuel is the biggest hope for this city."

Frederico Camello, president of the State Association of Industries, put it more bluntly. "We need electricity," he said.

.   .   .

For days I'd seen animals near the lake. A large deer, haunch muscles more powerful than anything in the United States, leaping into the trees. A giant anteater, big and woolly as a Newfoundland dog, lumbering through the swamp below the dike, fleeing Rosa's Volkswagen pickup on the dike road. A small golden anteater, helpless with confusion before the oncoming car, rearing and balancing on its tail, in defensive terror, hissing when I walked close, its little heart slamming visibly against its ribs.

Animals in the grip of a homing instinct. Animals looking at a lake where there had been only forest before.

"Most people think rescues are a good idea," Rosa said, "but I have my doubts. New animals can bring diseases into an area. And this dam's a problem anyway. It's backing up more than the engineers expected. When you plan a dam, you shouldn't need sixty miles of dikes. The reserve is shrinking."

We were in lowland rain forest, jungle receiving over fifteen hundred centimeters of rain a year. A copaiba tree ahead swarmed with tamarins, brown-white monkeys that travel in families and sleep in a group to preserve warmth and discourage predators. Rolled up, a tamarin looks like a termite nest.

Scientists are dazzled by the complexity of the rain forest. Vines twist like serpents. Epiphytes grow out of branches toward the ground. Leaves are shaped like fingers, hearts, arrows, blinds. Light changes simultaneously, rising toward the top. It's cool and dark on the forest floor, on ferns and herbs. Brighter but diffused midway up, on the shade-loving trees. Bursting into halos where leaves are hit by direct sunlight. Bright blue at the top of the canopy, where macaws sweep in pairs over the forest giants.

Rosa led the way across a crater as long and deep as a small truck, where a great Brazil nut tree had toppled. She stepped slowly, paused, one hand on binoculars, knee out, head back, nose up, concentrating in the morning's gray light.

The Amazon is so dynamic up to 450 species of trees can live in a single hectare (two and a half acres). A pond can contain more varieties of fish than the British Isles. A tree can house forty-three kinds of ants. Yet within the system relationships can be remarkably specialized. Only one kind of wasp pollinates one kind of fig tree. One species of ant lives in compartments in one plant, protecting it from predators. Without a certain bee, Brazil nut trees can't be pollinated, and they die.

"All animals have an impact on the ecosystem," Rosa said. "Some are pollinators, some seed dispersers. Remove them, and you may not have diversity any more." She sighed. "Nobody knows what happens when you put in a dam."

She balanced across a log spanning a stream. In the ten seconds we'd stopped, ants covered my boot. The forest grew swampy. Little pinprick stings in my fingers told me my maximum-strength insecticide shield was down. I whirled at a grunt, expecting a wild pig, but was amazed to see a hummingbird hovering a foot from my face. The sound came from the vibration of its iridescent green wings.

I asked Rosa if she ever gets bored on the same paths day after day. On the hot days when mosquitoes swarmed. Or the rainy days when she came home soaked. Or how much the logistic indignities bother her—the alcohol fuel for the car that comes watered down. The parts that never come at all?

Rosa smiled.

"I might walk one kilometer and see one group of monkeys, but that keeps me going," she said. "Most people never see the ecosystem we're part of. When I do, my heart beats fast. I get adrenaline. If you live your whole life in a city, you have no way of measuring the value of nature, and it is being destroyed."

Rosa ignored sweat bees crawling on her blouse.

"I get emotional in unspoiled places," she said.

.   .   .

Rosa Lemos was born in Bel Horizonte, 450 kilometers from Rio, 2,000 kilometers to the east. "The country used to be forest there. Now it's farms," she said.

Her father sold real estate; her mother was a housewife.

"If my mother saw a picture of a frog, she'd jump ten feet. She doesn't like animals. All I could have was fish because they weren't dirty."

In her Catholic high school, "we didn't study the Amazon much, except to learn it was part of Brazil. We learned that the first colonizers and explorers were heroes who opened up the country, and the Jesuits who taught Indians Catholicism were heroes too."

Rosa didn't know where her love of nature came from. She liked to watch "Wild Kingdom" on TV. In high school she started camping in the countryside. She thought she might like to make nature her career. "But I didn't know there *were* careers like that.

"I got out of high school and was working in an airline ticket office. My brother-in-law was an ecologist in the United States. He told me about a wildlife program at the University of Wisconsin."

Rosa got her undergraduate degree in Wisconsin, a masters in ecology at the University of Brasília, and went to the University of Florida to work on a Ph.D.

"I wanted to work on a whole community of wildlife, not just one animal. My professor said, try a dam. The work is important. Lots of dams are planned in Brazil. Nobody has done work on aspects of flooding. He talked to Electronorte, and they were interested in having scientists here. They said they'd give me full support.

"I always wanted to come back to Brazil. So much remains to be done here, and there are only a handful of people to do it."

It was dusk after a rough day. Rosa was back at the scientists' quarters, two corrugated-iron barracks enclosed by a chain-link fence. Her Volkswagen had run out of fuel on the way home. Two trackers and another researcher had walked ten miles on the dike before a rescue Jeep had come for them.

Other scientists at the dam studied bees. Snakes. Mammals as hosts for parasites. Fish adaptation in the lake. They threw a small party in a lounge beside a kitchen. Soft lambada music pumped from a recorder. The scientists boiled fresh fish and vegetables for dinner. Sergio Nogueira Cleto, a young biology student from the State University of São Paulo, poured shots of iced vodka. He studied differences in phytoplankton and zooplankton—one-celled plants and animals—in the lake "as a way of measuring the general health of the water, which is deteriorating," he said. "The decomposing trees put sulfuric acid into the water, and the trees consume oxygen as they deteriorate. There's a heavy dead soup on the bottom, but in a few years the water should clear."

Like Rosa, the scientists were unsure why Electronorte wanted them there. It was possible the power company was concerned about the environment, but possible also that scientists were no more than good public relations at a time when Electronorte approached international banks for more loans. And influential environmental organizations overseas pushed for environmental provisions in those loans. In Brazil, of the billions loaned for dams by the World Bank and Inter-American Development Bank between 1980 and 1990, less than one-tenth percent went for researching what the dams might flood.

The sky over the lake faded to bright lavender. Waves of white egrets flew overhead, as they did every dusk. Rosa returned to her room to copy notes into her computer. Her quarters were comfortable: a single bed, a camera on the sheet, extra batteries and stacks of color photos of birds on the desk, a box of chocolates, a tensor lamp. Her husband Paulo was back in Florida. Mosquitos flew so thick outside the scientists kept their doors closed. Electronorte workers sprayed the dam area regularly, but the insects still appeared in force each night.

By eight Rosa was typing the day's numbers, dates, and times into her computer. "Five saguinus," she wrote, meaning marmosets. They were small primates living in lower branches, dark brown with furry ear tufts, shyly peering back from behind trees. "Tamarins." "Capuchin monkeys." Named for capuchin monks, the black crown on their heads like monks' hats. "Cebus monkeys," which the trackers could call by whistling.

Rosa seemed frustrated. "It's too early to know what the results will be, just the first year," she said. "I thought the reserve would be a mess. But it hasn't been like that. The best I'll be able to recommend, if it continues that way, is the twenty percent release rate, a continuation of the system they used here. Maybe the rescue *was* a better idea. Electronorte provides the infrastructure and allows me to do the research, but I don't know if Electronorte will ever see it."

Rosa set the alarm for 4 A.M., to get back along the dike road.

.   .   .

Thirty to sixty million years ago the ancestors of Rosa Lemos's subjects lived in North America, not the Amazon. South America floated free, an island. Its wildlife was more primitive: giant saber-toothed marsupial carnivores, marsupial giraffe and deer. Sloths. Armadillos. Possums.

Scientists theorize that three million years ago the land bridge formed between North and South America at Panama. The wildlife of the continents mixed. The slower, less efficient southern animals died out. Big cats moved down from the North, faster and more efficient than the saber tooths. They evolved into the jaguars of today. North American deer ran faster, escaped better than the more clumsy marsupials of the South. Tapirs, the odd-looking evolutionary dead end, wandered down from Asia, across the Alaskan land bridge. Monkeys floated over on vegetative rafts from Africa. At the time Africa lay only a few hundred miles away.

"Eighty percent of the fauna in South America originated in the North," said Professor Gustavo Fonseca, who heads the ecology program at the University of Minas Gerais. "The only South American animals to survive up north were the armadillos, the possums. Sloths originated in South America and still survive today. Most rodents came down from the North.

In the rich, hothouse jungles of the Amazon, animal and plant species exploded. No winter existed to slow reproduction. Food and water were plentiful. Climactic shifts encouraged the formation of new species.

"We had several cycles of expansion and contraction," Fonseca said. "There would be islands of savannah and forest. When the populations fragmented into islands, new species evolved. Then the forest would expand and the species would interbreed. There would be a cycle of three or four expansions and contractions. The Amazon became a factory of species. For instance, these days you can find the same species in two different locations—different climate, different soil, different vegetation. In the detective way scientists work, reconstructing backward, we figure there were two different species in different locations. They interbred. The new species could live in both environments when the forest shrunk back.

"Now we're losing species even before we know what they are," Fonseca said. "About one and a half million species have been described: plants, animals, everything. But recent studies in South America . . . looking at one hectare of forest, everything there, found hundreds and hundreds of species that haven't been classified. Go a hundred meters away, survey another hectare, you find hundreds and hundreds of species that didn't occur in the previous spot. Extrapolating from that we might have as many as thirty to fifty million species in the world, eighty percent in tropical forests, and half of that in Latin America. So if we save a good chunk of Amazon rain forest, we save a good chunk of species."

In fact, tropical forests are disappearing so fast an estimated ten thousand species go extinct each year, says Harvard professor Edward O. Wilson. Conservation International estimates that twenty percent of the planet's plant and animal species live in the Brazilian Amazon. In terms of biodiversity, Brazil has the largest number of flowering plants in the world. The greatest number of amphibians. It's fourth in mammals. Third in birds.

And it was birds Rosa wanted to trap the next morning. At 4:30 we bumped across the top of the deserted dam in the unreal glow of powerful floodlights, up onto the narrow dike road for the forty-kilometer trip to the reserve. A predawn brightness seeped into the sky. Dead trunks rising from the lake had a ghostly, stake-like quality. Nighthawks resting by weeds bordering the road reflected the headlights in the red orbs of their eyes, and one, trying to flee, smashed into the windshield. Rosa stopped the car. The bird fluttered against the wipers, its wing broken. She slumped against the steering wheel, tears in her eyes. "This is going to be a bad day," she said.

Sweat bees poured through the open windows when she left the car in the road. "I want to study the understory birds that live below the canopy," she said. "When a dam is built we may be losing species that need a certain habitat. One way to find out is to see which ones can adapt to disturbance."

Build a dam. Do the birds move? Reports as far away from the United States indicate some migrating bird populations are dying out by as much as 4 percent a year as their winter habitats in the tropics are destroyed. Surveys conducted by the United States Fish and Wildlife Service concluded that between 1978 and 1987 the number of wood thrushes breeding in the eastern United States and Canada fell 4 percent a year. Two species of cuckoo, the black-billed and yellow-billed, were down an average rate of 5.9 percent and 5 percent, respectively. The ovenbird was down. The Tennessee warbler dropped 11 percent. Twenty-one species of birds whose numbers were dwindling in eastern North America wintered in the tropics.

"They get down to the tropics and find their winter homes gone," said a Survey spokesman. "They try to find a new habitat and they don't, or predators kill them, or they're thrown into competition with other birds in the new place. They die."

To catch birds Rosa used mist nets, closed at this hour to keep bats from tangling up in them during the night. We unrolled them in the jungle. They stood as high as badminton nets, but the mesh ran all the way to the ground; woven so fine I kept walking into them even when I knew where they were. The trackers had set up fifteen nets, pole to pole, along the trail. Rosa would check them every hour for birds.

"My guess is that I'll find two different communities because of the dam. One at the edge of the lake," she said. "A different one here."

Before coming to the western Amazon I'd visited a similar project near Manaus, in Amazonas. There, researchers from the World Wildlife Fund and Brazilian Institute of the Amazon tried to determine the minimum size a forest should be to fully sustain its ecosystem. Ranchers honoring Brazil's fifty percent law—a law ordering ranchers to keep half their jungle property as forest—allowed the scientists to work in plots ranging from one hundred to ten thousand hectares. Not surprisingly, the scientists found that larger areas sustain a fuller range of rain forest life. Like Rosa, they hoped authorities would use their results to plan development.

Perhaps the fifty percent law could be changed to make plots of jungle contiguous.

"Oooh," Rosa said, flushing with pleasure, spotting the first tiny bird in the net. It was a sparrow-sized Pipra, with a canary yellow underbelly, rose-colored legs, and a short beak. Cooing at the bird, Rosa painstakingly untangled it from the mesh and held it gently but firmly by its legs between her thumb and forefinger. It fluttered, trying to escape.

She blew on its downy head, used a wrench-shaped caliper, a kind of ruler, to measure its wings, beak, and tarsus, part of its legs. "In Peru the Pipra climbs trunks, ocacas and lianas, from the ground up. It has a weak, sneezing "Chief!", her book said.

She banded the bird. Freed, it stared at her dumbly, then flew into the trees.

A wood creeper fluttered, caught and upside down in the net. It pecked at her wedding band while she measured it. She couldn't find a picture of the next bird she caught in her *Birds of Colombia* book, so she gently tied it into a black cotton bag. She would bring it back to the dam, break its neck, and send it to the Museum Goeldi in Belém for identification.

"I hate that part of my work," she said.

The Amazon is shrinking every year. Between 1960 and 1989, twelve percent of a region the size of the United States east of the Rockies was destroyed, according to Landsat satellite photos. Just in 1989, a chunk as big as Kansas was burned by ranchers, cut down by settlers, bulldozed by construction companies and dam and road builders. Worldwide, an area as big as Austria is lost annually.

"There's a difference between deforestation and development," Rosa said. "Putting cattle or asphalt or corn down is not necessarily development. Development is the rational utilization of what you have. You must use it without destroying it. That's what I believe in."

After the last bird of the day, a wedge-billed woodcreeper whose little black eyes looked angry while Rosa worked, we rolled up the nets and headed back toward the dam. It was so hot the ink in my pen stopped working. My passport curdled in my pocket.

"I love what I do," Rosa said. "These birds are part of the same ecosystem we are. But we change it so much." In the backseat, the cotton bag with the bird in it was still. By the end of the summer Rosa would walk five hundred kilometers over the same one-kilometer trails. The Samuel Dam would be operational. Electronorte would already be surveying a site for another dam in Rondônia, less than one hundred miles away. Planners of Samuel had not taken into account population growth when they designed the dam. Samuel wouldn't even provide all the power Pôrto Velho needed any more, let alone power the whole state.

Back in town I accepted José Humberto's invitation for a Coke at his home in a special development that housed Electronorte executives: a fenced-in, guarded, California-style subdivision of one-story ranch houses with carports, mowed lawns, kids on bi-cycles or roller skates, and a big pool club that families could join for fifty cents a year. Friends of Electronorte, like the state secre-tary of the environment, could live in the subsidized town too.

"He's nice to us," José Humberto said. "He gives us political support."

At the pool club we had a beer. A boy on a new motorcycle drove up to a house, rock-and-roll music blasted from the window. Gray ash rained down on Electronorte town from an out-of-control brush fire raging in a valley outside the fence, sweeping through trees, popping leaves into the air. Nobody paid any attention. There was a good soccer game on TV. Men and boys watched Brazil play Uruguay at the club, dancing on tables when Brazil scored a goal.

"Anyone who criticizes Samuel has only to visit it. He'll never criticize it again," José Humberto said.

I walked out of Electronorte town and back into mainstream Pôrto Velho. Red dust rose from streets from a steady stream of traffic, and dirt roads led past cubicle homes in a slum near the town.

At dusk streetlights were coming on. I'd been invited to play Scrabble at the home of a friend named Rose. We set the board up and chose tiles. Judy Collins sang "Once There Was a Railroad" on the stereo. Tomorrow I planned to head into Pôrto Velho's worst slum to meet some of the thousands of poor migrants crowd-ing into Rondônia. But tonight there were lights, stereos, radios. All needed electricity. Rose made her first word, then the lights went out and the stereo stopped. Up and down the street the houses plunged into darkness.

Rose sighed and groped for a candle. She located her flashlight too.

"When are they going to turn on that *dam*?" she said.

The Invader

On a hot blue-skied Saturday morning, a few days after I left the Samuel Dam, I watched Bimarzio Fabio Filho kiss his wife good-bye, wave to his son and daughter, who were watching cartoons on TV from their hammocks, and step into the alley outside the tiny room where the family lived. "Today," he said confidently, "I'm going to find land."

A short, quiet man going to fat, Fabio waddled on rubber slippers down the narrow alley and emerged onto a wooden sidewalk at the corner of Pôrto Velho's most violent slum, Tancredo Neves, where many taxi drivers had refused to take me.

Housewives soaped pots at a well a few feet away. A bartender at the open-air bar, just four walls with rum bottles on shelves, set up a table under his tin awning. The wide dirt avenue stretched west through the new settlement, its choking red dust thrown up by bouncing trucks, pedestrians, and bicyclists streaming past the one-story storefronts.

"This place," Fabio said happily, "is so much better than where we were before."

Everything I could see in the sprawling shantytown of fifty-six thousand residents had been rain forest six years before. Rubber trees. Woolly monkeys. Orchids, jaguars. But with the forest gone, Tancredo Neves had the feel of a desert town. Dust coated our eyes and lips. I tasted dust when I breathed and risked hookworm just from breathing. An iron-red powder veneer covered the tin roofs, the barefoot children chasing each other, the stagnant water and snarling yellow dogs in drainage ditches, the water tower rising above the walled-in Catholic school, the jumble of hastily nailed third-hand wooden shacks stretching into the distance. Two women carrying bright yellow parasols against the sun picked their way through a pile of trash.

Fabio set off with a steady, placid pace away from the slum and toward its outer border, past the Good Jesus drugstore and combined storefront dentist/perfumery. "Someone told me the community center at Marco Frères neighborhood was giving away land," he said. The way he uttered "land," he meant more than just property. He meant a haven for a poor family that had lived as nomads until settling here three months before. Without land Fabio could be evicted at any time. He was burdened with $30-a-month rent. His wife went crazy from music blaring from the radio repair shop next door. His kids played in dirt in an alley.

Brazil has 12 million landless families, and is the biggest draw for poor settlers to the Amazon. In the forest, farmers displaced by agribusinesses in the East burn down trees to start new farms. In the towns, new arrivals flee the packed slums of São Paulo and the Northeast and Rio.

Urbanization is a leading cause of deforestation throughout the Third World. In 1950, forty-five percent of all people on earth lived in tropical countries, but by 2020 that percentage will grow to sixty-six percent, and the overall world population will double ten years after that. On any given day in Brazil there are millions of Fabios looking for land. Consider Rondônia alone. A population of seventy thousand in 1960 boomed to 2 million in 1990, with two-thirds of the new arrivals settling in cities, according to the World Bank's booklet, "Government Policies and Deforestation in the Amazon." And during parts of the 1980s, up to thirteen thousand people a month moved to Rondônia. Each migrant needed housing, medicine, food, clean water, a job, transportation, schools, a church.

"We're going to keep growing," Pôrto Velho's mayor, Chico Erse, had boasted to me. "I want to see new jobs, new factories for Rondônia's agricultural products. Coffee. Cocoa."

Land. In widening circles around the city, shantytowns were going up, and jungle being burned. Squatters died in land battles with hired gunmen and police. Malaria was rife. Shacks went up in hours. Settlers didn't know their neighbors.

I'd met Fabio at the Tancredo Neves Community Center, one of two hundred volunteer centers scattered through Pôrto Velho. With city agencies underfunded, the centers acted as liaisons between migrants and government, relaying needs to city hall, advising settlers on how to deal with the bureaucracy and get water, electricity, schools.

The Tancredo Neves center occupied a wooden hall on a sidestreet off the main drag. Visitors crossed wooden planks over ditches to reach it. Sunday was the most crowded day. Outside, workers for the Socialist presidential candidate, Lula, campaigned for an upcoming election. "Lula will make sure taxes go back to the people," they said. Men and women lined up behind the only public phone in the slum to make calls, but the line was short. There was no one to call. People had no phones in their houses.

Inside, Fabio was the only person not on a line. He stood in a corner beneath red-and-blue bunting left from Friday's dance, and beside pasted-up notices for the free Thursday night movie.

Short and anxious, he bore little resemblance to the tough peasants depicted in posters over his head. In the first, MOVEMENT OF PEOPLE WITHOUT LAND, muscular-looking men wearing bandoliers marched over a hilltop, fists raised. They were the idealized workers of Diego Rivera murals, Soviet art and paintings from the WPA (Works Progress Administration) period in the United States. Another poster in subtle reds showed a lone peasant silhouetted as he climbed over a barbed-wire fence: STIMULATE THE PARTICIPATION OF RURAL WORKERS IN THE POLITICAL PROCESS, the caption read.

Lines crammed the room. Men and women waited to see a secretary at a wooden desk. She distributed oil or rice on credit. Husbands and wives eyed sacks of flour being emptied scoop by scoop and sold at a special low price. Fabio never took his eyes off a third line that ended at a man in a chair carefully ripping stamps out of a book and handing them to applicants.

"The stamps are for free milk, government milk, real milk and not powder," Fabio said. "If all the people who signed up don't show by noon, I can get a month's supply for my kids."

"After the milk, I'll look for land," he said.

Fabio got the milk. Now I asked, as he walked, "How do you know someone is giving away free land at the other community center?"

"A man told me."

"What man?"

"I met him on the bus."

"Do you know him? Who is he?"

Fabio shrugged. "He said there was land."

I knew the mayor had announced that applicants for land should apply to the city at the Social Services Agency. The secretary of the Tancredo Neves Community Center had told me the same thing. "Community centers don't give away land," he'd said.

At 9 A.M. the sun was rising, boiling the slum. The ice cream vendors were out, wheeling their baby-carriage-sized two-wheel carts. Men wearing wide hats and shorts were playing pool at the open-air bars.

"What happens if you don't find land?" I asked Fabio.

Moving forward all the time, the short, pleasant man said, "Maybe I'll invade."

. . .

"Brazilian law recognizes two kinds of rights," said Lieutenant Angel of the state military police. "Deeds to land. And occupancy rights. If you settle on land and hold it for one year and one day, you have rights. People know if they invade, seize land, and resist eviction, they can eventually win. Lots of times title is unclear in the first place. The courts have to decide. In theory the system works, but there are charges of bribery."

I had told the police I was interested in the growth of cities on the frontier. They had offered to take me on patrol. Invasions weren't the only problem they had to deal with. Crime was up, especially on Saturday nights when the gold miners came to town. We cruised the slums, jolting up cramped dirt lanes past dilapidated shacks. Light glowed between gaps in the planking. Doors were open in the heat, and televisions were on. There was no order to construction, just a haphazard explosion of growth.

"Land and gold," Lieutenant Angel said. "That's why they come."

His commentary was a running record or urban problems. "Here is the bus station. Lots of drugs are sold here." We were driving along the major truck route through town, a four-lane dirt boulevard back near the Palace Hotel. I saw more hotels, shops, a tire store, the Rondônia tourist agency. The station was a huge open-air shed open around the clock and host to the expected contingent of seedy-looking characters. At 11 P.M. men and women milled on loading docks, by the taxi stand, and throughout a maze of closed shops behind the ticket booths. They didn't seem to be waiting for rides. They didn't seem to be doing anything. "We don't usually arrest people here. It's difficult to patrol," Lieutenant Angel said.

"These are gay prostitutes," he said a minute later. Five blocks from the station, we drove past trim figures in blond wigs and stiletto heels, beckoning drivers or climbing out of trucks. "It's not legal, but we don't do anything about it unless there's trouble."

We reached the cemetery near the main plaza downtown. "Cocaine and mescaline are sold on the street here," said Lieutenant Angel. The squad car turned up a zigzag road that paralleled the ten-foot-high wall around the cemetery. Dim figures bending into car windows recoiled at our approach and began walking away. The cars drove off too. "Usually we don't do anything here because there are too many little sidestreets. The dealers run away."

"What about murders?" I said. "Do you do anything about murders?"

"We are very good at preventing murder," Lieutenant Angel said.

"How about after the murder?" I said.

Lieutenant Angel made a sucking sound. "Afterward they are very difficult to solve," he said.

The car radio crackled to life. "He's got a gun!" shouted someone on the other end. The driver hit the accelerator but stopped for red lights. The problem turned out to be minor. Police had spotted a miner walking around downtown with a gun sticking out of his belt. The man had given up the gun peacefully.

Out of control. I remembered the words of the Brazilian consul general, whom I had met in his Rockefeller Center office in New York. "The government," he had said simply, "has lost control."

Opposite a chicken restaurant where the Chinese-Brazilian owner computed bills on an abacus, and across from a brightly lit snack bar blaring Beatles music at too slow a speed, the squad car drew past a steel gate set into another wall, this one topped with shards of broken glass. "Whorehouse," Lieutenant Angel said over his shoulder. "There are stag movies. Striptease. Prostitutes. We leave them alone unless there's trouble."

.   .   .

But there was something encouraging in the city too. A solid feeling of roots taking hold.

We drove past a university, a country club, new apartment buildings, ranch-style homes. Some new lives that people had started were turning out well. I'd met these people in the city too.

Rose Gannon, a petite, lively, three-year veteran from Rio, had moved west when her brother died, started a children's clothing store that failed and then a bookstore near the main plaza. The shop had evolved into a meeting place for visitors and intellectuals, university professors, Japanese sociologists studying Brazilian folktales, anthropologists from Brasília and Munich and Pittsburgh, reporters working on Amazon stories from São Paulo or New York. The armchairs in the middle of the store always seemed to be filled. Conversations and arguments went on after closing time, to be continued in restaurants around the city.

Miguel Nenevé, a thirty-year-old farmer's son from Santa Catarina state, a mild-mannered, shy man, had come to teach English literature at the university. His specialty was Robert Frost. "Do you know, 'His little horse must think it queer, to stop without a farmhouse near'?" he asked. Miguel invited me to dinner at his family's high-rise apartment. His wife made pizza. He rented video movies, Woody Allen's *Sleeper* and *Blue Velvet*. We drank Fanta soda and talked about sports. An average night in any city.

Urban dwellers. One night Miguel asked me to address an English language class he taught at a private school. The students included two doctors, an air force captain, the sixteen-year-old son of the state secretary of the environment, and high school students planning to spend a year abroad.

"Why did you move to the Amazon?" I asked the class.

"Because my husband was transferred here," said a doctor.

"I chose to. The Amazon is the future," boasted the officer.

The students all gave the same answer: "My father wanted to make money." "Is there more money in Pôrto Velho?" I asked them, remembering my cab driver's response. Yes. "Is life better here?" No. It's dirty and noisy, and there's no culture. "Will you stay?" Yes. There's more money.

When I was finished, the air force officer had a question for me. As the class nodded, prompting him, he said, "What surprised you the most about Pôrto Velho? What did you think you were going to find before you came?"

"Well, the international airport was a surprise," I said. Titters of amusement rippled through the room. "I expected to see fires everywhere," I added. The titters became laughter. "Everybody poor and sick," I said. "People walking around with guns." Sustained hilarity erupted.

"In fact," I confessed, sending them into the biggest paroxysms of the evening, "I was warned I might be in danger coming here."

"Did you really think it was that bad?" one girl asked when the class broke up. Parents were driving up in new Fords or Chevrolets, picking up their kids. They drove off, shaking their heads.

.   .   .

Bimarzio Fabio Filho and his wife Maria were born in the poorest, most crowded part of Brazil, the Northeast. The drought was so bad in the Northeast that recently Brazilian television news had shown newsclips of children in the Northeast using bones of dead cattle as toys, arranging them into little herds and naming them. The television reporter started crying.

But as early as 1970 President Emilio Medici returned from a visit to the Northeast so appalled by conditions there that he helped push through the first major Amazon highway, from Belém to Brasília, to help northeasterners move.

"Within five years, 2 million people lived along that road," said a United Press International correspondent who covered the project.

"Everyone from the Northeast wants a better life," said Maria Filho, a pale, intense woman whose academic air was accentuated by wide-rimmed glasses. She used to work as a lawyer's assistant in São Paulo when the family lived there.

"Fabio worked as a housepainter, a car salesman. He sold watches and sunglasses in the flea market. He always had three jobs," she said. Despite the hardship, Maria wanted to stay. "At least we had a real ceiling instead of a roof," she said wryly.

"São Paulo was crowded. We were robbed," Fabio told me.

The family sold everything and moved north, to the gold fields at Roraima. Fabio tried mining, caught malaria, and gave up.

"Then we came to Rondônia," he said.

They arrived by bus one night with no idea where to go. The hotel across from the bus station had no windows, no ventilation. Fabio slept in one bed with his son, five-year-old Tiago. Maria took the other with Fernanda, the two-year-old. They had so few possessions—suitcases and a small TV—that they all fit on the third bed.

The next morning they joined other recent arrivals fanning out from sleeping places, hotels and benches, to look for jobs or a place to live. The family walked for hours, buttonholing strangers. In late afternoon a bus let them off in Tancredo Neves. Maria hated it. It was hot and dirty, and she could tell in the rainy season the slum would be a sea of mud. A bartender on a corner told them a room was available down the alley.

"Radios were blasting from the repair shop next door," Maria said. "We walked around more, but the children were exhausted. It would only be for a little while. We moved in."

Before Fabio could look for land he needed food and rent money. He hit the streets again, leaving home at seven each morning, riding buses to better areas of town, knocking on doors and offering to paint houses. A dentist hired him to redo a waiting room. A rich couple traded a refrigerator for a new coat of paint on their home. They ordered Fabio to hurry because they were going abroad on vacation. A jeweler decided he wanted white walls in his shop instead of green.

"We saved a little money, but then the kids got sick," Maria said. "Fernanda started coughing. She had trouble breathing, had little balls in her mouth. The clinic gave me pills, but they didn't work. She stopped eating, and she was screaming at night. Her fever was going up. I took her to the government hospital an hour away on the bus. We never got in. The doctor wasn't there or only sees thirty people a day. I was really scared. At night I would boil water, put a towel over Fernanda's head, and make her sit in the steam. She wouldn't even eat Mabel Cream Cracker Biscuits, her favorite."

Finally Maria bought hypodermic needles and antibiotics at the pharmacy. A neighbor gave the injections, and they worked.

Fabio finished the refrigerator job two days ago. Now he had a little time to look for land. But when he stepped up to the Marco Frères Community Center, it was locked. It was a small square shack on the main road with no line waiting to get in. Nobody was here for land.

Nearby, a radio blasted the old Procol Harum song "A Whiter Shade of Pale." A naked boy stood in a doorway, scratching his scrotum. We moved to the side of the road as trucks and buses rumbled past. Fabio looked at the padlock a moment, shrugged, and padded over to two ice-cream vendors chatting in the street, their shoes up on the wheels of their carts. The placid, uncomplaining look on Fabio's face was unchanged.

"Nobody's giving away land here," said the taller vendor, who wore a straw hat and had holes in his sneakers.

"Try the San Francisco Community Center," said the other vendor, a boy smoking a cigarette. "They might have land."

Fabio started off again, a human tropism seeking land. The next community center was a half-hour walk. Fabio walked up to strangers along the way. "Do you know where I can find land?"

"I'm sorry. I just moved here last night," an old man wheeling a bicycle said.

A popcorn vendor with bags clipped to a broom handle over his shoulder paused, stroked his chin, and advised, "Go to social assistance. It's the only way to get land."

At a stand selling onions and bananas the proprietor jerked his thumb and told Fabio to keep going. "You can find land, but it's dangerous. If you invade, men come and destroy everything." He indicated a bare sandy area the size of a football field behind his shack. "Police came and drove all the people out." It was hard to hear him because a man was hammering, putting up a shed three feet away.

"Go past that, and you'll find invaders," he said. He admitted he did not own the stand. "My friend lets me sleep here until he sells it. He's afraid if no one watches it, someone might steal the land, the shack, everything."

Down the street. Across the sandy area. The sun was getting hotter. Fabio's pace stayed the same. He reached a section where the shacks seemed newer. Some had little grassy plots. A green paint job was new. A hand-painted sign warned trespassers from a wire fence: LOT 36. The sound of hammering and sawing were louder here. The air smelled fresher. The slum was becoming something wilder, reverting to a village. Streets became narrow lanes. The sky opened up—city power lines were gone, replaced by a primitive, homemade variety. Crosses made of tree trunks and two-by-fours tilted in different directions, like a line of Ku Klux Klan markers strung with every kind of electrical conductor. Barbed wire. Automobile, radio and telephone wire. Cables. Coat hangers. Masses of wire as thick as tumbleweeds, running off to the shacks.

A man in thonged slippers on a homemade ladder reached into a junction of wires with a wrench, hooking or unhooking his home from the pirated electrical supply. He either knew electricity or he was lucky enough to avoid electrocution.

"Do you know where I can find land?" Fabio asked a bald man leaning contentedly against the wall of his bar in the sun. But at the word *land* the man grew excited. "Land?" he said, getting to his feet. "*There,*" he said, leaning into Fabio's face as if daring him to do something, pointing twenty yards away, across a road. Beyond a barbed-wire fence that had been cut, three men clustered near the concrete lip of a well, their backs to a rickety shack. They worked the crank of the well, struggling to bring up a heavy load.

"He invaded two days ago," the bald men said. "He wanted it, and he took it! There's land right here!"

Fabio just stood there. A flush came over his face. He pulled at the bottom of his shirt, a nervous, unconscious gesture. Drawn, he began walking across the road. He couldn't believe he had really found anything. The bald man followed, still talking. "Invade," he urged. "You don't need to ask anybody. There's a lawyer in the city who owns ninety lots of land, *ninety,* and what do *we* own, huh? Invade, and then go to social assistance. You know what it's like in Brazil. Rich people have land, and poor people have nothing."

Fabio wiped his hands together. "I want to check," he said. When he strode through the gap in the wire, the men at the well looked up. A tall, thin man whose ribs showed on his bare chest and who wore khaki shorts stained with grease, broke away. "I invaded, it's true," he said at the prompting of the bald man, who interrupted, saying, "Do it! Invade!" The two men at the well nodded. The skinny man said, "I cut the wire. Nobody was here. My friends are helping me set up, and then I'll help them. We'll be stronger together."

The bald man started babbling again. "There's a lawyer in town—"

The thin man overrode him. "You can have land, too," he told Fabio. "We'll help you. If there are more of us, it's harder for them to dislodge us."

Fabio licked his lips. A song drifted from a radio at a corner bar. A soft calypso melody. "You can go to another place and meet somebody who wants to sing, too," a man sang. "Join together and transform your life in a happy way." A man at the well smoking a cigarette said, "Look for a place with bushes. If it's not clean, invade. If the owner comes, offer a little money. There's a corner lot behind this one. It's empty. I've been here two years."

"What about electricity?" Fabio asked.

"Hook yourself up!"

"What about wood for the house? Was it expensive?"

"Secondhand! Take a look!"

The shack seemed barely nailed together. Fabio saw a dirt floor, sunbeams shooting through gaps in the walls. Piles of brick bits. Coils of electrical wire and fencing. Styrofoam bedrolls with rumpled blankets on top. A new blue-steel hutch for glass cups and saucers. A propane tank of gas for cooking. A portable stove on wooden blocks.

Fabio stared into the shack.

At the well the weight the men had been struggling to pull up finally emerged, only it wasn't a bucket of water. It was another man, rising out of the earth, stepping away, dusting himself off. The man with the cigarette threw away the butt, drank a shot of rum from a bottle and grasped the bucket hook. The other men lowered him into the well until he disappeared.

"Digging for water," the thin man said.

"Don't go to social assistance," the bald man piped up. "They put you on their list and nothing happens. If you invade first, the city has to give you services."

Fabio stepped off by himself, and the men went back to work, glancing at him from time to time to see which way he would decide. His placid look was gone. Shrewd appraisal changed his face, deepened lines near his eyes and mouth. He scanned the area, mumbling to himself, "I could buy lumber." He walked off the property, his energy making his movements focused, exact. Everyone in Tancredo Neves understood that to invade was to invite reprisal. Fabio would be committing the whole family. Everything they owned.

The bald man stayed back with the invaders. Fabio walked silently for a few moments, drifting through squatters' yards, past a water trough, chickens, a woman slitting fish beneath a thatch-roofed shelter. He was heading in the direction where he'd been told he would find land. He halted before an unmarked plot overgrown with grass. It was the size of a two-car garage. For me, there was an unreality to the whole process. No real estate agents, contracts, or payments were involved. I'd wondered all morning if Fabio was even serious. Fabio stepped onto the lot and grinned like Balboa spotting the Pacific. "Abandoned!" he announced. "I was lucky to come!"

.   .   .

"In Pôrto Velho we have an invasion industry," Mayor Francisco Erse said. "Everybody knows how to invade. Afterward the city has to follow up with services, to buy the land in order to keep the problem from getting bigger. But I've stopped invasions. They don't go on anymore."

After only six months in office Mayor Erse was still confident, youthful and casually dressed in pressed white tennis shirt, jeans, thick-soled black ankle boots, and gold bracelet and necklaces as befitting the head of a gold boom town. Mayor Erse was the son of an engineer on the Mamoré-Madeira railway, built to carry Bolivian rubber through Pôrto Velho in 1912.

"In the 1970s the city was growing twenty-one percent a year, and we're still growing fifteen percent a year," he said. "Most of the migrants are poor. They expect an Eldorado. And our research shows a shift. Most immigrants come straight to the capital now, not the forest. In the United States you had two hundred years to convert from a rural to an urban population. Brazil has had to do it in twenty years."

In Mayor Erse's comfortable air-conditioned office we sat on a matching leather couch and sitting chair, a glass coffee table between us, an aerial map of Pôrto Velho on the wall, and lots of sports trophies and potted artificial flowers in crisp autumn browns. Autumn colors don't naturally come to this part of the world.

Mayor Erse repeated that the new social Services Agency provided a well-running alternative to invasions. Applicants signed up for land, and as parcels opened up—as the federal government donated jungle for settlement or the city purchased lots—they were allocated systematically, eliminating the need for invasion and violence.

At least that's the way the Mayor said the system had been functioning for the last six months. "But nobody knows when invasions will break out. You think they're under control, and they start again," a reporter at the city paper told me.

Mayor Erse leaned forward. "Before, people would organize into invasion groups, sometimes hundreds strong. And politicians encouraged invasions too. They would locate unoccupied land, often belonging to an opponent. They would encourage poor people to invade. They would promise that once elected they'd legalize all claims. When I came in I found thousands like that. I had to legalize it, buy the land for the city or swap it. Now we give settlers a "pre-deed" to keep them from selling the land, speculating with it. If they stay five years, they get a real deed."

"You say invasions have stopped," I said. "But next election, won't your opponents start them again?"

Mayor Erse grinned. "That depends on their morality," he said. He thought a moment, twirling a gold pen. "There's also a bit of cleverness on the part of landowners in this," he said. "Even though they lose, they win. Take my land," he said, and quickly changed it to, "Take someone's land. Let's say an owner's lots lie outside the city. If they were inside the city, they would be worth more. People start invading the lots. Well, that means eventually the land will be annexed by the city. So the owner wants his land invaded. That way it will be worth more. He'll make a bigger profit selling it."

"I don't get it," I said. "If he wants his land invaded, why does he try to evict the invaders?"

"Aha! He doesn't want *all* the invaders out. He likes the idea of a little invasion, just enough to get all the property rezoned. He wants to keep the rest of his land for himself. It's a game to see how much he can keep."

"By the way," I said, getting up, "didn't you start to say you were talking about your own land when you gave me that example?"

"Oh, not my land," the mayor said. "You must have heard wrong." We shook hands. The mayor told me I was welcome anytime.

·　　·　　·

The old woman came to the window and looked out at Fabio, who smiled back at her from her yard. Two younger women stood behind her, feeding babies with bottles, listening to every word. Despite the hot, bright day, the interior of the shack was filled with hanging wash.

"Excuse me," Fabio said, "but I am thinking of invading land next to your house. Do you know who owns it?"

The old woman nodded. "An excellent idea," she said. "I'd like to have a neighbor, then I wouldn't have to worry about being robbed all the time. Maybe I'll ask my son to invade the lot beside yours."

Fabio brightened even more. "Sure! If there are two of us, it's better! I'll help him, he'll help me!"

The old woman looked over both lots, which I had thought were one lot. "A lady owns the land, but she hasn't been here in a year," she said. "Besides, see the bar on the corner? She was angry when someone took over that land, but she couldn't do anything about it."

Fabio's brows shot up. "The bar owner invaded that land?"

"No, he bought it from the man who invaded it."

"Why is your wash hanging inside the house?" I asked.

"Because if I hang it outside, people will steal it." The old woman told Fabio, "I think you should invade the land."

Only three hours had passed since Fabio set out this morning. He borrowed a hoe from the woman and sat on her step, sharpening it with a rock. He strolled around the border of the lot, prolonging the instant when he would commit himself. The light hit the rusty blade when he swung it up, and then he was working, clearing knee-high clumps of weeds.

It was hard work. Fabio pulled off his shirt. His plump, pale belly jiggled over the waistband of his shorts. Sweat fell in sheets off his cheeks. "*Fazenda* Fabio!" he joked. *Fazenda* meant ranch. "This is wonderful! The bar will be in front and the house behind. Next time you are in Brazil you have to have a drink in my bar."

Fabio had inserted himself into the landscape. Nobody paid him any attention. A man invading land was simply part of the view, like the truck bouncing over potholes or the man pedaling a bicycle past, with beer cartons strapped to the fender, or the man playing pool at the corner bar. Throughout tropical rain forests, throughout the Third World, millions of men were chopping into the jungle, laughing with joy over finding a plot of their own.

"One billion of the 2.7 billion people in the tropics live in absolute poverty," said Peter Raven, head of the Missouri Botanical Garden. "They are unable to count from day to day on finding housing, fresh water or medical assistance for them or their families on a regular basis."

"You know," Fabio said thoughtfully, "they should *name* this street."

"What if someone tries to take the land away from you?" I asked.

Fabio straightened. "This is a piece of me now," he said, making a fist. "I won't permit it."

I saw smoke rising in the distance, a thin black stream from fire, and I excused myself and walked off to see what was burning. The road ended, and only footprints led between the shacks now. After a few more minutes the paths were gone too. The shanties were so recent, the grass around them hadn't been worn down yet.

I veered around a blackened lot where charred tree trunks lay smoldering in white-hot ashes. The air smelled like a fireplace. A chainsaw roared in the distance. There was a cracking noise that preceded the falling of a tree, but it was too far away to see it.

Over the tin rooftops the wavering line of distant canopy was a green retreating sea. The view brought to mind the words of Kenton Miller, a Washington, D.C., scientist with the World Resource Institute. A pleasant, friendly man who headed the Institute's forest and biodiversity program. We'd met on a rainy January day a few blocks from the White House.

"If you want to get a perspective on the occupation of the Amazon, imagine the United States after the Civil War," Miller had said. "There were a vast number of people who were landless, carrying weapons, and had a horse. The government set up the Homestead Act, a way of giving land title, and promoted the idea of people moving west to settle. And there were political reasons for that. We *had* to settle the West. In the Northwest the boundary with Canada was unclear. In the Southwest we had conflict with Mexico. There were political and agricultural agendas to get those people away from the East, get them settled and productive.

"Well, what did you expect to find? People grabbed land before the next guy. One person tried to do sheep and another cattle, and a third to plow. You can't do all that at the same time, so there was conflict. You had people coming in with wealth and people with nothing. Conflict. You had people trying to form groups to take over dominance of the regions. We eulogize this in Western movies. It went on for years. And during that period we had massive resource destruction: the bison. The vegetation of the Southwest by cattle. The great forest clearing. Wisconsin and northern Minnesota on fire, huge areas on fire, massive fires going faster than the trains to get people out of there. Finally guys like Roosevelt stopped it. It took years.''

For Brazil, the concern about borders had been present in the 1960s when the military government announced the push into the Amazon. After all, Brazil had won some of its borders from Bolivia and Peru, sometimes at the diplomatic table, sometimes by force. Politicians feared those countries might try to get land back, or invade forests. "I don't travel in western Brazil," one Peruvian World Bank official told me in Washington. "They might think I'm a spy."

Instead of the Homestead Act to coax settlers west, Brazil built roads, sixty-seven hundred miles in fifteen years. Fourteen airports were completed between 1976 and 1981. The government gave colonists land and provided loans and incentives to ranchers. It came up with the slogan, "Land without men for men without land."

The economic agenda was that Brazil needed foreign exchange to help pay off international debt. Any products that could be exported for dollars—soy beans, timber, minerals—would help.

The social agenda was to find new land for small farmers who had been kicked out of the South.

And overlaying the logical reasons had been the emotional one, the dream of Brazil's manifest destiny, its march to greatness, its desire to do the same thing every developed country in the world had done: harness its interior, plunge into the formidable jungle and emerge a world power. Already Brazil had the eighth biggest gross national product in the world.

The question was how well nature would withstand the patriotic onslaught. Instead of horses, settlers in 1990 had buses. Instead of axes, they used chainsaws.

According to satellite photos, a fifth of Rondônia had been deforested in the last ten years. Half of the Amazon's 15 million residents now lived in cities. Men like Fabio were still pouring in.

.   .   .

I had to take a detour to get back to Fabio. In the ten minutes I had been gone, someone had erected a fence blocking the path.

Fabio was leaning against his hoe when I returned, looking worried. "I'll have to get the house up fast. I don't want someone else to take the lot. I'll come here every day after work to watch the place, make sure I keep it."

I asked Fabio if he knew that the whole slum used to be rain forest. "Sure I do," he said. I asked him if that disturbed him, and he wanted to know what I meant. "Oh, you know," I said, "that there used to be animals here. Indians. Jungle. That these things are all gone now."

Fabio kept working. I was thinking that I would be visiting Indians next, west along BR-364, to see what happened to a tribe called the Karitianas as more settlers poured into the region.

The sweat flowed down Fabio's shoulders. Bits of red earth smeared the hoe. The lot didn't look weedy anymore, it looked prepared. A buildable plot for a new shack and bar. Fabio had even found a well hidden in the weeds while I was gone. He glanced around for loose planking. He wanted to cover the opening before he brought his kids to see the place, he wanted to protect them from falling in.

"Look," Fabio said. "You have to live."

Kilometer 50

The Indians

Before the sun was born the world was dark. The sun was a little Karitiana boy, very hot when he was born, and he gave off light. He was so hot no one could touch him. His parents said, our son is not a person, he's an animal. And the Karitianas isolated the boy. Then one day the boy got some bird feathers and put them around his face. And the boy started singing. "I'm going to wear these big, beautiful feathers . . . these parrot feathers. I'm going to wear them and leave this place." And that is how the sun got in the sky.

Cizinio Karitiana,
tribal shaman

Cizinio and Garcia both told me they were chief of the Karitianas. Garcia had led them for twenty years, since his father died. Cizinio was shaman, guide to the spirit world. They split because Garcia planned to sell wood belonging to the tribe.

"If we sell the trees, my son will have nothing. Nothing will be left," Cizinio said.

"We want roads. We want television. We want electricity," Garcia said.

I sat in a semicircle of Indians, on logs cut into stools in the shady part of a courtyard. It was late morning in the village.

Garcia looked enraged. *"I will sell the trees!"*

. . .

What happens to Indians in rain forests that get developed? Like other Amazon tribes, the Karitianas are likely descended from groups that migrated to South America between seventy and fourteen thousand years ago. Their three-continent trek took them from Asia across the Bering land bridge to Alaska, down the west coast of the United States, and eventually to the rain forest. Many tribes retain Asian customs, like penis sheaths and blowguns.

New arrivals adapted to the jungle. Stone for weapons was rare in the Amazon, so Indians used sharpened monkey bones or bamboo for spear and arrow points. They learned the medicinal value of plants, some of which now cure patients around the world. Scientists believe many plants once thought to grow haphazardly in the jungle are actually islands of food or medicine planted along trails.

During the rainy season Indians stayed in one place, growing crops like manioc, or fishing. In the dry season they traveled. Spanish explorers in 1541 described Indian cities that "glistened white, stretched five leagues without space from house to house." Up to 6 million Indians lived in the Amazon then.

But by the time Assis Dal Toe revved up his twin-engine Aztec for our fifty-minute flight to the Karitianas, Brazil's Indian population had shrunk to two hundred thousand, ravaged by war and disease. In the twentieth century alone, seventy-five tribes had become extinct. One hundred and thirty Karitianas occupied a two-hundred-thousand-acre reserve one hundred kilometers from the city, along BR-364 and down a currently impassable dirt road.

And from reports, their future looked grim. Roads like BR-364 might provide hope for poor migrants like Fabio Filho, but they made life hard for Indians.

"The Karitianas are in a high state of deculturization," read a Catholic missionary report I had. "Isolated and hungry. Their situation is grave."

"The Karitianas are in an aggressive phase," a nurse working with them told me in Pôrto Velho. "They armed themselves, went to Indian agency headquarters, and threatened to kill the head."

"Why do you want to visit the Karitianas anyway?" another

FUNAI—National Foundation for the Indians—worker said. "They're always asking for things. Visit the Uru Eu Wau Wau tribe instead. They're much more interesting since they've been in contact less."

He seemed to be saying that the recently contacted Uru Eu Wau Wau were going to become like the Karitianas. I wanted to see the end result.

From the air, the jungle mist cleared and the dawn was bright blue. The shadow of the plane crossed a panorama of Indian problems. The city oozed exhaust behind us. Smoke rose from the jungle where farmers cleared land. The brown Madeira River meandered through forest, dotted with gold mining dredges. And BR-364 pushed west below, a two-lane blacktop filled with trucks dodging potholes, flanked by new pasture bulging out on both sides.

"Contact is a death machine in operation," one anthropologist had said.

Assis Dal Toe was a private contractor for FUNAI. Like most Rondônians he was new to the state, having come from the Roraima gold rush in the North. Fifty thousand miners there had invaded land belonging to the Yanomami tribe. Dal Toe, thirty-six, carried himself with the casual independence of a freelance aviator. He wore tight jeans, mirror sunglasses, and a white peaked cap.

"I haven't been paid in six months," he said, reflecting FUNAI insolvency.

The village appeared as a brown rectangle topping a densely forested low plateau. As the Aztec rolled to a stop on a grass runway, children ran toward us, surrounding a heavier, powerful-looking man who turned out to be Garcia, the chief. His ironed blue shirt, trousers, and sandals were not what I expected to find in the jungle. His Asian features—cheekbones so high they flanked his eyes, long black hair brushing the top of his wide shoulders, monkey tooth necklace fixed with black twine—were.

But something was wrong. Garcia had given radio permission for a visit, but he seemed sullen, angry. His handshake lacked conviction. He led us back to the village, past a soccer field. I'd prepared myself for slower contact—lounging around, giving gifts, saying nothing for long periods of time. But Garcia seemed to be waiting for questions. He reminded me of celebrities on interview tours in the United States, tired of talking to journalists. I found myself filling the vacuum by asking questions immediately. He answered as if he had done so a hundred times before. With linguists wanting to know if the Karitiana language is part of the Tupi group. It is. With anthropologists asking if the Karitianas are polygamous. Most men have more than one wife. With historians trying to determine the Karitianas' first contact with whites. Written records indicate around 1910.

The path spilled us into the village. I saw squarish mud huts arrayed around a dirt courtyard. Women in flower print dresses swept dust into piles. A lone mango tree was so thin and sickly, its shade couldn't shield a child. A spider monkey tied to an ax handle dragged itself around in front of Garcia's house.

The *malocca,* or traditional community house where everyone lived and ate, had been replaced by single family huts. In one, belonging to a woman who'd been airlifted out for snakebite the day before, a naked blue-eyed doll lay on a lumpy velvet couch. A chained raccoonlike agouti ran back and forth on the dirt floor. An Esso pinup calendar hung from a wall near a water filter. The model on the calendar wore short shorts and leaned against a tire so big it filled the frame. Arrows leaned against the corner, but Garcia said they were for sale.

"We don't hunt with arrows anymore," he said. "We don't remember how. We use guns."

Back at his house he arranged little stools outside and brightened at the word *gifts.* I gave him machetes and shovel handles, which the head of FUNAI had suggested I bring. Later I learned he never distributed them to the other Karitianas. I gave plastic pens to the kids, and shiny postcards of London and Beefeaters at Buckingham Palace. "What will they do with postcards?" I'd asked the friend who gave them to me. She'd laughed. "Eat them, maybe," she'd said.

The children snatched the postcards and scribbled with the pens. And Garcia relaxed more when he began to complain. "In the old days we all ate together. In the old days we lived near a river and caught more fish. It's hard to shoot animals now because they're angry. They're frightened because when we learned to use guns, we didn't kill everything we shot. The animals have bullets in them now, and they ran away."

Still, Garcia had no interest in returning to the old days. "We didn't want to change at first, and we will never forget how we were, but changing is the best thing we ever did. I wouldn't go back. Nobody would go back. Civilization is better," he said, hand-rolling a cigarette. "We have clothes. Medicine. My children will speak Portuguese better than me."

I asked Garcia what he hoped the village would be like in ten years.

"Ten *years?*" He looked out at the reserve. Small fields near the village were surrounded by stockades against goats and wild animals. The Karitianas grew rice and beans there. A one-plank footbridge crossed a dry stream to the side of the village housing a FUNAI nurse and inoperable school. Garcia looked at the jungle beyond all of it.

"I want tin roofs. Modern houses. Chainsaws, and tractors to clear land. I want to plant soybeans. To have a generator for electricity. There will be farms all around this reserve, and we will be competing with them, doing the same thing."

He was starting to look angry again.

"How will you get the money for these changes?" I said.

The muscles on Garcia's face grew taut. He flushed. The Karitiana reserve occupied an exact rectangle that could have been delineated only by man, not nature. It was almost all forest. Sometimes Garcia spoke so loud I had the feeling he was addressing the Indians around us, not me.

"I will sell our trees!" Garcia hissed.

.   .   .

It was hard to get permission to visit Indians in Brazil. Even after Minister of Interior João Alves Filho guaranteed me access, it took weeks for it to come through, and when it did, I had a cold. Indians could die from colds. And my cold, with its coughing, headache, and fever, was contagious. My translator had caught my cold.

Civilized diseases had killed more Amazon Indians than war. Indians had no resistance to illnesses common in the rest of the world. "Before contact there was no flu, TB, malaria," a FUNAI doctor had told me.

"Hug them, kiss them, shake their hands, and they get germs as deadly as bullets," authors Brian Kelly and Mark London had written.

I had read how the first Kayapo band contacted shrank from 350 people to 85 within six months. Other Kayapo groups had dropped eighty percent from a single viral epidemic.

White man's diseases could be so virulent, they had even wiped out uncontacted tribes. Long before explorers penetrated certain Amazon areas, tribes there were decimated by yellow fever, typhus, and malaria spread along trade routes. When whites finally reached the areas, they found corpses dressed in western clothes, with pots or guns nearby.

I had tried to cure the cold before visiting the village but had also hidden it from FUNAI. I was afraid if FUNAI knew I was sick, they would stop my trip. Each time I went to regional FUNAI headquarters I took antihistamines, kept from coughing, and talked as little as possible so people would not hear that I was hoarse.

After a while I grew disgusted with myself. A debate raged in my head: "You'll kill the Indians," one side said. "You're only going for a day. Don't exaggerate," said the other.

The debate came to a head when a Pará-based anthropologist retorted to me, "Everyone wants to say, oooh, I saw Indians, I gave them a pen, I got my picture taken with them."

I confessed to Amaury Viera, regional Funai head. I told him I didn't want to endanger the Indians and asked what he thought I should do.

"The Karitianas have been in contact a long time," he said. "Go."

So now I sat with Garcia on the little logs while Garcia recounted the history of the tribe.

"Rubber tappers were killing us, so we moved away," he said. Garcia coughed.

He was talking about the turn of the century: "The whites came and burned our village, but we were lucky. There was no one in the houses. Then they came at night and burned our houses with families in them. The third time they kidnapped our children. If they take our children, we don't care if we die, so we fought them. We killed farmers and *seringueiros*."

Garcia coughed.

Seringueiros were rubber tappers. Around 1890, the start of the first world rubber boom, rubber barons needing cheap labor enslaved and tortured Indians, according to British government investigators who came to the region.

"Some of the most sordid atrocities on record were committed in Julio Cesar Arana's rubber empire on the Putumayo River at the turn of the century," Alex Shoumatoff wrote in *The Rivers Amazon*. "Men were shackled in chain gangs and if they failed to gather a certain quota of latex were burned alive or strung up and quartered or had their testicles shot off for the amusement of Arana's captains. Women were herded off to "breeding farms. . . . Fifty thousand Indians died along the Putumayo."

Garcia coughed. A single, quick convulsion. I'd only been here an hour, and the translater and I looked at each other.

"Finally we found our children," Garcia said. "They were in clothes, working for the whites. We didn't recognize them at first. The *seringueiros* hit them, whipped them."

The Karitianas and the *seringueiros* made peace, and the children returned to the tribe. A more cordial period followed where Indians drifted voluntarily between the work camps and the forest, bringing latex for money, staying home if they chose.

Garcia doubled over, hacking.

"Do you think he's getting sick?" I asked the translater when Garcia went into his hut.

"No."

"Me neither. It's impossible, so fast."

"Actually, I do think he's getting sick," the translater said.

"Me too," I said.

Garcia came out and blew his nose by pressing an index finger against his right nostril and expelling mucus on the ground. His own first contact with whites came when he was fourteen years old, he said. On a hunting party. Karitianas had stumbled on two whites fighting in the forest. Unnoticed, the Indians surrounded the men.

"My father whispered, 'Let's kill them.' I said, 'Let's see if they have salt. If they have salt, we won't kill them,' " Garcia said.

"They had salt."

What followed was a crossroads for Garcia and the tribe since his father would die soon. One of the white men turned out to be a *sertanista,* an advance man for the Indian agency. *Sertanistas* contacted new tribes and pacified them. The *sertanista* invited the hunting party back to Pôrto Velho.

"He gave us gifts and took us to the city. It was so different from the forest," Garcia said. "No one spoke our language. There were too many whites. We were afraid. We thought they would kill us. But when nothing bad happened, I decided whites were okay.

"I was the one to make the people understand about the city and about whites," Garcia said. "I was dreaming something new. But the people resisted. They used to ask me for explanations all the time, about white people. How should we act, they would ask. How should we behave about whites? At every meal I had to explain about whites."

"What did you tell them?" I said.

Garcia had to stop talking because he was coughing violently.

"I told them, don't leave the village. Stay here. Whites will bring gifts," he said.

.　　.　　.

Valdemar and Epitacio were going hunting and asked if I wanted to go along. Valdemar, forty-eight, carried a single-bore shotgun over his shoulder and wore clumpy, calf-high rubber boots as protection against snakes. Epitacio disdained the boots for black Puma sneakers. We walked across the high plank footbridge to the side of the village where FUNAI had located its worker housing, and into the forest on an overgrown track.

"We never used to get sick before white people came here," Valdemar said when I coughed.

In the forest, mid-sized trunks rose from ferns and brush thick on the ground. Rotting logs felt spongy as mattresses. Palms unfolded from the earth like fans. Vines squirmed toward the canopy. A spiderweb glowed in a sunbeam. We passed over a black pool swarming with mosquitos.

Valdemar, leading, almost unconsciously snapped the ends off twigs as he moved. He hacked at thicker brush with a long knife. The trail was so narrow I wouldn't have noticed it unless he went first.

After ten sweaty minutes he asked, "Have you ever been in the jungle?"

I realized that, to him, we had not been in the jungle yet. Valdemar plunged off the trail. I lost sight of his blue cap, and by the time I caught up, sweat drenched my armpits, but Valdemar was dry. We balanced across another log. On the other side he froze, then snapped the shotgun into position. Thirty yards off something big and black fled down a trunk. A woolly monkey ran off on the ground.

The roar of the shotgun echoed in the jungle. Valdemar missed.

A tree was riddled with shotgun pellets. Epitacio appeared behind it, where the monkey had been. I had not realized he'd gone.

Ten minutes later Valdemar froze. Missed a monkey again.

He missed the third time.

"Out of shells," he said, looking bored. He gazed at the sun. "We like to be back by five," he said.

When we reached the village, Garcia was worse. He'd unbuttoned his shirt, and sweat poured down his chest. His breathing was hoarse, wheezy. His forehead was drenched.

Two of Garcia's daughters, who had stood beside him all morning while we talked, were coughing too.

Garcia raged against FUNAI. Without a decent road to BR-364, the Karitianas had no way to bring crops to market. "They promised trucks but gave nothing," he said. "We want a better road. When they arrived here they had lots of money, but once we learned Portuguese, there was no money."

"The only reason we keep FUNAI here is for medicine," Garcia said. "I will break with FUNAI!"

I asked if I could visit again. He turned depressingly meek. "If you get FUNAI permission," he said.

Suddenly he looked beyond me and straightened. A group of Indian men I had not seen before filed into the clearing, led by a lean, handsome man with a machete. The men spread into a semicircle around Garcia and me. The leaner man remained silent, just stood beside a pole. He and Garcia eyed each other. Assis Dal Toe called with forced cheeriness, "Time to go." I asked one or two more questions, but Garcia's answers were monosyllabic, and he shifted in agitation on the stood, concentrating on the other man.

At the plane Assis said we would be taking a sick infant to town. A frightened-looking Indian mother carried the child into the backseat. We took off. Below, Karitianas watching us grew smaller. I could see Garcia coughing in the high grass by the runway.

Assis Dal Toe adjusted the lever, and the Aztec banked left, the sun red at dusk. Fires curdled up from the forest in spots. Pôrto Velho grew closer. The tension in the village left its residue in the plane. No one spoke for a while. The woman stared out the window. The infant lay quiet. The pilot and I passed a water bottle.

Cizinio, it turned out, had been the lean Indian with the machete.

"They have two chiefs now," Assis Dal Toe said. "They're fighting. The tribe is divided."

Assis Dal Toe told a story about a Uru Eu Wau Wau who had killed a *sertanista* when the *sertanista* ran out of gifts.

"Indians are like children," he said.

The moon was the sun's brother. He raped his mother. He went into the forest with her one night, to eat fruit. She picked lice off him, and then he raped her. She couldn't fight him because men are stronger. But he knew he had done something wrong, and that the Karitianas would kill him. He climbed up a tree, and took off his legs. He threw them down to his mother. He started to rise into the sky. He told his mother, every month you will bleed when the moon goes in the sky. That is why women bleed every month.

—Cizinio Karitiana

Brazil's Indian Protection Service, originally called SPI, was founded in 1910 by the hero-explorer Candido Mariano da Silva Rondon, for whom Rondônia is named. Rondon opened up the Amazon laying telegraph wires in the late 1800s and early 1900s. His motto was, "Die if you must, but do not kill Indians." He helped push through a 1911 law guaranteeing Indians their rights and customs.

SPI was supposed to mediate arguments between settlers and Indians, to contact new tribes, and to soothe the transition of Indians into Brazilian society.

Some SPI workers, like "Luiz," the *sertanista* who brought Garcia to Pôrto Velho, took their mandate seriously. Others took advantage of Indians to get rich. In 1967 the whole organization was dissolved when its head was charged with forty-three crimes, including complicity in murder, embezzlement, and theft of Indian lands, wrote Alex Shoumatoff. The head of SPI was implicated in bombing and dropping poisonous food to Indians in order to clear their land for miners or sawmill operations.

The National Foundation for the Indians, FUNAI, replaced SPI. It had a similar job and the same problems. Brazil's Indian laws are extensive but not always enforced. As of 1989, for instance, only 7.91 percent of so-called Indian lands were actually registered with the government. Even in reserves that had been registered, miners, squatters, colonists, and ranchers cut down trees. Just in 1986, the government granted 537 mining claims in 77 out of 302 indigenous areas in Brazil, reported the Brazilian National Anthropological Association.

Part of the problem with the government's Indian policy lay in the Darwinian nature of the bureaucracy. Different departments often had conflicting jobs. INCRA, the National Institute for Colonization of Agrarian Reform, which gave land to poor colonists, often put them in or beside Indian land.

Then there were money shortages. "The only way to control invasions is to have posts in Indian areas," said Amaury Viera. "Last year the Uru Eu Wau Wau reserve was invaded by squatters. We kicked them out. Now it is the dry season, and they will be back."

Another part of the problem was FUNAI's vision of its role. Was it designed to shield Indians from society or integrate them into it? Was it possible to do both? "We think the ideals of preserving the Indian population within its own habitat are very beautiful but unrealistic," Minister of the Interior Rangell Reiss said in 1974. FUNAI was run under the Ministry of Interior. "We are going to create a policy of integrating the Indian population into Brazilian society as rapidly as possible."

To accomplish this, FUNAI set up the "Indian income" plan. FUNAI helped tribes settle near posts, then taught them how to grow traditional Brazilian crops, like rice and beans. The income from these crops was supposed to go to the Indians. But often it went to FUNAI, charged David Mayberry-Lewis, anthropologist and head of Cultural Survival, a Boston-based nonprofit group.

On the freewheeling frontier, even when FUNAI did its best to balance the different aspects of its job, it had to contend with graft within its own ranks. Mining or timber companies wishing to operate in the Amazon require a document from FUNAI affirming that no Indians live in the area to be developed. Companies bribed workers to falsify papers. One regional FUNAI head had just been fired for selling wood.

Still, many FUNAI people were dedicated and chafed under the budget restrictions. Sydney Possuelo was an ex-*sertanista* who had started working for FUNAI without pay for an opportunity to spend time with the famed Villas Boas brothers, Nobel Peace Prize winners for establishing Xingú National Park. He'd spent five years with the brothers before working elsewhere as a *sertanista*. When I met him he had just been put in charge of contacting new tribes in all of Brazil. Trim, warm, outwardly friendly in jeans and half-laced workboots, he stood out against the more formally dressed bureaucrats in the halls of FUNAI's Brasília headquarters. He showed the wistfulness of a field man whose success has elevated him out of the wild he loves and into an office. He was still moving into his office, so we had to clear away souvenirs—arrows, spears—to sit on a couch. Rows of photos of smiling *sertanistas* with Indians lined one wall. The Indians in the pictures were always naked. Painted. Holding arrows. They were never the clothed, acculturated Indians like the Karitianas.

He smiled encouragingly at my bad Portuguese, used his hands to make points, always looking into my face even if his translater was speaking. I had the feeling he acted the same way with Indians.

"There are eighty-six tribes in Brazil that we know of that have not been contacted yet," he said. "Twelve in Rondônia, four in Acre."

The tribes had been spotted by pilots, miners, settlers. Possuelo showed me a book listing the latitude and longitude of uncontacted Indians, their fates sealed by rows of numbers pinpointing them. Possuelo said FUNAI tries to put off contact with the Indians for as long as possible, but when the arrival of civilization becomes inevitable, as it was for the eight thousand Indians affected by BR-364 and the Polonoroeste project, *sertanistas* spearheaded the contact.

"But generally speaking, every contact with isolated Indians is bad for the Indians," said the man in charge of contacting them.

Just now Possuelo was readying to fly to a Para tribe with medicines. Missionaries had contacted the tribe two years ago and "by the second time I visited them they were dying of colds and flu," he said. "Now they all have conjunctivitis. Probably from the missionaries."

Sertanista procedures for meeting new tribes are remarkably similar, considering how different tribes can be. First *sertanistas* build a base as far as sixty miles from a tribe, equipped with radios and surrounded by floodlights to discourage attack. The noise of a generator keeps Indians from attacking too.

They walk trails looking for signs of Indians. "We hang gifts on trees," Possuelo said. "Knives. Pans. Plastic airplanes. Sometimes we take Indians from another tribe. That improves our image. We come back days later to see if the gifts are still there. Sometimes the Indians haven't touched them. We leave more. Sometimes they destroy them, stamp on them. Finally they take them and leave gifts. Arrows. War clubs. That means we can approach."

"We spend a few months visiting each other," Possuelo said. "Then the first phase is over. The *sertanistas* leave, and doctors come."

For *sertanistas*, early stages can be fatal. The photographs of the smiling men on the office wall turned out to be murdered *sertanistas*. Possuelo's photo album contained more graphic shots. A *sertanista* whose decapitated head lay six inches from his torso on the bamboo floor of a hut. A bare-chested *sertanista* with arrow shafts protruding from his shoulders. A *sertanista* in underpants being hauled by ropes from a river where he'd been drowned.

My eyes were drawn to a picture on the wall of a grave with a

bottle of wine at its base. And back to those other pictures. In all
of them the *sertanistas* concentrated their attention on the lens,
like anyone knowledgeable about photography, posing. The Indians beside them seemed out of place, wrecking the symmetry of
formal photography. Small, unclothed men holding arrows, tat-
toos across their cheeks, forest behind. Inexperienced with cam-
eras so their attention was elsewhere even while the *sertanistas*
posed them. Take the Indians out of the pictures on Sydney Possuelo's wall and I had the feeling the rest of the photos would
congeal in the empty space where they had been, filling it in,
eliminating the vacuum.

I remembered in Brasília I'd met João Alves Filho, minister of the
interior. A tough-talking man angered by criticism of Brazil's treatment of Indians. He had said Indians in Brazil were "better off than
at any time in Brazil's history." More land had been allocated for
them under the current administration than in all the years before.
"Indians own more than five percent of Brazilian territory," Filho
said. "Each Indian has an average of four hundred hectares,
twenty-four hundred for a family. That's twenty-five percent more
land than United States Indians."

The governor of Rondônia had also boasted of new, benevolent
treatment of Indians: "*We* didn't have Colonel Custer," he had
said disdainfully in his office, surrounded by aides. "*We* had Colonel Rondon."

I asked Sydney Possuelo if he thought there was a big difference
between the way Indians were treated in 1989 and the way they
had been treated before.

"No," he said, smiling.

"Then why do you work contacting them?"

The FUNAI translater burst out laughing. "Because he likes it,"
she said.

Possuelo shifted in his chair. Outside in the capital it was dusk.
The rush hour sounds of traffic drifted through the open window
from five stories below.

"There are 140 million Brazilians," he said. "It would be better
for the Indians if we didn't exist, but we do. Only through FUNAI
is it possible to protect the tribes.

"We don't have to contact Indians to protect them," Possuelo added. "My dream is to block access to their areas. Install listening posts. Keep invaders out. That is already the law."

"The law is in effect?" I asked.

Syndey Possuelo never stopped looking into my face. "Between my dream and reality are many blocks," he sighed.

.   .   .

Back in Pôrto Velho I visited the Karitianas at the Casa Dos Indios, FUNAI's house for Indians. Sick Indians received medical attention for minor ailments there. Healthy ones stayed there when in town. Twenty Karitianas were at the Casa Dos Indios, led by Cizinio.

The compound—its dormitories, health clinic and outhouses—was contained by an adobe wall topped with barbed wire, on a dirt residential street within sight of the Madeira River. Indian boys played soccer in the street. Elderly Suruí, Cinta-Larga, and Karitiana Indians in their best pressed clothes; a button-down striped, ironed shirt and tie, a floral print dress and shined high-heel shoes—sat disconsolately on a wooden bench outside the gate, gazing across the street at a corner bar where Indian men played pool in the heat of the afternoon. Inside, two Karitiana men slouched against the bar, guzzling fist-sized glasses of Antarctica beer with both hands. "I . . . am . . . the . . . chief. I . . . need . . . money for food," one said.

A woman snatched a boy from the room, out of a knot of children watching the drinkers with big eyes.

Back at the gate, the old people grasped my hand and asked for money. In the compound I saw three one-story dormitories on concrete foundations, raised against the rainy season. Hammocks were strung from poles supporting overhanging roofs. Lambada music drifted tinnily from a radio atop a broken Toyota, the overall effect one of rural destitution. As in the village, women used straw brooms to sweep debris, chicken bones or pieces of garbage, into conical piles in the dirt. One woman in shiny new high heels and a torn print dress fed a baby on a porch.

The day nurse, Celia, invited me into her infirmary office. She spoke no Indian language and used mime to communicate with patients, she said.

"Pretend I'm an Indian," I said. "What do you say?"

Celia jabbed a finger at herself, giggling good-naturedly at play-acting. "I am Celia, Celia," she shouted. "What hurts?"

Dr. José Ferrari was a rotund, bearded man who had left a more lucrative São Paulo private practice to work with Indians and the poor on the frontier. He spent mornings at the Indian House and afternoons at the public hospital. I offered him antibiotics I had brought from the United States for myself: erythromycin against infections. Metrozenine, for amoebas. He brightened at the offer, but the infirmary was stocked with both. "Nothing else?" he said, disappointed.

Dr. Ferrari took me on his rounds. He'd spent three years in the interior and two more in town. "All the tribes have the same problems," he said. "Malnutrition. TB. Measles. Much of the problem comes from diet. In 1969 when the Surui were contacted, they'd never heard of rice or beans. After contact they stopped hunting and fishing. Their food was substituted by rice and beans that lumberjacks gave them. No protein. The Indians even hunted and sold the game for money to buy rice, candy, milk." Dr. Ferrari seemed depressed.

Dr. Ferrari spoke to most Indians we passed, gently raising an infant's ankle, inclining his head to concentrate as another man told him symptoms, lifting a little boy's striped polo shirt and touching red spots across the belly. "Clothes make them sick," Celia had said. "You need to wash if you have clothes. They have no experience with that kind of hygiene."

Dr. Ferrari stopped a woman carrying a small boy. A thin child with swollen limbs. "Look at him. He doesn't play. Lackadaisical. He's losing his hair. A sad child."

With each room the sense of gloom thickened. A figure out of the movie *Freaks* sat on a corner bed, on a concave mattress. It looked like an old woman's head protruding from a sack containing a baby-sized body. Only when the doctor pointed out tiny swellings where the knees touched the fabric did I realize she'd folded her legs beneath her, but they were so shrunken, I had to look hard.

Her wide eyes were frightened, feverish. It was clear she understood no Portuguese.

"TB," Dr. Ferrari sighed.

It was easy to snipe at FUNAI, but like Dr. Ferrari and Celia, even with her lack of language, many who worked at the Casa Dos Indios were dedicated.

I found Cizinio, the Karitiana shaman, in the third dormitory with the other Karitianas. But the force I had felt emanating from him during his confrontation with Garcia seemed absent here. At the Casa Dos Indios, Cizinio was a sad, gentle presence, visibly weighed by problems that turned out to be a son with pulmonary tuberculosis.

The shaman, or *prajé,* could see ghosts of departed Karitianas, Indians told me. He could make himself invisible. Could make you see a loved one far away, but just at night. He mediated disputes in the tribe. A couple of years before, two Karitianas had fought over a woman. The husband had gone hunting in the forest. The lover had followed and shot him in the back.

"I didn't do it," the lover told the enraged Karitianas. "My arm did it." The Karitianas left the man alone, but days later the dead man's spirit came to Cizinio. "The spirit said the other man had murdered him," Cizinio said.

Cizinio sent the man to live with the Uru Eu Wau Wau in the south, but they didn't want him either. The man lived with Funai on the Uru Eu Wau Wau reserve now, Cizinio said.

"If a Karitiana is sick, I can call the spirit back," Cizinio said. "When a person is sick, it is because his spirit has left his body. It is near heaven but not in heaven. I have the responsibility and knowledge to call the spirit back. I have a party for the spirit. I drink Chi Cha, alcohol, and offer food."

Cizinio sat on a log in the middle of the compound, waiting for visiting hours at the hospital so he could see his son. Children played around us. Cizinio was a calm, gentle man who looked younger than his thirty-eight years, with a taut muscled body, an unlined face, and jet black straight hair to his shoulders. But viewed sideways, his shoulders stooped.

Cizinio sang a song he used to draw errant spirits back to earth.

A four-note melody that came out so softly I had to put my ear near his mouth to hear. In its repetitive cadence, in sharps and flats, it reminded me of Jewish chants on high holy days.

> I am going to give you this food
> I brought you this food
> You're a very nice person
> Please come and take the food
> This food is for you
> You're going to be saved if you take this food.

Cizinio's jaw clenched off the last note of each line, as if to propel it into the void. "Sometimes the spirit answers," he said. "It says, I am angry. I want to be in paradise. But if the spirit is brave, it will come back and face the problem."

"I'm sorry your son is sick," I told Cizinio. "Have you tried to bring his spirit back?"

Cizinio shook his head. "I don't have Chi Cha in the city, our alcohol. Or wild meat—not cows like here."

Then we drove to the hospital. Cizinio gave directions to the outskirts of town. We passed trucks heading for the riverfront, to be loaded on barges and shipped to Manaus. The much-heralded Trans-Amazon Highway, completed ten years before, was impassable from lack of maintenance. Goods from São Paulo or Rio had to be diverted hundreds of miles. Whole trucks were shipped upriver.

I was surprised in the car at how small Cizinio was. Face-to-face he had seemed larger, more commanding. He was a sad, worried father going to visit a sick son. But I knew he was capable of violence because it was he who had led the club-wielding Karitianas to Amaury Viera's office two years before. He'd been grief-stricken then when another son died from lack of medical attention. It was a time when doctors, unpaid for months, had stopped working for FUNAI.

"We surrounded Amaury," Cizinio said. "He was scared." Cizinio chuckled. "If he had shouted at us, we would have killed him. But he was gentle. And spoke softly. So we left."

On that occasion, as often happens when Indians are pushed

over the edge, they got relief—a visiting doctor. Now we parked outside the hospital, and Cizinio invited me in but said he wasn't sure if the doctors would allow me to visit his son. We walked down a bare, long, dark hallway, musty smelling from age and heat. Sick-looking people leaned against walls, eyeing passersby if they were healthy enough to be curious. A guard waited at the end of the hall, inside a steel gate. He let Cizinio through but barred me. The place felt like a prison.

"What makes a spirit leave a person's body?" I asked Cizinio through the gate.

"A spirit abandons you because it is angry or sad. I am sad because my son is in the hospital. My spirit could leave me. It doesn't like when I am sad."

.   .   .

One day while Cizinio's group was at the Casa Dos Indios, Ailton Krenak came to visit. Krenak was an Indian political activist from Brasília, and national coordinator of the Union of Indigenous Nations. His last name, Krenak, was also the name of his tribe.

None of the Karitianas had heard of Ailton. He stood in the middle of the dormitory, a big man with long hair, looking at the flies, the ragged bags of clothes squeezed in shelves, the dog under the steel bed frame, the boy standing beside him with his infant sister in his arms. Blisters covered her stomach.

"You people live like dogs," Ailton Krenak said.

The Indian House erupted. "It's not our fault."

Ailton told the Karitiana, Surui, Cinta-Larga, and Uru Eu Wau Wau present that a new plan might bring millions of dollars to the Indians. The World Bank was considering funding the completion of environmental work begun under the old Polonoroeste project, calling the new project "Planaflora," but the Indians had to organize and push for participation or they would lose out. The money would be squandered, like before.

Ailton invited the Indians to a meeting at the Federal University outside of town.

They all packed into a Toyota Bandeirante driven by another activist, a United States doctoral student working with the Union of Indigenous Nations.

In many places in Brazil Indians were organizing. The Garaio tribe had helped get a dam diverted by flying members to Washington and imploring legislators to cut funding for the project. Acre's Indians were joining their traditional enemies, the rubber tappers, to fight off ranchers in the forest. Leaders from dozens of tribes had attracted world attention the year before at a big meeting in Manaus, increasing foreign pressure on the Brazilian government to make good on environmental provisions in multilateral loans.

Indigenous people were organizing to halt rain forest destruction in other parts of the world too. The Penan, a hunting and gathering tribe in Borneo, were blockading logging roads after failing to get protection for their rain forest from the Malaysian government. Other tribes in Southeast Asia had formed the Indigenous Peoples Network to begin fighting projects they said damaged forests in their areas.

These movements were young and weak, but attracted funds from abroad. In Brazil they provided rallying points for ecological groups in the big eastern cities. They aroused the ire of developers who claimed Indian rights were a front for foreign designs on the Amazon. Foreigners wanted to keep Brazilians from developing the region so they could get rich from it themselves, the argument went.

Elsewhere, Indians as well as rubber tappers were exploring ways to market rain forest goods for profit without cutting forest down. Ecologists called this "sustainable development," the utilization of standing forest for income so that it could be preserved and generate money at the same time. The Shavante Indians sold forest fruits abroad. The Surui had contracted with Cultural Survival to supply Brazil nuts for Ben & Jerry's ice cream in Vermont. Cultural Survival had also brought back samples of 350 potentially commercial rain forest products—products that could not be grown in plantations, that could only be gathered in the wild—for testing by interested companies.

The Body Shop, a London-based cosmetics company, had plans to release a line of rain-forest–based cosmetics within months: shampoos, face creams, lotions, soaps, and massage creams. And

Ralston Purina Company planned to test-market a breakfast cereal that included ingredients from the Amazon forest.

Over fifty years, harvesting of forest products could provide twice as much money as cattle ranching—$6,330 compared with $2,960 for each hectare, according to a study of the Peruvian Amazon by Charles M. Peters of the Institute of Economic Botany at the New York Botanical Garden.

But the marketing strategies were new and untested. "We don't know if they will work," said Cultural Survival's field contact in Pôrto Velho, a Dutch ecologist named Vim Groeneveld. "Among the Indians there's growing opposition to the idea of selling wood," he said, "but gathering nuts requires work, compared to doing nothing and getting paid for it, and any human being finds that more difficult. Nuts don't pay well. And Indians have different values. Rubber tappers are used to western capitalism. Indians aren't. You're starting from scratch."

At the university, Ailton told the Indians there would be a big meeting in October. He wanted all the tribes to send representatives, to attract press coverage, and invite Brazilian politicians to attend.

"Each chief should appoint someone to go," Ailton said.

The Uru Eu Wau Wau wanted nothing to do with Ailton's idea. "Nothing good comes from any contact with whites," they said. The Surui and Karitianas argued with them. "We should find out what the plan is about," Cizinio said. "We don't want to miss out like last time," he added, referring to the lack of benefits the Karitiana had gotten from the Polonoroeste project.

Cizinio decided he would go to the October meeting and take along Sebastion, a teenage Karitiana who had learned to read and do math at the Catholic school in Pôrto Velho.

Garcia heard about the meeting back at the village. He said *he* would represent the Karitiana.

"We want to run our own lives," Cizinio said.

.   .   .

"The indigenous population of the Amazon states along Rondônia are highly vulnerable to the expansion of the project," the

World Bank paper said, referring to "Planaflora,"the new environmental plan. "They are tribes without political organization to support them. They speak little or no Portuguese. They have no numerical knowledge. They are illiterate," read Sebastion, a Karitiana, holding up the report.

We were back at the Casa Dos Indios, on a verandah, in late afternoon. Cizinio wore mustard-colored shorts and listened intently, picking at his toes. I'd gotten the report from the American graduate student, who told me he had gotten it from someone sympathetic at the World Bank. Neither Ailton Krenak nor the activists had given copies to the Indians.

"The majority of the aims of Polonoroeste have been achieved," Sebastion read. "The Indians are receiving much better equipment and care than at the beginning of Polonoroeste. Eleven thousand Indians benefited from Polonoroeste. Indian lands were demarcated. Ninety percent of the Indian population lives in preserves, and the majority of these people have health, housing through FUNAI, and cars and boats where FUNAI works. Most posts have agricultural machines."

Sebastion's face seemed to close in on itself, his eyes growing blacker. He flushed. Cizinio just said, "We don't have boats."

"They say they have posts with nurses and pharmacies," Sebastion said. "There's hardly any medicine. When there is good medicine, FUNAI people bring it to their own families."

"The money went into their pockets," Cizinio said.

Indian criticism of past use of World Bank resources is echoed by anthropologists working in Brazil. "The bank people haven't been to Indian areas," said one Pará-based scientist who asked not to be named, fearing revocation of his Indian visiting privileges if he were identified. "They land at the post. There are some trees there. A building. An Indian might drift in. The people advising the bank don't know what to do."

David Price, a Cornell anthropologist hired by the bank to advise it on Polonoroeste, concluded his report to the bank: "It is hard to understand how FUNAI could present the World Bank with such a project. Does FUNAI fail to realize that its program is divorced from reality and likely to prove counterproductive, or does it suppose the World Bank will fail to notice? Either FUNAI is hopelessly incompetent, or it cynically assumes the World Bank does not really care whether the project is effective. . . . To entrust the Indians' welfare to FUNAI as it is now constituted would be criminal."

The loan went through.

"Of the $26 million that should have been spent on the Indian component of Polonoroeste between 1980 and 1985, $19 million remained unspent while field personnel constantly noted the lack of resources," wrote Environmental Defense Fund anthropologist Stephen Schwartzmann who spent years in Brazil with tribes. "Sources close to FUNAI say FUNAI spent money to cover operating expenses."

Sebastion flipped over the report and scribbled numbers on the other side. One dollar equals ninety cruzeiros, he wrote. Five million dollars equals 450 million cruzeiros. The enormity of that sum, to people eking out their lives shuttling between the FUNAI village and the squalid Indian House, portioning out cupfuls of rice for food, was earth-shattering.

The report said, "The federal government and the government of Rondônia will be working together to demarcate Indian land, support FUNAI in its work of contacting isolated Indians and improving protection of Indian areas."

In light of complaints I'd been hearing for weeks, I asked Cizinio what he thought of the idea of contacting new Indians. It was one of those stupid journalism questions when the asker knows the answer. Of course he was going to think it was a terrible idea. But once again the huge gap between the way we thought loomed, when he nodded and said peacefully, "Good idea."

I figured he'd heard wrong. I asked again.

"Very good idea," Cizinio said.

For days I had listened to him say, "In the old days my cock was free. I didn't have to wear clothes. In the old days we were happy. In the old days we didn't get sick."

"Don't you think the same thing will happen to other Indians that happened to you if they're contacted?" I said.

But Cizinio didn't look at his condition as permanent. To him it was part of an evolution. Contact itself had not been objectionable to the Karitiana, it was the way contact had been carried out.

Cizinio might not want to sell the Karitiana wood, but his dream of the future was the same as Garcia's.

"When you have a wild animal, you want to domesticate it. But as soon as FUNAI domesticated us, they left us alone," he said.

Cizinio asked me if I knew anyone who might help the Karitianas get a tractor. Those little shovels and machetes I'd brought, charming gifts reflecting a western concept of Indian agriculture, were the tools of peasants. Cizinio said, "We want to grow soybeans. We want to show the government how hard we work."

Somehow the conversation worked its way around to sugar. The first time Cizinio had eaten sugar, he said, "Worms came out of my nose and mouth. I almost died." Sugar was one more example of white ways that damaged Indians. "Sugar rots our flesh," Cizinio said.

"Well, why don't you stop eating sugar?" I said to him.

He and Sebastion thought it was a funny question.

"We like sugar," Cizinio said.

.   .   .

But Cizinio was in the best mood he'd shown in days. "My son is getting better," he said. "My brother cured him, but not the way you think. My brother is dead."

During a day-long trip to the village, Cizinio had seen the spirit of his brother. The spirit had said, "Don't be worried. Your son's illness is small." "When I went back to town my brother was in the hospital," Cizinio said. "He put his hand on my son's forehead, and my son began to get better.

"You probably don't believe that." Cizinio said.

I didn't know if he'd seen his brother's spirit or not. I've never seen a spirit, but that doesn't mean they don't exist. Once when I lived in Washington, D.C., the oddest feeling had come over me whenever I got into my Volkswagen Rabbit. It was that the car was dangerous, that my dead grandfather Willie was trying to tell me to stay away from it. I'd had the car for five years without trouble. I hardly ever thought about my dead grandfather. And I never thought about spirits at all. But the feeling lasted two days, kept getting stronger, and at the end of that time the car caught on fire.

I told Cizinio that I didn't know whether he'd seen his dead brother or not. I said I supposed it was possible. He nodded, pleased, but burst out laughing when I asked him how his dead brother had gotten to town. "Did he come in the FUNAI truck?" I said.

"Oh," he roared, holding his stomach. "The truck!" He couldn't talk he was laughing so hard. He forced out, "And I thought you understood." He had to stop talking because more laughter rocked him. Gasping, he explained, as if talking to a five-year-old, "Look, did you ever see an escalator?"

"Yes."

Cizinio's hand moved diagonally into the air, miming an escalator. "That's how spirits travel, without moving their legs." A fit of hilarity seized him. "The truck!" he gasped.

I told Cizinio and Sebastion about my wife's Italian-American family in Rhode Island who said they saw ghosts of dead family members walking around upstairs where we slept when we visited. Uncle Brownie in particular was alleged to have appeared many times over the years. I had always wanted to see Uncle Brownie. Whenever I visited I called upstairs, "Hey! Uncle Brownie!" But I never saw anything.

Cizinio and Sebastion sat cross-legged, nodding with professional interest. "Those spirits in your wife's family, they're not Indian spirits," Sebastion said.

"I know," I said. "They're her family."

"They *couldn't* be Indian spirits," Sebastion said, "because Indian spirits live over there"—he pointed to the sky—"and white people's spirits live *there*." He turned his hand ninety degrees.

Cizinio corrected him gently. "No, white people's spirits live *there*," he said, pointing about five inches from where Sebastion had indicated.

They were into a technical conversation. "There?" Sebastion said.

"There!"

"Oh," Sebastion said. "There."

Then we started telling growing-up stories. Cizinio laughed at himself relating times he had screwed up as a kid. There was the time his father took him into the forest to teach him to shoot monkeys with arrows. "Hit it in the eye," Cizinio's father said.

Cizinio hit the shoulder, the monkey pulled the arrow out and ran away. Cizinio's father said in disgust, "You are bad."

There was the time Cizinio had missed a bird with the arrow, too, but on that occasion a better marksman behind him had finished the job. There was the time Cizinio's father told him to put his hand in a big wasps' nest. The wasps started stinging him all over, but he wasn't supposed to pull his hand out. He had to keep his hand in the nest even though the wasps were all over him.

"After a while I fainted," Cizinio said. His father put a salve on him. All the boys had to put their hands in the wasps' nest. Cizinio and I were the same age, thirty-eight and as boys, while he'd been shooting monkeys, I'd been learning to use the subway turnstile in Brooklyn. I asked Cizinio why the boys had to put their hands in the wasps' nest.

"Because that was our pain. Because we had to be tough. Because we lived in the forest," he said.

"Do boys still put their hands in the wasps' nests?"

"As a punishment," Cizinio said, "if they're too curious."

The old ways were dying. In Acre, the adjacent state, I had gone into a classroom where Indians sat at little desks while anthropologists explained something to them. My Portuguese wasn't good enough to understand the lesson, so I'd asked one of the teachers what the class was about.

"The Indian language," she'd said.

"They're teaching you their language?" I'd said.

"No, we're teaching them their language."

"Their own language?" I said. "Why are you teaching them their own language?"

"Because they don't know it anymore," the anthropologist said.

.　　.　　.

I left Cizinio and Sebastion, and went to dinner at the FUNAI doctor's house. He lived in a small, neat bungalow in a guarded compound on the outskirts of the city. He was washing his car when I arrived, and we spent hours looking at snapshots of the doctor and his wife, a nurse, with different tribes in the interior. Sometimes, in the snapshots, gold-mining dredges floated in the background on Indian land. Many times, the doctor told me, Indians sold rights to their land or timber to mining companies.

"But the companies cheat them, pay for one amount and take another, and after a while there are no more trees," he said.

The doctor knew about the fight among the Karitianas. He knew that both Cizinio and Garcia said they were chief. I asked the doctor who he thought would be chief in the end, and the doctor shrugged as if it didn't matter. It was a hot night, and we had gone across the street from the compound to an open-air bar. The owner kept pouring cold, flat beer into glasses he washed in a dirty sink. The doctor leaned back, sipped, and said, "All the tribes are like that now. They all have two chiefs. They're all falling apart."

The doctor wasn't an optimist. "And it's always over wood," he said. "One always wants to sell it. One doesn't."

The doctor looked into his beer. "Tell the story of the Karitianas," he said. "It's the story of every tribe in Brazil."

All animals and people are descended from Karitianas. This is how white people came to be. There was a Karitiana who knew he was going to die. He told the tribe he would come back looking different, wearing clothes. The Karitianas said it was all right to leave, but they asked him, when he came back, not to be a bad man. And the man died. A few days later he returned but nobody recognized him. He had white skin and green eyes. Karitiana hunters killed him. When they went home the chief was angry. The chief said, "Don't you remember? Now he will come back with a weapon we can't fight." And the whites came and started killing Karitianas.

—Cizinio Karitiana

The Rain Forest and the Cancer Patient

New York University Medical Center fills four square blocks on the East Side of Manhattan. In its five hospitals and cancer clinics, over five thousand patients a day are treated for ailments from cuts to cancer. Many of these people, as well as millions of other patients everywhere, receive drugs that come from rain forests.

Reserpine, used against high blood pressure, comes from the Indians of South America, who process it from snakeroot and coat arrows with it for poison. Pilocarpine, against glaucoma, is derived from the jaborandi bush of the Amazon, which is going extinct in the wild. Glaziovine, an antidepressant, comes from the rain forest. So does cissampeline, a skeletal muscle relaxant. Diosgenin, a contraceptive. Bromelain, an anti-inflammatory.

In fact, twenty-five percent of all prescription drugs sold in the United States come from plants, and since scientists have analyzed only one percent of tropical plants, the other ninety-nine percent will provide new, powerful cures, they claim, *if* they can discover the plants before they become extinct.

It's a Catch-22 argument. The medicines haven't been discovered yet. The only way conservationists can argue for saving them is to point out the medical superstars that have come out of jungles so far. And the biggest of these, vinblastine and vincristine, come from a tiny shrub in the rain forests of Madagascar. A shrub conservationists say demonstrates all the potential of the Amazon to provide medicines in the future, and a shrub that would determine whether Darlene Huertas would live or die.

Now, as I stepped from the elevator at New York University, a boy in pajamas shuffled toward me, moaning, "What did they do to my tongue?" A tube ran from a needle in his wrist to a plastic bag suspended from a tripod. He rolled the tripod as he walked. I passed the recreation lounge where a boy with stitching across his skull played Nintendo, his father slumped a few feet off, crying.

Darlene Huertas had warned me she might be in no condition to talk. She had Hodgkin's disease and a sixty percent chance to live. Her room lay beyond the nurse's station and a glass display case filled with dinosaur cutouts and kid-made "record albums"—magazine photos of rock stars glued to colored paper.

She slept beneath a gauzy pink blanket, her window overlooking the East River a block away, tennis courts on Roosevelt Island, and the Queensborough Bridge that would glow at night.

Sixty percent seems like good odds in poker or blackjack. In cancer it doesn't seem good enough.

Darlene gagged, and I saw the needle going into her wrist at the fringe of blanket. She was here for her weekly chemotherapy. She said, "Uh, uh, uh, uh." Her mother, whom I had not noticed behind the curtain room divider, scooped up a plastic basin and moved smoothly toward the bed.

"I guess I'll come back later," I said.

Outside in the hall, I could hear a doctor telling a parent, "We put a needle in him. He drifts peacefully off to sleep."

Darlene threw up in the basin.

.   .   .

Darlene's doctor was a children's cancer specialist named Aaron Rausen. I'd met him at his NYU complex office and told him I was researching connections between tropical plants and the medicines they provided. He'd told me he would ask one of his patients, who turned out to be Darlene Huertas, if she would talk to me.

"Nobody knows how Hodgkin's disease starts," Rausen had said. "Stress may be involved. The disease is a cancer in cells normally found in the glands of the body. These glands usually swell up when you're sick. They're a filtering system to trap bacteria, but if the white blood cells in the glands go crazy, that's Hodgkin's disease. It travels from one gland to the next. Usually it starts around the neck, then spreads to the glands around the collarbone, armpits, the glands around the heart, lungs, middle. It can go into the belly and the back of your abdomen. To your spleen, liver, lungs, and bone marrow."

Rausen was a fast-talking, uncle-ish man with tufts of white hair sprouting from both sides of his bald pate. He said doctors used a category system to rank the seriousness of Hodgkin's cases. "One means it's in the lymph gland system. Two is when it's still in one system but has spread to both sides of the diaphragm. Four is the most serious, when it's gone to places other than the lymph glands."

"What number is Darlene Huertas?" I asked.

"By the time we got her? Four."

. . .

Darlene Huertas's neighborhood, Parkhill Avenue, seemed a million miles from any rain forest. Bars ran down her sixth-story windows, and windows across the street displayed bedsheets as curtains. Plywood boards plugged spaces for air conditioners. Boys in hooded sweatshirts—drug dealers, police said—never seemed to move off the street, and a jagged line of broken glass littered the road a foot from parked cars which had been broken into. Police had told me that the neighborhood had the highest crime rate in the borough.

Upstairs, Darlene lay on the quilt on her canopy bed, at home between chemotherapy treatments. She was a petite, quiet girl conservatively dressed in a green plaid jumpsuit, bow tie, and crisp white blouse. It was the outfit she'd worn to school today.

Sometimes she seemed younger than her seventeen years, scared, slipping her thumb into her mouth. At other moments she looked older, a young woman in pain behind cute red-framed glasses. There was a Scorpio calendar on the wall and stuffed bears and animals on the white maple dresser. Monkien, the white monkey. Mama Doo, the brown teddy. Big Boy, the polar bear. Blue Man, the little blue bear. Teardrop, the French porcelain doll.

"I hug them and I love them. I tell them they'll always be with me," she said.

Her apartment was a neat three-bedroom with fish tanks, ferns, and a brass relief in the living room of a conquistador in armor astride a leaping horse.

Her mother Carmen was a night postal clerk, her stepfather Ray a telephone company operator. She had a boyfriend, Ramone, who lived with his mother in Brooklyn. She liked to rollerskate, play Pac-Man, read books like *The Call of the Wild*, and watch Kung Fu videos with Ramone. She attended a special Manhattan high school for business careers and planned to be an accountant. "I was always good with math."

Her biggest problems were Ray, who she said called her "fat" and "lazy," and played loud music when she was trying to study, and her weight. At four feet nine inches, she was bone thin now, but Darlene said before the disease started she weighed 160 pounds.

"I love Ring-Dings," she said, licking her lips.

Boys called her Gumby.

"Every word was like a barb in my heart," she said.

Then a terrific thing happened. She started losing weight.

"I thought my body was changing," Darlene said. "I thought, that's what happens when you're seventeen."

·   ·   ·

Ask a doctor about Hodgkin's disease, you'll hear all the symptoms at once. As if they appear that way and make it obvious Hodgkin's disease caused them. But Darlene fooled everyone.

It was spring when her pleasing weight loss started, the thinning of her cheeks, legs, waistline. Then something happened that took away a little of her fun.

"My mother was brushing my hair. She pulled back a ringlet, and there was a scaly patch on my skin."

"Ringworm!" Carmen cried.

"I do not have ringworm," Darlene shot back. "I wash every day!"

More patches appeared, on her elbows, arms, and stomach. Since Carmen worked nights and slept days, Ramone's mother brought Darlene to a skin specialist in Manhattan. He took samples of the rash but didn't know what caused it. He suggested she use a medicinal cream, which didn't work, and he told her to cut out fried foods and Ring-Dings.

"Some doctor," Darlene said. "He didn't even know what the rash was. And I wasn't going to give up Ring-Dings."

Her weight dropped to 150, 135.

"Honey," men she didn't know called to her on the street, "you look good."

Her weight fell to 125.

"Are you sticking your finger down your throat after you eat and making yourself throw up?" Carmen demanded.

"No."

"Darlene, did you have a baby or something?" kids in school asked.

"I did not have any baby."

Proud of her figure, she started wearing slinky, body-tight clothes. "Little tank tops," Ramone complained. She also noticed, as the school year neared its end, that she was having a little trouble getting out of bed in the morning. The sunlight would be streaming past the bars onto the Scorpio calendar. She would hear the honking of the private taxis downstairs that took commuters to the ferry for bus fare. She'd hear Ray's music out in the living room. And she'd roll over and go back to sleep.

"I told you she was lazy," Ray told Carmen triumphantly. "She'll never finish school."

"Crackhead," whispered the boys in hooded sweatshirts outside when she walked by, just loud enough for her to hear.

"I am not a crackhead. Do I look like a crackhead?" Darlene told them, chewing them out. "You are so immature."

"I figured I was depressed," Darlene said. "I always had to take care of my baby sister. I was fighting with Ray all the time. It was like my whole body was rebelling over the stress. Or maybe Ray was right and I was lazy. Maybe all girls went through weird body changes at seventeen."

Alone and in her room, she'd put "Daddy's Home to Stay" on the record player and sing along. She could swear at those times she heard her real father's footsteps in the hall.

"You're not gonna kill me like you killed your father!" Ray would yell.

Her stomach hurt, but that was from tension, she thought. Then she started feeling sick when she ate. Ramone's mother, Gloria, nicknamed "Mom" by neighborhood kids, grew worried. "She was always upset. She'd cry for no reason. Her grades started going down, and she's a good student. I told her mother to get her to a therapist. I was afraid she was going crazy. Now I know if she hadn't been sick, she would have been able to handle what was going on at home.

Ramone and Darlene started fighting. She thought he liked other girls.

"She had an attitude," Ramone said. "She'd be watching TV, squeaking with pain and holding her stomach. I'd say, 'What's the matter?' and she'd say, 'Nothing.' "

The fighting got so bad Darlene and Ramone broke up. She figured that was why her stomach pains got worse.

Finally Carmen took Darlene to Dr. Bernard Visconti, the soft-spoken family pediatrician who had taken care of Darlene for years. Visconti, who bears a slight resemblance to the actor James Coco, was surprised at how pale she looked. "I thought she might have mononucleosis," he said. Visconti ordered a blood test and a sonogram, but both came back normal. He asked Darlene to come back for more tests. She didn't.

"You know when you say you're not afraid of something but inside you really are?" Darlene said. "Inside I was afraid of going back."

. . .

It was only a small shrub, a pretty ornamental used for decoration around the world. Two feet high, with a magenta, glowy color, the rosy periwinkle's bell-shaped flowers had five petals with purple-red eyes. They blossomed all summer.

For hundreds of years the periwinkle amassed a powerful reputation as a folk healer among native people in the tropics. In Madagascar it was said to cure diabetics. In Jamaica doctors used it as a medicinal tea. In India juice from the plant was applied to wasp stings. In Hawaii healers boiled it to stop bleeding.

In 1949 two teams of North American scientists decided to test the periwinkle's reputation against diabetes. At the University of

Western Ontario a group headed by doctors C. T. Beer and R. L. Noble injected rats with a compound from the plant. They wanted to see if the rats' blood sugar went down. But the rats died. Thinking the compound had been too strong, the scientists diluted it for a second test. The rats died. Beer and Noble were intrigued. They autopsied the rats and found to their surprise that the animals had been killed by a common bacteria found in animal labs. The rats' blood sugar level remained unaffected. Other animals in the lab hadn't been killed by the bacteria, and the periwinkle compound, when Beer and Noble analyzed it, contained no bacteria at all. So where had the bacteria come from? Beer and Noble theorized that something in the compound had lowered the rats' natural resistance to bacteria which had been there all along. Something had killed off the rats' white blood cells and made them susceptible to the bacteria.

Excited, they wondered if they had an anticancer drug on their hands. After all, anticancer drugs were toxins that attacked out-of-control white blood cells.

A few hundred miles away, in Indianapolis, a team at the Eli Lilly Pharmaceutical Company tested the periwinkle too. Dr. Gordon Svoboda, who headed the effort, ran a periwinkle extract through a routine "screen"—a test against several forms of cancers. The extract killed off P-1534 leukemia in mice.

The two teams joined up to test the first human patient, a Canadian machinist with terminal Hodgkin's disease. Like Darlene Huertas, he had lost weight, fifty pounds. He had a nine-inch tumor in his windpipe and was in agonizing pain. In the spring of 1960 the machinist received his first injection of vincristine, the compound the Canadians had isolated, at an Indianapolis hospital. Within two weeks the tumor was shrinking, the patient walking. Doctors gave him biweekly injections, and the disease disappeared for two years. Then it became resistant to the drug and returned.

But by then Svoboda had isolated a second compound from the periwinkle, vinblastine. Chemically, vinblastine differed from vincristine by only a single molecule, but medically it attacked Hodgkin's disease in a totally different way.

The machinist was cured within a few months.

He never got Hodgkin's disease again.

Eli Lilly patented vincristine and vinblastine, selling them as Velban and Oncovin.

In 1962 the National Cancer Institute hailed vincristine and vinblastine as miracle drugs. A year later the American Medical Association called the new drugs outstanding advances of the time.

By 1980, Velban and Oncovin, in combination with other drugs in chemotherapy, produced an eighty percent cure rate against the rare childhood cancer, Wilms' tumor, a fifty percent rate against Burkitt's lymphoma, and a seventy percent remission rate against gestational choriocarcinoma. Children who contracted childhood leukemia, who formerly had a twenty percent survival rate, now had four times as good a chance of living.

Sales of Velban and Oncovin topped $100 million a year by 1985. The two drugs even helped Rausen choose his career. As childhood cancer patients lived longer, they needed doctors to care for their special kinds of complications.

Over the years new drugs against cancers came into existence, but Velban and Oncovin remained the backbone of chemotherapy treatments for Hodgkin's disease and childhood leukemia.

"I wouldn't even think of not using them," Dr. Rausen said.

.   .   .

Schoolbooks lay on Darlene's hospital bed since she insisted on studying during treatments. She kept insisting she would go to college next year, that she would graduate. She told me she hated the chemo. She went pale and gagged just thinking about it. "As soon as they put the IV in me, I throw up. I can taste it in my mouth."

She said her night sweats had started a few months after she'd visited Dr. Visconti, but didn't go back. She'd wake drenched in sweat. She was so tired she missed days at school. She dropped to 110 pounds. Her math teacher failed her for absence and poor performance. Her English teacher became worried. During "Macbeth" quizzes, when other kids were busy answering questions like, "Macbeth says he fears only (a) MacDuff (b) Ross (c) Banquo (d) Donalbain?" Darlene would just put her head on her desk and seem to drift off.

The teacher, Michael Marantz, wrote a memo to the guidance department.

> Darlene has been my student before, and I know her to be a good-natured, conscientious, and responsible young lady. For this reason I was surprised to find she was falling behind in her homework and seemed somewhat less courteous than I knew her to be. . . .
>
> *Today I noticed that she looked rather ill, stressed, her eyes clouded over. We had a fairly long talk, and she revealed to me that she has been moving in and out of her home due to a long-term conflict that she has with her stepfather.*
>
> *As this family conflict appears to be having powerful effects on Darlene emotionally, I thought I should apprise you of it. PS . . . I should mention that Darlene expressed that she has angry thoughts of doing violence to her stepfather (though knowing her personally it seems unlikely to me).*

The guidance department assigned a youth counselor to Darlene, but her problem wasn't mental.

By December, Darlene had lost fifty-five pounds. Finally, she visited Dr. Visconti again, coming in with her sister Venus for Venus's checkup. Visconti took one look at Darlene and told her to go home, pack a suitcase, and wait for the ambulance.

"I didn't know what she had, but it was bad," he said.

Visconti told the admissions staff at St. Vincent's Hospital in Staten Island that he was admitting her for "dehydration," but in fact his purpose was to try to figure out what her problem was. "I wasn't taking any chances," he said. He ordered a battery of tests. On her X ray the radiologist spotted a small glandular enlargement near her aorta, the main artery looping off the heart. A shadow too big by the size of a fingertip. Tumor, the radiologist thought.

"Well, now that you ask, I wasn't getting up in the morning, and I did sweat a little," Darlene told Visconti. She'd not connected the symptoms before.

Visconti had never met Rausen but knew his reputation, and he called the NYU cancer expert. Rausen asked him to send Darlene to Manhattan immediately in an ambulance, sitting up. "All I knew was that there was a tumor in her chest," Rausen said. "If it's a non-Hodgkin's disease mass, I've seen people die by lying down." It was after normal working hours. Darlene got CAT scans of her chest, abdomen, and pelvis. She had a lymphangiogram, where small radioactive substances were circulated through her lymph channels. Doctors checked her blood count and did a liver and spleen scan. They came into her room with something looking like an apple corer to break off a piece of her bone. "You're not putting that thing in me," she said.

The surgeon made a small incision between her ribs and took a biopsy of marrow.

Rausen was surprised by the result. Although Darlene showed none of the outward signs of the disease, no swollen glands that he could feel, the marrow biopsy was positive.

Rausen prescribed a four-drug regimen: vinblastine, adriamycin, bleomycin, and dacarbozine. She would receive twelve injections, two weeks apart, and radiation treatment after that.

"We use four drugs because it's like being hit by four different people at the same time," Rausen told Darlene. "It's much more effective than being hit by one."

The odd skin rash Darlene had, had nothing to do with the disease. It was a fluke.

Everyone sat back to see if the drugs would have an effect. They would have to kill every single cancer cell in her body.

"In the old days, she would have been dead in months," Rausen said.

.   .   .

Dr. Norman Farnsworth looked more like a Chicago ward boss than a professor of pharmacognosy. He wore a flashy red tie over his ample stomach, and he smoked big cigars. He described a sixty-year-old guest at his own recent sixtieth birthday party, a man who had come with a young date, by saying, "Maybe he's got a corkscrew dick." He held up his wrist and said, "Hey! Whaddaya think of my new Rolex! Twenty-five bucks in Bangkok, and it hasn't lost or gained a second since November!"

But Farnsworth was one of the most respected authorities on plants and medicines in the world. He'd been president of the

American Academy of Pharmacognosy and had written papers on the discovery of vincristine. He ran a research program at the University of Illinois to try to locate tropical plants that might heal AIDS and cancers. He'd designed a new computer system to cross-reference folklore, chemical structure, medicinal value, and scientific experiments on over eighty thousand plants.

Farnsworth leaned forward in a university dining room and attacked his steamed scallops. I'd gone to Chicago to talk to him in between visits with Darlene.

"Whaddaya wanna know?" he said.

I told Farnsworth I'd been researching the history of vincristine and vinblastine and that I was curious about whether other valuable medicinal plants came from the tropics. Farnsworth sighed. The list was that long.

"Quinine against malaria," he said. "Morphine and codeine against pain and coughs. Nicotine for antismoking. Scopolamine for motion sickness. Theophylline for asthma and lung problems. Digitalin and digitoxin, drugs of choice against heart disease. Emetine, an amoebacide; neoandrographolide, against bacillic dysentery."

In Farnsworth's co-written essay, "Tropical Rainforests: Potential Source of New Drugs?", he'd included a chart of thirty-nine tropical plants, drugs they provided, and uses for the drugs.

"Prescription drugs sold in the United States from plants are worth about $12 billion a year," he said, adding, "With deforestation rates as high as they are, within a decade or so, large numbers of plants species will be gone forever, lost to humanity."

The reason tropical plants were particularly potent in terms of the toxins they contained was that in the savagely competitive world of the rain forest the plants needed poisons for self-protection. "Plants stand still," wrote Dr. Dan Janzen, who studies rain forests in Costa Rica. "They can't run or fight or flee. They can't bark or rear up. So they develop defenses."

"One hundred million years ago seed plants began their great rise on the planet," said Dr. Michael Balick, director of the New York Botanical Garden's Institute of Economic Botany, which was participating in a National Cancer Institute search to find useful medicine in the tropics. Later I planned to go into the jungle near

BR-364 with a Botanical Garden researcher looking for cancer cures. "Coevolution meant battling back and forth between predator animals, or insects, and plants. An animal would learn to eat a seed and eliminate a plant population. Then the plant would evolve a compound to make the animal sick if it ate the seed. So the next generation of animals would leave the seeds alone. Plants developed millions of compounds this way, and there are more of them in the tropics because the tropics don't get cold. Look at the 270,000 seed plants on earth. We know everything there is to know, chemically and medicinally, about only 1,100 of them. And out of those 1,100 have come our medicines, our pesticides. The other 268,000 are still big questions. Burn down rain forests, and you lose potential cures."

Even rubber, the sap of the *Hevea brasiliansis* tree, had evolved as a defense. "When a boring insect drills into the tree, it gets a lungful of sticky, congealing liquid," Janzen wrote.

Now Farnsworth drained the last of his iced tea and waved away the dessert cart. "I'll show you the computer," he said.

He walked briskly despite a recent ankle injury suffered during a plant-gathering trip in Thailand. We moved through windy Chicago streets past throngs of white-jacketed pharmaceutical students.

Farnsworth said just now one of his researchers had brought back some plant samples from Brazil for testing against cancers and AIDS, but he wouldn't identify the plants because new discoveries could be worth millions. Any profits would be split by the university, Farnsworth, and researchers.

"If we find a valuable compound, we'll take it to a drug company," Farnsworth said. "If the plant is from Brazil, we'll set up a factory there to process the stuff, and Brazil will get revenue too."

Scientists and conservationists had long criticized drug companies for not sharing profits of medicinally valuable plants with host countries. Income sharing would encourage preservation, they said. Madagascar, original home of the rosy periwinkle, had never gotten a penny of the vincristine or vinblastine profits. "They've been bitching about it for years," Farnsworth said.

But then he drifted from the more generous view to one that was more mercenary. "If I were a researcher, as soon as I found activity that looked interesting from a plant that grew in Brazil, I'd look in every country where that plant might grow for the same plant. And if it didn't grow there, I'd find a way not to have to rely on a sole source of supply, like sneaking out seeds."

Brazilian officials are understandably touchy about losing the commercial rights to their own plants. They point to one example where a United States–based researcher was granted authority to collect an Amazon fungus for research and later abandoned the research and started up a company to sell the fungus to laboratories.

Farnsworth's offices, which were being moved, were a mess. Papers and reports lay in piles in a central lab area. There was a skeleton in a glass case in a corner. Farnsworth said his NAPRA-LERT, "natural product database," had come into existence after "a million man hours" of researchers culling through scientific journals for articles on medicine and plants.

Doctors, patients, pharmaceutical companies, governments, parents whose children had accidentally swallowed exotic plants, even a California man contemplating a sex change operation, curious about the use of steroids, accessed the system for $10 a question.

"You can request information by plant or country or chemical compound or even by potential curative property," said Mary Lou Quinn, managing director of the database. Randomly she summoned up a sample on the humming amber screen, all information available on a small tropical plant called *Osterific sanctum*.

The printout that emerged went on for pages. Folk healers in India used *Osterific sanctum* to alleviate protracted labor, it said. In South Korea the plant was regarded as a contraceptive. In Java people believed it increased milk secretion. In Nepal it was given against rheumatism. Ailments it supposedly combated included colds, gastric ulcers, phlegm, diarrhea. The plant was dried in parts of Asia, then ingested to bring down fevers. Its leaves were steamed and fed to children to ease digestive complaints. It was said to be an aphrodisiac, a poultice, an anesthetic. *Osterific sanctum* was used to ease irregular menstruation and stomachache.

And the printout wasn't finished. It went on to describe scientific tests that had been run on *Osterific sanctum* and results. Scientists wanting to discover what groundwork had been done on the plant could learn, studying NAPRALERT that *Osterific sanctum* had been tested as an antiaggressive in rats and found active. That it had shown antitumor activity in rats, too, but had not shown antifungal activity in an agar plate in a lab. Tested on guinea pigs as an antispasmotic, it had shown inconclusive results. In rabbits it had relaxed muscles. In female cats it had failed to stimulate the uterus. Tests went on for pages. *Osterific sanctum* had been tried as a skeletal muscle relaxant on frogs. It had been studied for antibacterial properties, anti-inflammatory properties, spermicidal effect.

"We're adding six thousand plants a year to the system," Farnsworth said.

With so many potential cures to be found, Farnsworth was angry at pharmaceutical companies he accused of foot-dragging.

"Until three years ago, no company had a regular program to look at plants," he said.

Now three programs had started. At Merck in New Jersey. And at British and German companies.

"Why did the companies wait so long?" I said.

"They're assholes," Farnsworth muttered.

Farnsworth said drug companies prefer to try to synthesize new drugs than to locate them in plants. "At first it seems synthesis is easier, in a way," he said. "It's a more controllable process. It's schedulable, at least on paper. The company's idea may be, 'Well, we know a certain molecule has a curing effect, but it's too toxic. And we know that with other toxic compounds, if we add this X-group, we can decrease the adverse effect. So if we add it to this compound, we'll get that effect here.' With plants, drug companies say there's too much variability in the wild. The second time you collect a plant it may not have the same chemical compounds as the first time. Bullshit! The people who make excuses are ignorant of the field of natural resources. They're chemists and marketing people and research people who haven't been in the lab for thirty years. They say things like, What would happen if you found a cancer cure that only grows in Uganda? And Uganda said, you can't take the plant out of here?" Farnsworth shook his head. "Pharmaceutical companies wanna control the material. And you can't always do that."

Authorities at Merck declined to say what plants they were testing when I called them.

"If the companies feel that way, why are they starting plant programs at all?" I asked.

Farnsworth smiled. "Because in the end synthesis isn't working," he said.

. . .

I visited Darlene in the hospital again. She had four chemo treatments to go. She was putting on weight, "looking like Buddha," she joked, but it was too early to tell if the improvement would be permanent. "Only one cancer cell has to stay alive for the whole thing to start again," Rausen had said.

Then we talked about Tennessee Williams's play, "The Glass Menagerie," which Darlene loved.

"A lot of people wouldn't even have noticed those little pieces of glass," she said, "but that girl thought they were beautiful."

Suddenly a boy's voice spoke up from behind me. "Nice wig you got on, Darlene."

"It is not a wig," Darlene said, looking over my shoulder.

The voice went on smooth. "It really covers up those bald spots."

Giggle. "Get outta here," Darlene said.

"You're gonna look like me soon," the boy said.

I turned but couldn't see his face. A baseball cap covered the top of it and a surgical mask the bottom. I saw a thin nose, a swath of dark skin, a blue vein down the bony edge of forehead. A plastic tube ran from his wrist to a bag of saline solution attached to his wheelchair.

The boy told Darlene there was a party in the recreation lounge. Then he rolled out of the room.

"Andrew is a pain," she said, rolling her eyes.

Andrew Von Bassion had osteogenic sarcoma, a bone cancer that attacks the marrow. His thighbone had been removed a year ago and replaced with a cadaver's. When he rolled up his pajamas, his right leg looked more like a woody vine than a human appendage, with no knee contours, just an unbroken smooth surface. Pale, enlarged track marks from stitching ran down the side.

After the surgery Andrew's cancer had gone into remission. Dr. Rausen said the disease had come back. No miracle drug like vinblastine existed for Andrew's form of cancer. Rausen was trying experimental therapy as a last resort.

"Andrew is probably going to die," Rausen told me.

Andrew and Darlene had become friends at the hospital. Andrew and his roommate Minotta had taken the frightened girl under their wing when she arrived. Andrew had shown Darlene where the extra linens were. He'd warned her about the hospital food. Told her interesting medical facts: "Your nails'll get harder during chemo. You can grow 'em long. They won't chip. And your mouth will get dry. Like the morphine I take? It dries my mouth."

If Darlene was in pain but too shy to call the nurses, Andrew would tell her to do it and then call himself when she refused.

They'd share food their mothers brought, rice and beans. And talk for hours about boyfriends, girlfriends, Rausen, families. "Dr. Rausen's lying about me being sick," Darlene would cry when she couldn't stand the chemo anymore. Andrew would say, "Come on, Darlene. You know that's not true."

Once, when they were both home, Andrew came to Parkhill Avenue and cooked lunch for Darlene. "He burned everything," she said. But they ate it anyway.

Now Andrew was getting worse and Darlene was getting better. She was up to 120 pounds. She wished she didn't have to get fat again.

"I'd give anything to be as fat as you," Andrew told her, joking but wistful. "You have a gorgeous figure."

·   ·   ·

In August, almost a year after Darlene had started having trouble waking up in the morning, Dr. Rausen told her the good news: She was in remission. The four-drug anticancer regimen, headed by vinblastine, had done its work. There would be no need for follow-up radiation. Darlene would have to come for checkups every couple of months for two years.

Thanks to her hard work and the sympathetic helpful staff of Murry Bergtraum High School, Darlene graduated with a B average. In September she was waking at 5:30 again, in the 109 bus again, winding her way down the crooked Staten Island streets, past stores and clapboard homes, toward New York Harbor.

Darlene boarded the mustard-colored Staten Island ferry, and it chugged off, past the Statue of Liberty, toward the twin towers of the World Trade Center, which marked the southern tip of Manhattan like a border checkpoint. On the other side she rode the subway to City Hall and walked four blocks west, merging into a stream of college students. As the Hudson River came into view, so did a spanking new complex of low, modern-looking buildings. Darlene moved up a concrete ramp and beneath words sandblasted into the entrance reading MANHATTAN BOROUGH COMMUNITY COLLEGE. Her plan to enroll at a four-year college had been set back by the illness, but she intended to transfer later on.

At the same time Andrew Von Bassion was back in the hospital. Surgeons had removed a football-sized tumor from the area near his spine. "Touch my back. It feels like jello," Andrew said.

Because of the operation, chemotherapy, and a leg he'd broken on Halloween when he fell through the rotting roof of an abandoned building, Andrew had trouble moving. Each time he shifted position in bed, which he did by hauling himself backward with his elbows, his mouth jerked into a line of pain before relaxing back to geniality.

We talked about a trip Andrew had taken to Portugal with his father, a retired Army sergeant. They'd visited a town where before a bullfight he'd joined a crowd of people dodging bulls running through the streets. Then he'd eaten the best shrimp he'd ever tasted at a waterfront restaurant a cabdriver knew. He asked lots of questions about Brazil, especially about a gold rush going on near Pôrto Velho. Andrew hoped he might be able to do more traveling soon, to go to Panama, he said. He had relatives in Panama. In Panama, he liked to sit on the dock by the sea and fish.

Darlene had told me, "Andrew said when you're sick you get a wish. Like if you want to go somewhere or meet a famous person, you get to have that because you have cancer. I never liked to think about the wish. It was for people who had to be in the hospital for a long time."

Andrew's hair was back, full, black, and wiry. But beneath the blue fuzzy blanket he looked thin.

Darlene visited him sometimes and brought food: pizza, burgers, anything but the hospital food. "He's like my brother," she said. "He's the only one who really knows how I feel."

They talked regularly on the telephone. He had a stuffed tiger he'd been given as a gift, and Darlene tried to coax him into giving it to her. "Forget it," he said. "He's my tiger."

"Darlene is a very positive person," Rausen had said. "Unusually caring. She tries to pull other people out of the doldrums. She's a maternal kind of hopeful person, and with Andrew she feels an innate obligation to help him get over his clinical depression."

"I know Andrew's going to die," Darlene told me as we strolled around her neighborhood one day. "But maybe they'll save him. Maybe they'll find one of those flowers . . ."

The Gold Rush

On the boat Rooster had to be careful. "So very, very careful." A miner fell into the river, and an alligator bit off his arm. A miner came down with malaria but was diagnosed wrong. He was buried near a rubber tree. A crew slept peacefully one night while their anchor cable snapped and their dredge swept into the rapids. No one ever saw them again. Two men got into a fight over a woman. Rooster watched as they shot each other.

"Sure there are dangers, but now for the payoff," Rooster said. "Gold."

It was near dusk on the Madeira River, a silty Amazon tributary longer than the Mississippi. From the air the gold rush had looked peaceful: bright splashes of blue or yellow, tarp roofing on the mining dredges. And green jungle on both shores. But frantic activity marked the river close-up.

Sixty thousand miners hunted for gold, washed down from the Andes in Peruvian and Bolivian tributaries. Rooster's double-deck *draga,* or dredge, was one of six thousand boats anchored between rapids, in calmer but still swiftly moving stretches of river. *Dragas* were primitive factories, wooden shacks on steel pontoons, rafts cluttered with pumps and sluice boxes, homes for miners, drilling platforms for pipes.

Minerals are a big reason Brazil wants to develop the Amazon. Amazonas, the state to Rondônia's north, has natural gas. Roraima and Mato Grosso have gold rushes of their own. Pará, easternmost Amazon state, houses the most impressive find. Back in the 1960s pilots flying over the Carajas Mountains noticed their compasses going crazy. A Brazilian geologist landed a helicopter there and found a mountain of iron ore estimated at 18 billion metric tons, enough ore to supply the world's needs for over two hundred years. Other geologists located gold, manganese, copper, bauxite, and tungsten nearby.

"Cities of boats, of noise and light," Rooster said now. Off the port side I saw the floating whorehouse, powder blue and sagging in the middle, with old LPs hung for decoration on the walls. And floating restaurants, cabarets, gas stations. *Dragas* pushed slowly against the current, nosing like dinosaurs near shore, dropping suction pipes sixty feet to the bottom of the river. *Dragas* anchored in midstream, lashed together for safety, or lay half-smashed on rocks after being swept through rapids a hundred yards upstream.

"Every day comes the buildup, the expectation," Rooster said. "Every day we get gold."

Prospectors and independent operators in the Amazon produce seventy tons of gold a year, five times the output of Brazil's industrial mines. Since the bulk of Rondônia's take is smuggled to Bolivia or Uruguay, officials say no one knows for sure how much gold is brought up by the independent miners on the Madeira, but estimates run between six and ten tons a year. The officials hope gold will help develop Rondônia, lure settlers and industries to the frontier. But conservationists fear it will mean destruction of some of the most diverse rain forest on earth, and charge miners will just move away when the gold is gone.

Garimpo has no corresponding word in English. It means more than just mining camp. It means the whole area where independents operate, the whole state of mind; the thousands of men crawling over the river or earth, the boom or bust tales, the intoxicating anarchy of living on the edge.

And of the sixty thousand men at the Madeira *garimpos*, Rooster was one of the lucky ones. He worked on an automated boat. More at risk were divers who carried vacuum pipes to the bottom by hand and stood there for hours in the dark, breathing through thin rubber hoses, dying in claim fights when the hoses were cut. The poorest miners stayed on shore, panning for gold in streams that fed the river.

I had come to the *garimpo* with warnings fresh in my mind.

"Gold miners are like AIDS," a curator at the Museo Goeldi in Belém had told me. "When they leave an area it's destroyed. Indians dead or on the run. Nothing alive on land or in the water. You can't have a little AIDS. You either have it or you don't."

Miners invaded Indian land in Rondônia, Roraima, Mato Grosso, and Pará states. They polluted Amazon rivers with mercury. They attacked and burned automated machinery designed to do their jobs. They used *dragas* to launder cocaine money.

"In the Amazon," Brazilian Consul General Carlos Augusto Santos Neves had said in New York, "the government has lost control."

And in Brasília I'd met Foreign Ministry Secretary General Paulo Flecha Tarso de Lima, a deep-voiced man whose plush office seemed as far away from the *garimpo* as Trump Tower in New York. We sat on leather couches near an antique Portuguese tapestry of Indians in a jungle. A servant poured cups of hot, sweet coffee into china cups.

"The government has been accused of being lenient with miners," de Lima lamented, "but the miners are desperate and have nothing to lose. There are one million gold diggers in this country. They challenge all laws. They resist police. We've developed ourselves into an important gold producer in an unproductive way," he said, referring to estimates that for every ton of gold legally brought out of the Amazon, four tons are smuggled out. "If politics had allowed, we could replace the men with machinery," he said, sipping slowly, "but these people vote."

But Rooster didn't resemble the demons of these stories. He was a calm, pleasant man, slow moving with an exacting patience that suited him for work on the *draga,* where a mistake can mean death. Rooster's lifelong nickname had probably come from his physical appearance. From the short, stocky body and wide chest. The crown of dirty-blond hair that fell from the center of his forehead to the tips of his shoulders. Jagged scars on his ankles marked where he'd suffered mishaps on the *draga,* and the nail of his big toe was falling off after a bucket fell on it.

"What I want is a farm," he said. "A little farm where I can have a quiet life. Three more years," Rooster promised, "and I'll quit."

The whole boat vibrated from operation twenty-four hours a

day. Gold extraction was a straightforward business. The pipes brought silt up from the bottom. The silt roared down floor-to-ceiling wooden ramps called sluice boxes, aft in the boat. The boxes were covered with thick synthetic carpet that trapped heavy gold particles and allowed lighter water to run back to the river. Every twenty-four hours the crew rolled up the carpet, shook the collected sand and gold into steel buckets, and Rooster separated out the find.

"Two *dragas* can be next to each other," he said as the dredge jerked from the drill smacking into rock below. "One gets two kilos (worth $24,000 on the black market) in a day, the other nothing. One day *we* got two kilos. The next day . . ." Rooster shrugged to indicate fate.

Shirtless from the heat, Rooster disappeared into a supply closet and brought out on deck a jar of silvery mercury. He poured the mercury into the silt-filled buckets as diesel smoke blew into his face. "The mercury fuses with the gold and keeps it in the bucket," he said. Shoulders jerking like a pneumatic drill operator's, he used a long-handled electric mixer to churn the mercury, silt, and gold. The sense of movement never stopped. The deck rocked as the pump operator changed the direction of the drill. The river rushed past below between gaps in the plank deck. The anchor cable quivered from the pressure of the current. Swift steel outboards, "flying boats," brought crewmen to other *dragas*.

Rooster inserted a garden hose into each bucket. The water washed excess sand onto the deck and back to the river. Soon all that remained of twenty-four hours of operation was a drinking glass half-filled with mercury and, Rooster claimed, gold. The whole thing looked like mercury to me.

"What will you do with the money you earn?" I asked.

"Save it, save it."

Crewmen had said they didn't get excited when gold was tallied, but they drifted over or hung from wooden railings outside sleeping cubicles upstairs or watched from hammocks strung over the sluice boxes.

There was José, an ex-bus driver from Rio Grande do Sul, a tall, bearded man who dreamed of buying houses and land. Luiz, young and thin, who got malaria a lot and just wanted to have something, anything, because "like me, he comes from nothing," Rooster said. Marcilio, from the drought-stricken northeast of Brazil, had come to the *garimpo* because his girlfriend mocked his poverty. "I'll go back and make her proud," he said. But he spent all his gold on drinking and women.

"I never had a farm, but on a farm, well, even a little farm," Rooster said, "there's rest. A quiet, easy life."

He didn't notice the butterfly that landed on his shoulder as he poured the mercury-gold onto a T-shirt. He squeezed the T-shirt until mercury ran through his fingers into a pan. When he opened the shirt a ball slightly larger than a marble lay inside, grainy hard and putty-colored. It still didn't look like gold.

But Rooster grinned with a practiced eye. "It's going to be good."

For the final step he brought out a spindly-looking machine, just a steel compartment mounted on a tripod with a spigot coming out the top.

"I light a fire under the compartment," Rooster said, sealing the ball inside. "The mercury evaporates into the spigot as steam and drops back into a pan. The gold remains inside the compartment."

Twenty minutes later Rooster shut off the fire. When he lifted the lid, I caught my breath. There was gold inside, an irregular chunk barely larger than a silver dollar, thick as a potato pancake, with a pitted surface. Rooster put it on my palm. It was heavy. A beam of sunlight sliced between the sluice boxes and played on the surface. I realized, feeling the surprising coolness of the precious metal against my skin, that I had stopped noticing the din some time ago.

Everyone was smiling. Rooster brought the gold upstairs to his room, a space the size of a shipping crate that he shared with his wife, Elizabe, the cook on the *draga*. He weighed the take and recorded each man's share in a ledger: six percent for operators, ten percent for Rooster, the manager. He locked the gold in a safe upstairs. "The owner will come tomorrow and collect it and ship it to São Paulo," he said. It was too tempting to robbers to let gold sit on a *draga*.

"For gold," Rooster said, shoving the scale against the wall beneath a soccer poster, "I postponed my life."

．　　．　　．

One miner paid six thousand cruzados, over five years' salary for a rubber tapper family, for four hours with a prostitute. Another took over a whole hotel, just kicked out the other guests, and lived there until his money ran out. A miner tied cash behind him with a string, and everywhere he went, the money trailed behind. When people asked him why, he said, "All my life I chased after money. Now let it follow me."

Flush with cash, miners flew to Manaus, Brazil's duty-free city in the jungle, and came back with stereos, televisions, watches, scotch. Miners turned the cemetery and bus station into drug supermarkets, Lieutenant Fabio Angel of the police told me. We were driving his beat on a Saturday night. "Crime goes up when the river goes down," Lieutenant Angel said. "The miners aren't working."

Gold washed down the Madeira and changed every aspect of life in Pôrto Velho. At the bookstore I watched an anthropology professor buy textbooks and pay with gold flakes she took out of a bag. At City Hall I eyed the gold necklace the mayor wore as he argued with aides over installing traffic bumps in new neighborhoods populated by miners' families. After an interview with the president of the state Association of Industries, during which he delivered the usual speech on the need for "new investment in Rondônia," he pulled a plastic bag from his desk filled with gold bars the size of Milky Ways. "From my *draga*," he bragged.

Afterward I took a walk down Seventh of September Street, the main commercial thoroughfare in Pôrto Velho. Every other shop seemed to advertise: WE BUY GOLD. Hawkers stood in doorways crying out the day's price for a gram: "Thirty-four cruzados!" A Ford pickup pulled over and unloaded two women miners, tough-looking in skin-tight jeans and black shag haircuts. They refused to sell their gold to the owner of one shop after he weighed it with lead weights and matches. They thought he'd doctored the scale. They grudgingly accepted an offer from another man, but before he handed over cash, he melted down their nuggets with a blowtorch to make sure *they* weren't cheating *him*. Nobody took their eyes off the flakes for even a fraction of a second. Men had been killed for stealing gold dust under fingernails.

Amid the anarchy came feeble attempts at order. At the Miners Union I met Secretary Nillson Ferraira, a hardworking ex-diver who carried a gun when he went out of town. Nillson had started work at the *garimpo* teaching new divers about the dangers of narcolepsy, and pilots about deaths caused by flying out with patients with too much oxygen in their blood. Nillson was always running out to a *garimpo* on emergencics. Miners had illegally roped off an area to outsiders near the river, and police wanted Nillson to talk him out of it before there was a fight. Miners were opening a new *garimpo,* and Nillson was heading out for the all-day beer party.

"We have about twelve thousand members along the Madeira," Nillson said. "They get a fraction of health care paid for, a little legal help if they're in trouble. They get a union card they can show *draga* owners to show they're in the union. But the truth is, we don't really know anything about the men we give the cards to. One man got a card on Friday, and on Monday he was killed robbing a bank in Cuiabá."

I also visited the Miner's Cooperative, another organization, which was funded, under a law being challenged in court, by mandatory donations from mine owners. The Cooperative was supposed to provide aid for the men too, but I felt like I'd walked into the union scene from *On the Waterfront.* President João Wanzeler doodled while we talked beneath a photo of himself in a red shirt and black tie. The paperweights on his desk were giant copper bullets. There was a willowy blond in the office who had won the "Miss Nugget" competition at the Festival of Gold during the rainy season. "I won half a kilo of gold and a job here," Miss Nugget said.

"What is the job?" I said.

"What *is* the job?" Miss Nugget asked Wanzeler, while Cooperative officers chuckled and nudged each other on a couch.

"Public relations," Wanzeler said. Miss Nugget smiled. "Public relations."

Wanzeler asked me how he might be able to "raise money to help the miners" in the United States, but asked me to keep the request secret from politicians or environmentalists in Rondônia. "They'd try to get some of it." Then a vice president of the Cooperative drove me to a *garimpo* a hundred miles from town, down BR-364. On the way he chain-smoked cigarettes and rolled his full-length trousers up beyond his knees, against the heat. He said he had owned *dragas* himself once, in the South, but had been forced to leave.

"How come?" I said.

"Oh," he said, waving the smoldering butt to indicate unimportance, "a little problem."

"What little problem?" I said ten minutes later.

"I got in a fight with someone. Actually, I killed him."

"What was the fight over?"

The vice president laughed. "Pussy."

"And the police were after you?"

"They weren't really *after* me," he said. "I was an owner and he was just a worker, so they believed me. But they were getting suspicious."

The conversation lagged as we reached the *garimpo* and spotted a corpse lying on the ground, surrounded by lit candles. "Hey," the vice president called to people nearby. "What happened to him?"

"Nothing," they said, scattering fast. "He just ate lunch and died."

The incident reminded me of Nillson Ferraira's answer when I'd asked him if there were any floating churches on the river. Nillson had thought the question pretty funny.

"Miners remember God when they get a bullet," Nillson had said.

.   .   .

Rubens Machado Lemes, Rooster's real name, grew up in the southern state of Rio Grande do Sul. With only a primary school education, he had trouble finding work but finally got a job driving a city bus. He met Elizabe at a snack bar where she worked, and they married and planned a family.

But Rubens hated the bus. "I hated the uniform, the white shirt, black shoes, blue pants. Six days a week, twelve hours a day. Always the same route. From the bus station to the police station.

From the police station to the church, then back to the bus station. With the passengers yelling, 'Hurry up!' "

For seventy-two hours a week of labor, Rubens received less than $100 a month. "I got more and more exhausted. I quit two or three times, but they asked me to come back. There was no other work."

"One time two blind men got on the bus," he said. "One wanted to get off at the bus station, the other at the church. I mixed them up."

Then one day Rubens met a man with a suitcase at the bus station. "I'm going to Rondônia," the man said. "I'll get rich, come back, and buy houses and snack bars." Rubens wished the man well and forgot about the conversation until three years later when he saw the man again. He *had* gotten rich.

"I talked with other drivers, and we decided to go," Rubens said. "I told Elizabe, let's delay having a family a few months. I knew I would have rough hands at the *garimpo,* but I knew I would get gold."

Rubens, José, and João rode a bus over a thousand miles to Rondônia. But lots of other men had the same idea, and they crowded into camps along the Madeira. Rubens spent a month hitching rides on the flying boats, calling to passing *dragas,* asking for work. At night the friends strung hammocks from trees. Their big break finally came when a *draga* broke, and the owner needed someone who could fix engines. "I knew how, from the bus," Rubens said. He worked three more weeks without pay, just for food and lodging. But when the *draga* was launched, he became an operator at six percent. "The first day I made more than I did in a month driving the bus."

Dragas ran twenty-four hours a day, seven days a week. "You don't know if it's Sunday or Monday," Rubens said, uncomplaining. "One day a month I'd go to town, walk around, phone Elizabe, but the rest of the time it was three hours on, three hours off. Sometimes we'd buy whiskey from Bolivia and drink it on the boat. Play music on the cassette, lambada or country-western. Read *Playboy.* You could go crazy on that boat without a woman."

After six months Elizabe asked to join him. "I told her, men will offer you money a hundred times a day to sleep with them. But I was glad she came."

Time seemed to spread out on the *draga* or compress itself into brief spasms of emergency activity. Rubens relaxed in a hammock, off work as we talked. A minute later he was charging between the sluice boxes with a wrench, trying to untangle the flying boat from a cable threatening to turn it over. He went back to the hammock. But then one of the logs that regularly shoot down the river (*Madeira* means wood) smacked into the *draga* and floated brush piled up behind it, endangering the mooring from the extra weight. Rubens wedged himself through a trapdoor on deck, legs submerged in the river, kicking at the mass to free it.

"A few months ago the anchor cable broke. We went downriver, smashing into other *dragas*. I tied a rope to myself and swam ashore. We were scared," Rubens said.

Much of the danger could come from other miners. There was a dredge near Rubens's where the crew stole gold from the owner. And there was a new man on board who was paid only three percent, not six like the rest. One day the owner came to collect his gold, and the new man asked for six percent. The owner refused. The new man said, "But I'm the only one here who's not stealing from you." A crewman heard this, got a gun from a sack, and went up to the new man. "What did you say?" he said. The new man said, "You heard me. You're all stea—" The other man shot him in the head. He fell on deck, spurting blood, still trying to talk. The gunman told the owner, "This is none of your business." The body lay on deck awhile, then it was gone. The *draga* pulled up anchor and moved away. No one told the police.

"At the *garimpo*, you have to be friends with everyone," Rubens said.

But his reward was in the ledger he kept. He could open the thick book and count his share mounting up. In the neat, orderly column, under Rubens's name, twos grew into threes, tens into twenties. The book recorded loans to miners, who paid them back out of their cut. Rubens's odometer for wealth. Anytime he wanted, he could ask the owner for his gold, and he would be paid in bullion, not cash. It made no difference whether the price of gold had gone up or down in the interim. Rubens would get the exact amount he'd recorded in the book.

"I've got almost four kilos saved," he said. A kilo was worth almost $13,000.

"How much does a little farm cost anyway?" I asked.

It was morning on the river, a bright blue day. The *draga* had been running without emergency for the last six hours. José swished a pan back and forth in the sluice box to get an idea of the richness of the silt. Elizabe scrubbed battered tin pots in the open-air galley until they gleamed. Marcilio stared at the blowup poster on the wall of Roberta Close, the famous Brazilian TV personality and transsexual. They'd bought the poster because it was the only sexy art for sale that day in Pôrto Velho. Beggars can't be choosers.

Rubens said he didn't know exactly how much a little farm cost, but I had a feeling he knew he could get it for less than $52,000.

"In five years I'll quit and go home. I want to buy a *draga* first," Rubens said.

"Five years?" I said. "Last time you said three."

When Rubens smiled, the lower half of his face widened and his teeth gleamed. "I had nothing before," he said. "Here, every day I receive money."

.　　.　　.

Rondônia is the third largest gold supplier in Brazil and the leading supplier of tin. Almost sixty percent of the state's income comes from mining. Bom Futura, a huge tin *garimpo* lying five hours east of Pôrto Velho, ships over $200 million worth of the metal around the world annually. Brascan, a Canadian company, operates a mechanized tin mine nearby.

"There are enough minerals in the Amazon to pay off Brazil's foreign debt and still erase the entire United States deficit, which is over a trillion dollars," geologist Orestes Schneider dos Santos claimed in *Veja* magazine.

No country on earth has made a policy of leaving their mineral wealth in the ground, and Brazil isn't any different. Minerals in the ground are worthless, Minister of the Interior João Alves Filho told the Brazilian congress in a fiery speech in 1989. Get them out fast! Filho warned that valuable metals could even become obsolete if they weren't exploited quickly. Japanese car manufacturers, he said, would soon be making engines out of ceramics, lessening the need for steel on the world market.

Proponents of mineral development in the Amazon claim that mining destroys less jungle than other commercial activities. "To generate a million dollars of profit in a year, you have to destroy only .017 square kilometers, as opposed to 100 square kilometers for cattle," reported *Veja*.

But the argument is slightly inaccurate in the sense that mining brings new settlers to a region. Rubens's *garimpo* was small, gone in the tick of a clock as I passed overhead in a jet, but many miners there had brought their families to Rondônia. They needed housing in town, electricity, food, health care. And each road built to a mine or *garimpo* soon carries squatters into the jungle, who burn forest for farms or pasture.

Even the best-planned projects can go awry. After the initial discovery of iron ore at Carajás, the Brazilian government announced a development scheme that would encompass an area exceeding Texas and Oklahoma in size. Almost $70 billion was to be raised in Brazil and from banks in the United States, Europe, and Japan to fund mines, dams, roads, and ranches. The core of the project would be the mine and a 550-mile-long rail line to the port city of São Luís. A Brazilian mining company, Companhia Vale do Rio Doce (CVRD), won the concession and finished the facilities with scrupulous attention to the environment. CVRD replanted deforested areas. It controlled wood extraction and blocked squatters and independent miners from invading. Even diehard conservationists had nothing bad to say about CVRD.

But CVRD's core area was only six percent of the project. Outside the concession, things went out of control. Invaders poured down the new roads. The government funded cattle ranches, agribusinesses, and colonies that failed because the land was poor for farming. Most alarming, it approved a series of pig iron plants to process ore, plants that would use the rain forest as fuel.

The plants would need an estimated 1.5 million metric tons of charcoal annually to keep running, Brazilian government agencies reported. That charcoal would come from trees.

The well-protected CVRD project could become "a green island surrounded by semidesert," wrote journalist Roger Stone. Maritta Koch-Weser of the World Bank described a "stunning panorama of deforestation" around the well-managed island. And ecologist Philip Fearnside, who works for the National Institute for Research in the Amazon (INPA) likened the pig iron plants to cuckoo eggs in a nest.

"When a cuckoo lays an egg in another bird's nest, the unfortunate host soon finds itself diverting all its efforts to providing food for the enormous cuckoo chick," Fearnside wrote. "In the same way, the forests and the entire economy around the pig iron plants will be irresistibly drawn into feeding the plants with charcoal, regardless of the local population's own interests."

"Economic viability exists in the short term, using the natural forest," said one official of CVRD. "International banks who financed Carajas may be worried about their image, and so are we. But while there's a market for timber, pig iron, or meat from cattle ranches in the Amazon, there's no solution. Demand is encouraging devastation."

"People think the Amazon will always take care of itself," Fearnside told me in his Manaus office. "But it won't."

Other INPA researchers were looking into effects of mineral exploitation in the Amazon. One of them, Dr. Bruce Forsberg, had just returned from measuring mercury pollution near the Madeira. Forsberg, native of Washington State, sipped herb tea from a clay cup and sat in a special backless chair designed to alleviate back strain. The thirty-eight-year-old scientist explained that the bulk of the pollution occurs during the final state of gold separation when fused gold and mercury is burned. "Most *dragas* don't have the machine to save mercury," he said. "The miners burn the mix in a pan. The mercury rises into the atmosphere as steam and comes back to earth when it rains. Half the fish we examined in the Pôrto Velho market were contaminated."

In the rain forest, probably the wettest environment on earth, water seems the most fundamental element, and an act poisoning it assaults the basic building block of life. You have only to fly through an Amazon rainstorm to see incredible varieties of simultaneous condensation. Huge anvil-shaped thunderheads, cumulus and cirrus clouds, all seething in a soup of mist that turns the earth hazy and indistinct. The humid air seems more liquid than gas. Water pours from you as sweat when you step outside in the jungle. It comprises the bulk of the insects you squash. It can even account for most noise in the forest. The sound of rain often lasts for hours after a storm has ended. The drops take that long to work their way down the canopy. "In the Amazon," said a curator at the Museo Goeldi, "water is the name of life."

Forsberg poured more tea. To figure how much mercury gets dumped in Amazon rivers, he said, take the amount of gold recovered, then multiply by 1.32 kilos of mercury for each kilo of gold. If eleven tons of gold had come from the Madeira in 1988, as Nillson Ferreira said, that meant as much as fifteen tons of mercury had gone back into the ecosystem.

"Mercury poisoning is a progressive disorder," Forsberg said. "Some people can withstand a lot. Others go wacko. First you lose feeling in the ends of your toes and fingertips. Then you get the shakes. Lose motor coordination. Have problems hearing and seeing. Mothers with no visible defects can give birth to deformed fetuses. In extreme cases, you get spasms and die.

"If a person eats two hundred grams of fish a day, not a lot for a poor person in the Amazon, they're susceptible," he said.

Although Forsberg reported seeing very few of the mercury removal machines on the *dragas,* my own experience was different. Every boat I boarded had a machine, and managers cited different reasons why. "I don't want to breathe the stuff," said one. "I care about the environment," said another. Rubens, who saw most things in terms of economics, was the most pragmatic. "It's cheaper to use the machine. Mercury costs money, and the machine saves it."

Draga owners, mining union officials, and politicians were sensitive enough to the mercury issue to pay at least lip service to environmental concerns. State Environmental Secretary Chico Araujo showed me pamphlets his office distributed to miners, explaining how the machines work. The head of industrial development for the state displayed a machine in his office. Governor Jerônimo Santana said, "Most *dragas* use the machine now."

Their concern seemed genuine until I met the whistle-blower. He was a short, fat, shy-looking former clerk in the environmental secretary's office, and we talked on the street in a downtown area of the city occupied by barrack-style state government offices. The whistle-blower clutched a new attaché case. I had a feeling something interesting was inside.

"When I worked for the office of the secretary of environment, we commissioned a report on mercury poisoning in the Madeira. The conclusions were pretty bad, but nothing was done with it. It was put in a drawer."

"I wish I could see the report," I said.

The man brightened. "Oh, you can see it," he said, unsnapping the case. The report was inside. Brazilian scientists conducting the study had concluded that in some places mercury levels in the Madeira exceeded safe standards. For instance, the World Health Organization had estimated that in humans mercury poisoning begins with a concentration of six milligrams of mercury in a gram of hair. Miners at the *garimpo* had been found with twenty-six milligrams in each gram.

Some fish in the river contained mercury levels four times higher than the maximum permitted by Brazilian law for safe consumption, the report said.

"Mercury pollution in the air of the city is increasing," the report said, "especially near the gold shops. Emergency action is required."

"Why was this suppressed?" I asked. A slow smile spread over the whistle-blower's face. He rubbed thumb, index, and middle finger together and shoved them in his hip pocket to make his accusation.

"What happened to you when you pushed to have the report released?" I asked.

The man blushed. "I was transferred to another agency. But I'm going to send the report to Brasília, to IBAMA [the Brazilian Institute for Forest Development]. Maybe they'll do something about it."

All around us, government employees who didn't make waves strolled in and out of buildings holding reports or chatting with each other, looking relaxed and contented. I asked the whistle-blower why he bothered. "You have another job now. Why pursue the issue?"

The man looked surprised. "This is our water," he said. "I have a family. We drink it. We bathe in it. What do we do if our water is poisoned?"

. . .

Every job comes with little side expenses that sap profits, and in Rubens's case the problem was malaria. "I've had it five times," he said. "I spend eight percent of my income curing it."

We were in town nursing Fantas because Rubens had malaria again and couldn't drink alcohol while he was being treated. The disease turned his eyes red and his movements lethargic. Zero Hour, the bar in which we sat, was frequented by miners from the Setauma Hotel across the street. The owner was a *garimpo* success story. Paulo Sacks had parlayed his fortune into the hotel, a *draga* shipyard, and floating cabarets and restaurants. Photographs of his empire hung in the lobby, along with a poster of Marilyn Monroe.

"Everyone wants to be like Paulo and own *dragas*," Rubens said.

Elizabe was in Pôrto Velho, too, in a private hospital. She had *falciparum* malaria, which had been misdiagnosed as *vivax* strain. She could barely move and lay in bed with tubes running into her arms. The treatment was quinine and antibiotics.

"She says she wants to go home," Rubens said. "But I think she'll change her mind when she's better. I did. The first time I got malaria was the worst. I thought I was going to die. The pain in my stomach was awful. I had the shakes. I couldn't eat. If I had had money, I would have gone home, but I was broke. I'd been at the *garimpo* only a month. A friend took care of me in a hotel."

Malaria is rampant in the Amazon, and most miners get it. Health officials watched the number of reported cases grow from eighty-nine thousand in 1975 to seven hundred thousand in just the first six months of 1989. Fifteen hundred people a year are killed by the more severe strains. Malarial mosquitos normally live at treetop level and feed on monkeys, but knock down trees and the mosquitos move to the ground. I met miners and colonists who had caught malaria as many as twenty-six times.

In the bar Rubens made a gesture common to malaria sufferers—an odd, quick, almost involuntary clenching of fists, as if to say, "I beat it." Two nights later I understood the gesture better. I was lying in bed at 2 A.M. when I realized the night was chilly. Amazon nights were usually hot, but I had an extra blanket in the room, and I covered myself. The chill didn't go away. It occurred to me that the cold might have nothing to do with the temperature outside.

Suddenly my body went crazy. I was freezing, convulsing, and I started to black out. I made it to the bathroom, but my vision was blurred and my hands were yellow and covered with enormous goosebumps. I cursed out loud in an effort to stay conscious. I'm stronger than you, I thought. I realized I was making Rubens's gesture, clenching and unclenching my fists.

I spent the rest of the night freezing and burning. In the morning I went for a malaria test. It was negative, but I began taking antibiotics. Two days later I was better. A doctor had no idea what had happened to me. "Maybe it was food poisoning. Maybe it was a single attack of malaria since the preventative medicine you were taking was new. Maybe it was something that doesn't have a name yet. There's plenty of that around here."

Rubens was well enough to return to the *garimpo*. Elizabe was still hospitalized, but he planned to come back to see her in a few days. He paid the hotel bill in gold and found a ride to the Madeira. He squeezed into the backseat of a friend's new fire-engine-red Ford Escort.

With rock music blaring from the stereo, they headed west on BR-364 toward the gold. The car whipped around the traffic circle marking the edge of town, shot past the line of grimy miners hitching to the river or waiting for special "*garimpo* taxis." They nearly sideswiped a Mercedes flatbed weighed down with pontoons. Time seemed to compress, fold in on itself, with the music exploding in the car. They passed the university and the private housing for engineers on the Samuel Dam. The miners whooped and pounded on the dashboard. They spilled mercury into my palm and laughed as it rolled down my lifeline toward my wrist. Vehicles moving at average speed seemed impossibly slow, already receding in the rearview mirror. The highway billboards, GARIMPO TOOLS or POWER SAWS, disappeared. The car rocked over fresh holes in the pavement, bounced across railroad bridges, bypassed overpasses being constructed, cattle ranches, small shacks and farms. Dusty cars filled with more miners came from the other direction, barreling toward town.

Rubens seemed calmer heading for the *garimpo*, but the frantic sense around him grew as the Escort arrived and parked in a mud field where paid guards watched cars. We couldn't see the actual river yet, just the channel where flying boats churned past and miners hammered on *dragas*, losing money for every second they were being repaired. Sparks flew from welders' torches. A little girl carried a section of tin roofing on the deck of a docked family *draga*. Dogs snarled over chicken bones on a mud embankment practically paved over with discarded bottle caps and trash.

"There are one million gold miners in the Amazon," Foreign Ministry Secretary General Paulo Flecha Tarso de Lima had said, "and they vote." Knee-jerk gold rushes and land rushes and cattle rushes had already deforested twenty percent of the state.

Any grand plan to build facilities in the Amazon would have to take these hundreds of thousands of independent operators into account, or it would fail. Not only miners but colonists and farmers, all the poor people who rushed in when new areas opened up. Any neat projects on paper describing mining ventures or dams or roads or colonies would backfire into a joke if the Rubenses of the Amazon weren't taken into account. Most miners pouring into the region didn't plan to stay there, didn't have a stake in preserving the region. They wanted to get their money and go home. The lines of authority between formal government and the occupiers of the Amazon are not clearly defined enough for investors, meaning foreign funding banks, to assume the government controls the region.

The truth hit me. Rubens *liked* the psychotic jolting back and forth, lethargy to emergency, quiet to crisis.

Rubens looked happy.

In a flying boat spurting geysers of water from improperly welded repairs, Rubens watched the Jairo y Marcos *dredge* grow closer. It was anchored near rapids, and diesel smoke wafted into his face as he climbed on board. He scanned the *draga* for jobs to do. The plank walkway on the port side needed shoring up. The pipe bringing silt from the bottom was getting rusty and ought to be replaced.

"I'll stay at the *garimpo* until I'm forty," Rubens said, "then I want a farm, a little farm."

I looked at him. He was home. "First you said you'd quit in three years, then five, now seven," I said. "Do you really want to go live on a little farm?"

Rubens looked out at the city of boats on the river. He smiled.

"Lots of people never leave," he said.

The Vigilante, the Physicist, the Mets, and the Rain Forest

As miners, squatters, ranchers, and developers knock down rain forests, the greenhouse effect worsens and climate changes as far away as New York. There's nothing new about the greenhouse effect. In its original form it has existed on earth for millions of years. It's caused by carbon dioxide in the atmosphere and a few other gases like methane, and chlorofluorocarbons. CO_2 is only one-hundredth of one percent in the atmosphere, but it forms a blanket around the Earth, letting sunlight in, keeping heat from drifting back to space.

Without the greenhouse effect, scientists say, Earth would be twenty degrees colder. Covered with ice.

But starting with the industrial revolution 150 years ago, and recently as whole-scale rain forest burning began, humans have released so much carbon into the atmosphere that they have changed the balance of gases above the earth. The greenhouse blanket has thickened, and according to climatologists, temperatures have begun to rise.

In 1988, James Hansen, the director of the Goddard Research Institute of NASA (National Aeronautics and Space Administration), shocked the Senate by testifying that the greenhouse effect was here. Computer simulations indicated it raised the probability of summer heat waves and wildly swinging weather. The Earth was warmer in 1988 than at any time in the history of atmospheric measurement. The five warmest years on record occurred during the late 1980s. But the heat would keep rising in 1990 and 1991.

Hansen's team predicted that CO_2 in the atmosphere could easily double within fifty years, raising Earth's average temperature between one and five degrees. If that seemed like a little, Hansen said, during the last ice age average temperatures were only four degrees colder. "And ice covered New York."

"Global climate change will have significant implications for when, where, and how we farm, for the availability of water to drink and run our factories, for how we live in our cities, for the wetlands that spawn our fish, for the beaches we use for recreation, and for all levels of government and industry," said a report on the expected climate change from the Environmental Protection Agency.

"And remember," said Dr. George Woodwell, director of the Woods Hole Research Center in Massachusetts, "after CO_2 doubles, it doesn't stop. It keeps going."

"We're building a time bomb without knowing its destructive potential," James Hansen said.

.   .   .

"Hot, hot, it's so hot," the old woman moaned. Paramedic Danny Blum told her not to worry, she'd be in the hospital soon. We were in a cramped East Side walk-up on an August afternoon. Outside the temperature was 90 degrees, but inside at least 105. "Get ready for a four-day heat wave," Deborah Norville had announced on the "Today Show" that morning, against a weather map filled with smiling suns.

To get an idea what New York might be like if James Hansen's predictions were correct, I was spending time with paramedics, police, the New York Mets, commuters, lifeguards, and energy workers at Con Edison on ninety-degree days. The number of days like that would skyrocket if Hansen was right.

Now Blum prepared the IV needle. His partner Diane Sentra unfolded the wheelchair. The eighty-eight-year-old cardiac patient sat gasping in a lemon-colored nightgown, blinking through bottle-thick glasses at a peeling wall eight feet off. Her chain-smoking daughter talked nonstop while the emergency crew worked.

"She can't breathe! All night she doesn't sleep!"

"Do you know where we are?" Blum asked the patient gently. "Yes."

"Where?"

"Here."

Blum smiled. He was a mild-looking, bespectacled twenty-six-year-old whose wit kept the mood up during his double shift today, trip after trip to stifling old people's residences too small to deserve the name apartments.

"Twenty-five percent of the cases coming in today are probably heat-related," Dr. Robert Newborn had told me at Blum's home base emergency room, New York Hospital, Cornell Medical Center, on 65th Street. The acute treatment room had been filled with asthma patients, cardiac patients, patients who "felt funny" jogging. And Newborn's boss, emergency room chief Dr. Alexander Kuehl, had said, "You tell me the temperature, I'll tell you how many ambulance runs the city will have. On an eighty-degree day, two thousand. On a hundred-degree day, three thousand."

Kuehl ought to know. He'd run New York's Emergency Services between 1981 and 1989.

Blum and Sentra carried the patient in the wheelchair three flights down. They loaded her into the ambulance double-parked in front of a Jaguar repair shop and hit the siren, but on the side streets traffic wasn't moving. Buildings far away looked hazy, even though the weather bureau had called the day "clear."

"On hot days my heart goes out to old people," Danny Blum said.

"If the number of ninety-degree days ever doubled, it would be disastrous for us," hospital chief of paramedics John Delaney had told me in the paramedic office off the main emergency room, a cramped, hectic walk-up with radio dispatchers in an alcove, near posters saying JOIN THE NEW ACTION ARMY. SEE BEAUTIFUL DOWNTOWN BAGHDAD.

"You'd have more fires," Delaney said. "Lots of old buildings can't handle extra electricity. Air conditioning works for a day or two, then there's a problem. Older people tend not to eat in the heat. In longer heat waves they collapse in their apartments. Plus motors are burning out in elevators, people have to walk up stairs."

"We walk upstairs with seventy-five pounds of equipment," Blum joked, "and we need the oxygen on a hot day, not them."

When we arrived at the hospital, nurses wheeled the old woman into the emergency room. Fifteen minutes later the paramedics reached the next patient, a seventy-five-year-old saxophone player in a basement studio on the West Side. The man sat limply on a bed against the wall, shirt unbuttoned, chest heaving, flecks of spittle collected on the slack corner of his mouth. Around him the room was cluttered with piles of sheet music, old reviews, glasses, records. And in the center of it, like an energy source, a gleaming, butter-gold saxophone on a stand.

Blum prepared the IV needle. Diane unfolded the chair. Outside on the steamy streets, a rainstorm began.

"Hot," muttered the old man, a gleam of sweat on his face.

.   .   .

James Hansen had risked his reputation as a careful scientist when he appeared before the Senate subcommittee. He'd defied government orders to keep quiet about his findings. His work and his delivery itself, a mix of plain speech and mathematical analysis, had moved the climate issue to the world's front pages.

In person, Hansen's collegiate aspect was enhanced by an argyle vest sweater, matching socks, and Top-Siders. His high forehead and thinning straw-colored hair gave him an intent, vulnerable look. We were at the Goddard Research Institute on 112th Street, near Harlem, an odd location for a facility specializing in outer space. His office, done in dark woods and black leather, seemed more like a study. We stood at a window looking down on Broadway below.

"I've been trying to figure out how to ask you this without getting into numbers," I said. "If your predictions are right and the CO_2 doubles, what will the street down there look like in forty years?"

He didn't answer while he considered the question. Below, a truck from the Bronx Terminal Market delivered frozen food to a grocery. I saw a "Flowers by Valli" store and a green awning on Cafe 112. A light, muggy drizzle swept Broadway's median strip and empty benches. In February, the heart of winter, the temperature was sixty-one degrees.

Hansen said, getting started, "There would be more traffic on Broadway, more cars."

"Why?"

He looked up, the answer obvious to him. "The West Side Highway would be underwater," he said. With greater global heat, greenhouse theory went, the Antarctic glacier would melt and oceans expand as they warmed.

"You might see Dutch engineers down there, to build dikes," Hansen said. "The Dutch could sell their expertise in New York, Florida, Louisiana."

"Dikes," I said.

"Uh, you might have traffic jams on Riverside Drive. It would be a mess. As the warming progresses and droughts get more frequent, you might see signs in restaurants, 'Water Only By Request.' Hurricanes and thunderstorms will be more frequent. Remember, we're talking about increased frequency of severe events. So you might see tape over windows across the street."

Hansen's shelves were piled with scientific papers. With doubled atmospheric CO_2, the Goddard team predicted, the average number of ninety-degree days a year in New York would jump from fifteen to forty-eight. In Washington, D.C., from thirty-six to eighty-seven. Denver, from thirty-three to eighty-six. Chicago, sixteen to fifty-six.

Also, Washington's one hundred-plus degree-days could jump from one to twelve. Omaha's from three to twenty-one. Memphis's from four to forty-two.

Hansen wasn't the only one making predictions. In the grim executive summary of the Senate-commissioned Environmental Protection Agency report on climate change, the EPA said that with doubled CO_2, rising seas could flood a coastal area as big as Massachusetts. Diseases like Rocky Mountain spotted fever and malaria could move north. U.S. forests might not adapt. Less snow and faster evaporation might shrink the Great Lakes. More electrical power would be needed everywhere. And California, already subject to crippling water shortages, would suffer many more.

Now Dr. Hansen gazed down 112th Street, a narrow gauntlet of rain-washed brownstones leading to the Hudson River a few blocks away. A whiff of precipitation came through the opening in the window. "Sometimes," he said, "I see migrating waterfowl, ducks or geese, over the river. I guess I wouldn't see them so often, as their watering holes dry up. You might find different trees on the Broadway median strip. You know our climate model indicates the greenhouse effect magnifies extremes in the hydrologic cycle. Dry regions get drier and wet regions wetter. I was stupid enough to plant birch and white pine in my yard in New Jersey, we're in the southern end of the limit of those trees, and I'm having a hard time with them. The climate doesn't kill them, but they get more susceptible to fungus and insects."

As he talked I remembered a comic strip I'd seen on a wall outside Hansen's office. It showed a dinosaur skeleton in a museum, and a guard reading a newspaper nearby. The sign on the exhibit said, "Extinct from climate change." The headline on the paper read, "Greenhouse Effect." The caption under the whole cartoon was "Deja Vu?"

We left the window and sat near a blackboard on which he'd chalked, "Sea Level. Pressure patterns. Global cloud distribution."

Even as we spoke, Goddard's computer downstairs was simulating climate, assigning mathematical values to weather influences like wind, volcanos, tide movements. Then it used the laws of physics to predict how in the future those influences would interact. It might be February in New York City, but it was spring on the computer. Wheat grew in Russia and Kansas. Ice melted in Switzerland. By tomorrow it would be summer.

Hansen leaned forward on his leather chair, lights on in the office because it was so dark outside during the day. The concentric lines creasing his forehead intensified his concerned look.

"Do you think this sounds like science fiction? In a way it *is* science fiction," he said. "But my wife and I used to go to the beach when we were married. I'd look at the waves. Nature seems so powerful," he said wistfully, "you have to wonder. . . . These gases people are sending into the atmosphere. Can they *really* compete with the powerful forces of nature? Even as a scientist you wonder. But after being involved in these studies for over a decade, checking the models, looking at the Earth's climate, figuring out what kind of force is necessary to really change nature," he said, sitting back as if he wished the truth were otherwise, "you come to the conclusion that, yeah, man can change it."

. . . .

"Empty your pockets," Mega ordered. "If you don't do it in three seconds, I'll turn you upside down."

He and two other Guardian Angels eased into a semicircle around a stoop in Hell's Kitchen at midnight. The girl sitting there protested, "I didn't do anything wrong." She was a petite, pretty blonde in a red blouse and tight cutoffs. A boy who had been talking to her edged sideways, walked off.

"One," Mega said. "Two . . ."

His real name was Reggie but Guardian Angels used nicknames. "Ninja." "GI Joe." They were poor kids in red berets and white T-shirts. Volunteer anti-crime patrols, called vigilantes by civil libertarians and saviors by block associations, worried that police protection wasn't enough.

"Three," Mega said.

The girl spat, dug into her pockets and threw a crack vial on the stoop. Mega crushed it. "Get off the street," he growled. Cursing, the girl sulked off, looked back longingly at the vial. So far, every time the Angels had confronted someone, they'd come up with drugs.

On hot nights, crime rose in New York City. I'd patrolled with Angels in winter, when the same streets had been deserted. Now, with the intense heat, people were everywhere; drinking, talking. Tension seemed enhanced by the 90-degree temperature. A palpable edge of violence moved west with the Angels down 46th Street, patrol leader Mega looking side to side, checking basement steps and hallways, his beret pulled low. Mega—shy, softspoken Queens teenager when he wasn't with Angels. A bouncer in a discothèque. A bodybuilder who helped support his mother and sister. In uniform, a fearsome presence in hobnailed boots.

"What are you doing here?" he growled at two men sharing a hypodermic in a hallway. The Angels crushed the needle and kicked the men down the block. They broke up a deal between a prostitute and a john. They confiscated a Bic lighter and crack pipe from an older man hiding down basement steps.

At break time Mega's patrol returned to headquarters, an out-of-business French cafe on Restaurant Row. Across from Broadway Joe's and next to Orso's the boys bivouacked, an army on the move, sprawled in booths beneath wallpaper depicting dancing French peasants and chowed down on donated fried chicken and Cokes.

Thirty-four-year-old founder Curtis Sliwa leaned against the empty bar near a display of confiscated Bic lighters. He was a tough and articulate high school dropout, called "Rock" by the kids, married to a fashion model. He said the number of Angel recruits always skyrocketed in summer.

"Heat is like the full moon, the effect it has on people," he said. "The violence level is up. The senses are bombarded. It's a dirty city to start with. People have urinated, defecated. The heat warms up those smells. With the street people out there, the smell goes up. Crime goes up. People's flashpoints go up."

Police statistics confirm the theory. Between the cooler summer of 1987 and the broiling one of 1988, crime skyrocketed in New York. But even within the year of 1988, crime went up during warmer months.

Between 1987 and 1988, for instance, felonious assaults rose in New York by 7.2 percent. But during August, they rose 8.2 percent. Felonies during the whole year rose 9.8 percent. In August, they skyrocketed 16.6 percent. And while misdemeanors fell 2.8 percent, in August they only dropped 0.1 percent.

I noticed the difference when I went on patrol with Manhattan police. First on a cool April night, in a squad car out of the Ninth precinct on the lower east side. A pleasant, eventless evening with officer Brian McCullough and his partner on the four-to-midnight shift, cruising past bodegas, street people living in Tompkins Square Park, crackhouse lookouts on Eighth Street, NYU students and shoppers on lower Broadway, restaurants on Second Avenue.

Then on the four-to-midnight shift on a hot August night, in the back of Scott Maher's car being tossed side to side as we rocketed from one real distress call to another, interrupted by more calls in between.

"One at a time," moaned Scott, hitting the accelerator. Pedestrians crouched on Houston Street, pointing in the direction a mugger had gone.

Now, back at Guardian Angel headquarters, Mega finished his fried chicken. He made sure his donated walkie-talkie was working. He adjusted his black-studded wristbands on both wrists and led his three-man patrol back down 46th Street.

Near Tenth Avenue, seven or eight drunks lay on the sidewalk, backs against a chain link fence enclosing a small concrete park. Mega walked up to a drunk. "Get up," he said.

"Hell with you," the man said.

"Get off the street," Mega said, leaning down.

The drunk wielded an empty bottle by the neck. His friends tried to restrain him. He and Mega stood nose to nose.

"Fuck you," the drunk said. "I was in Vietnam."

Mega roared, "Off. The. Street!"

At 2 A.M., the temperature was still ninety degrees.

·   ·   ·

Rain forest destruction contributes about ten percent of the greenhouse effect, scientists say, and pumps between 1 and 2 billion tons of carbon into the atmosphere every year. Left standing, rain forests cleanse the atmosphere of carbon in two ways: through photosynthesis, they suck up carbon dioxide and release oxygen. Then they store the CO_2 they absorbed.

Burn down rain forests, you not only end the photosynthesis, you release hundreds of years of stored-up carbon.

Just clearing one acre of Amazon forest releases one hundred tons of carbon into the air, say published reports. And in the Brazilian Amazon, eighty-seven thousand square miles of forest were burned in 1987. Brazil alone accounts for at least five percent of the greenhouse effect.

"Although global temperature changes attributable to Amazon clearing may appear modest, they are added to an environmental strain on a system very close to breaking," wrote ecologist Philip Fearnside of the Brazilian National Institute of Amazon Research.

"The Amazon is not just 'some acres,' " said Brazilian ecologist José Lutzenberger. "It's an enormous stretch of forest bigger than the continental United States. And it sits right on the equator. A cooling effect from this fantastic forest affects the north and south hemispheres."

Take away the cooling effect, he was saying, and watch the weather heat up. A reporter asked if he was saying that some day rain forest destruction could help turn Kansas into a desert.

"Nobody knows, but it's possible," he said.

Lutzenberger was taken so seriously as a scientist that in 1990 newly elected president Fernando Collor de Mello appointed him environmental secretary.

But for Brazilians and other rain forest countries, there are much closer ramifications of rain forest destruction than Kansas drought. Like rain drying up over their own forests.

"Half the rainfall in the Amazon is generated internally," said Tom Lovejoy, assistant secretary for external affairs of the Smithsonian Institution. "You can see the recycling, plumes of moisture rising from the canopy after rain to form clouds. There are projections of major drops in rainfall in the atmosphere if deforestation continues."

Which would mean dying crops, higher food prices, more erosion in rain forest countries.

"Forest and climate are inseparable partners," said Eneas Salati, Brazilian climatologist.

Still, many Brazilians grew enraged at North Americans when they heard talk like Lovejoy's. The same scientists who charge rain forest countries with causing ten percent of the greenhouse effect say that just U.S. cars and factories produce twenty percent. A single car driven for a year can spew as much as five tons of carbon into the atmosphere.

I asked Lovejoy about it when we were driving past ranches in the Amazon, near Manaus, bumping on mud roads past cows grazing in fields that used to be forest. Rain fell in a downpour.

"How are environmentalists going to stop the big part, the U.S. part?" I said.

Lovejoy sighed heavily. "That's going to be the big fight," he said.

.　.　.

The heat wave persisted and I moved around the city. New Yorkers seemed more angry, more strained.

"The heat changes our response time," said lieutenant lifeguard

Michael McCauliff, a Coney Island lifeguard and Brooklyn College senior, a four-year veteran on the beach. "We've got a pier here. People fall in or jump when it gets hot," said McCauliff. "They get dizzy or hot and don't realize how deep the water is. Last year a guy fell in one morning. We got him out, and he was okay. But in the afternoon another man fell in. Our response time was slower. We got him out, but he had brain damage."

"Power usage goes up in the heat. You find fewer people outside," Gus Preschle, operations manager for the World Trade Center, told me. "I've got sandbags stored for the vehicular ramps for flooding. I might need more of them in the future."

"Aircrafts perform differently in the heat," said Ralph Kearns, assistant manager of the Kennedy Airport tower. "With the hot, thick air, planes get from the ground to five thousand feet in twice the time. If the numbers are doubled, you're going to encounter delay."

"You'll have more choking smog. With the oceans rising, salt water would back up the Hudson into the city's water supply. It wouldn't be a city I'd like to live in," said New Yorker and Environmental Defense Fund physicist Dr. Michael Oppenheimer.

"Little things can go wrong with the equipment in a heat wave," said Walter Johnson, shift superviser on Con Edison's Waterside power plant in Manhattan. "The system is pushed to the limit, so much so that word comes down not to test equipment. All testing is stopped."

But I didn't need experts to show me my own city. All I had to do was walk down any street to see changes in a heat wave. I tried jogging in Prospect Park during an air pollution alert, and stopped, heaving, sick. I rode my bicycle through Brooklyn streets, and hydrants were open everywhere, the city's water flooding away. When I walked the subway to ride out to Shea Stadium, my trousers stuck to my thighs from heat, and the air seemed browner.

The Mets trailed the Pirates by two games, with a week in the season to go. It was a warm, pleasant evening when I reached the dugout, and the Mets were warming up on the field.

"I'm writing about what happens in the city when the weather gets hot," I'd written the front office. They gave me permission to be here tonight.

As I watched, pitching coach Mel Stottlemyre gave rookie Julio Valera batting practice. Valera hit a line drive, and the infielders stretching on the grass near the backstop cheered.

Manager Bud Harrelson sat on the dugout steps, surrounded by reporters. Would he play Carreon or Boston in center field today, they wanted to know. Would Ojeda or Darling be in the pitching rotation? Nobody was asking about the greenhouse effect, and I felt a little silly doing so.

"You want to know about what?" Harrelson said when my turn came. I wanted to tell him I was a thirty-nine-year-old man who could still put himself to sleep at night dreaming of playing center field for the Mets.

"When it gets hot, we cut down on batting practice," Harrelson said. "Anything over 90 degrees is sapping. We keep ammonia water in the dugout. Pitchers put it on their face. I've seen guys put their whole head in it. And AstroTurf," he said, shaking his head, "absorbs heat. When we play on AstroTurf on a 90-degree day, it could be 130 on the field."

"When it gets hot we have a lot of problems," said trainer Steve Garland. "Especially in prolonged heat. With muscles. Legs. The upper body. Several times this year we had problems with guys having to leave the game. They missed three or four games at a time. Daryl Boston," he said, naming a center fielder. "During a very hot day, eighty-eight to ninety-two degrees, high humidity, he was coming around third base and he scored, but he came up lame. It was a cramp. There's no question in my mind it was because of heat. Darryl Strawberry," he said, naming the right fielder in his last year with the team, "is very thin and muscular. He doesn't have much water in his muscles. With prolonged heat he's subject to hamstring. In football they do a lot of IVs at halftime. Football, with all that equipment, you'll have real problems if it gets hotter. *Real* problems."

.   .   .

Big changes happen in a thousand little ways. A few more robberies. A broken elevator. A plane backed up. A man with a heart attack. I stood with Jim Hansen at the scientist's window, looking out into the middle of the next century, through his eyes. "You could end up with more pollution," the physicist was saying. "You'll need more power plants to keep cool. You might see more sun hats shading people's faces. If you're a commuter, portions of Roosevelt Drive could be underwater. Maybe there'll be more helicopters taking businessmen to work. Wealthier people won't want to deal with traffic."

I asked Hansen if he ever felt lobbied or pressured to quit talking about the greenhouse effect.

Hansen chuckled. "Lobbied isn't the word," he said. He said sources of funding had stopped coming through.

Meanwhile the computer kept running downstairs, churning out predictions, and Hansen kept giving talks. But he felt a little misunderstood lately. Ever since he'd appeared before the Senate subcommittee he'd been attacked by some scientists who said his conclusions were wrong or premature.

A few researchers claimed cooler weather in 1989 and 1990 showed Hansen hadn't known what he was talking about. Others claimed sunspots or the El Niño Pacific current had caused the brief warming trend. One team at the Massachusetts Institute of Technology went back and researched a hundred years of British sea captains' temperature recordings, taken on ships all over the world. They concluded that global warming had simply not taken place.

Hansen seemed frustrated by reports of these studies. "There's nothing in recent U.S. temperatures that casts the slightest doubt on the greenhouse theory," he said. "Every drought can be related to antecedent atmospheric conditions. Last summer in the Senate hearings they asked me if I thought the current drought was caused by the greenhouse effect. I told them it's impossible to say. What our model suggests is that the frequency and severity of droughts are increasing."

Hansen had made up cardboard dice to illustrate his conclusions. On the first die, two sides were red for hot days, two white for average, and two blue for cool. That die represented the temperature between 1950 and 1980, Hansen told audiences. Roll the die, and there would be a two-in-six chance that a summer might be hot.

But the die for the 1990s had four red sides.

"If our calculations are correct, greenhouse warming in the 1990s will be sufficient to shift the probabilities so the chance of a hot summer will be fifty-five percent to eighty percent," he said.

In the fall of 1990, a four hundred-scientist UN panel reported that greenhouse warming was indeed changing Earth's climate. They recommended reductions in carbon emissions from industry and rain forest destruction if the trend was to be slowed.

Now Hansen rummaged on shelves to find reports to give me, and he said the uncertainties in global forecasting involved predicting regional climate changes, not global ones. To come up with more practical recommendations for policy makers, the Goddard team was altering their climate model, changing mathematical values in the computer for factors like storm speed. "Storms move too slowly in the model now," he said. "If we're going to simulate specific droughts realistically, we have to do a better job simulating storms in the model."

Outside, the rain picked up and battered against his window. Hansen liked to tell a story about a colleague who'd given a speech on climate change to a society of automotive engineers. Afterward the man was approached by an engineer from Honda, who discussed engine designs the company was testing to improve efficiency. He was also approached by an American manufacturer, but the American wanted to talk about why greenhouse theory was probably wrong.

But ultimately Hansen said he thought positively. "Some changes are already inevitable," he said. "They'll be bad but not disastrous. I don't worry. I'm optimistic if we get the information out, people won't follow the business-as-usual path."

The rain eased a little, and flocks of pigeons circled the rooftops. I unbuttoned my winter coat and sweated out on the street. The sun had come out. Men and women walked on the bright, wet sidewalks, with ties loose and jackets under arms. When I got home to Brooklyn, I found my wife in the bedroom with the air conditioner on.

"It's too hot to go out," she said.

Kilometer 220

Hamburger Tax
Shelters

Sometimes, on BR-364, it was hard to imagine the pastures lining both sides of the highway had ever been jungle. Ranches were everywhere. Bigger ones had wire fences running along the road and lots of healthy-looking white cows on the rolling land inside. Chewing or lying around. Looking like cattle in Vermont. These ranches had names like the "Ponderosa" and the "Chaparral."

Smaller spreads were announced by hand-scrawled signs on fence posts—FABIO'S FARM. There would be a couple of shacks on stilts, a pig disappearing into the shadows, a woman half-visible in an open window with the shutter open. A vision of rural poverty throughout the Third World.

Sometimes 364 looked like the kind of country road city dwellers enjoyed on Sunday afternoons. A few palm trees bending in the fields. The forest sitting back, green and benevolent at a distance. Drivers bought Cokes or candy at gas stations. On the surface it wasn't so different from Wisconsin or Minnesota.

But to ecologists the peaceful scenes were a kind of genocide. Of the 135 million cattle in Brazil, half lived in the Amazon, eating the place to death. Each bull needed one hundred times more pasture to live here than in the South of Brazil where the soil was better. Just to produce a 125-gram hamburger, ranchers had to destroy 6.5 square meters of tropical forest.

"Cattle ranching is a principal factor in eliminating forests of Central and South America," said Ira Rubinoff, head of the Smithsonian Institution's Tropical Research Institute.

"Cattle ranching destroys twenty thousand square kilometers of

Latin American rain forest a year," wrote Norman Myers in his *Primary Source*. "Between 1966 and 1983, over one hundred thousand square kilometers of Brazilian Amazon were burned to make pasture."

They weren't just worried about Brazil. By 1990, Costa Rican ranches covered a third of the country, up from an eighth thirty years before. In Nicaragua, Guatemala, and Salvador, the story was the same.

"It's the hamburger connection in Central America," charged Peter Thacher, a Distinguished Fellow at the World Resources Institute in Washington. "Forests are destroyed to lower the price of a U.S. hamburger a nickel."

The worst part was that the ranches weren't even profitable, not in the long run, many scientists said. Cattle would eat and trample pasture, compact soil, and cause erosion. Then ranchers would move to another place. They could do it and still make money because of a government giveaway scheme, a tax shelter program called SUDAM.

In fact, according to the World Resources Institute, by 1987, 37 million acres of Amazon deforestation could be traced to government-financed programs and subsidies. "The fiscal burden has been heavy, the environmental consequences serious, the contribution to Brazilian development dubious at best," the report said.

Going east from Pôrto Velho along older portions of BR-364, I'd seen many abandoned farms and ranches, with weeds growing where pasture had been.

Now the highway left Rubens Lemes's *garimpo* to curve down through swamp. Trees were shorter. Grass grew out of black water as the road proceeded west on a dike. The swamp ended, and a ranch came up on the left. As soon as I saw it, I knew it was the one I wanted to visit. It had the biggest, proudest sign I'd seen since Pôrto Velho. As big as a billboard. Ten feet high: SANTA CARMEN RANCH. SUDAM RANCH, it said.

I stopped the Volkswagen on the steel cattle grid and slipped the barbed-wire loop off the gate. Nobody saw me enter the ranch. I wondered if I could find what the ecologists had predicted. Wrecked pasture. Eroded land.

Ahead, beyond the field and cows, a cluster of pastel-blue shacks hugged a dirt road. The road continued up a hill, passed a sawmill, branched straight and right, and disappeared toward the back of the ranch.

Smiling people came out to greet me. A man with a beer belly named John Evangelista. A little blonde girl. I saw an old couple silhouetted behind a screen on a porch. There was a teenage boy who introduced himself as Claudionei. They were all related, all family. They had moved to Rondônia at the request of the manager, the old man's son-in-law.

"What do you raise here?" I asked.

"Cattle."

"How many cattle have you sold?"

"None."

"How long have you been here?"

"Three years."

"Then how does the ranch make money?"

"We cut and sell the trees," someone said.

I started to take notes, but the people became nervous. If I wanted to visit, I needed permission. José Evangelista, the owner-manager, lived in town. He was the brother of the man with the beer belly. He spent three days a week at the ranch. Call him and come back, John Evangelista said.

"You sell wood?" I repeated.

"Talk to the manager," they said.

I went to town and called José Evangelista. He was "out." Then he was "sleeping." Then he was "at the ranch." Then he was "back from the ranch but out."

"I don't think he wants to meet you," said Miguel Nenevé, the English professor and translator who took many trips with me along 364.

We called José Evangelista again. He was home.

"I don't want to talk to you," he said. He hung up.

·   ·   ·

On a Saturday morning when José Evangelista was in town, we got into Miguel's Volkswagen and drove 150 kilometers to the ranch. Everyone seemed surprised to see us. "We talked to the owner like you wanted," Miguel said, smiling. "Now we're back."

They didn't believe us, but they were too polite to disagree. Claudionei took us deeper into the ranch on the back of a tractor to see José Evangelista again. As we clanked along he told us the ranch was twenty thousand hectares (fifty thousand acres)—so big he'd never seen the back of it in the three years he'd lived here.

He was a shy fifteen-year-old, lean, with a dirty plastic-brimmed hat perched backward on his black curls to protect his neck from the sun. His shirt was unbuttoned to his pectorals. "Every Monday the lumber trucks come, lots of trucks, so many trucks that sometimes one is leaving and another coming," he said. "They come from all over Brazil—Rio, the *garimpo*. Soon we'll be building another sawmill to cut wood faster."

The area through which he drove had an ill-kept, overgrown appearance. Grass grew in wild clumps. Most of the trees had been cut. There were no cows. Claudionei said he worked six days a week. Woke at six each morning, breakfasted on coffee, drove the tractor. The hardest part was clearing brush because the tractor grew hot. In the rainy season Claudionei wore a poncho. In the dry, he plowed, making sure the steel blades bit into the earth deeply to hold the seeds, but not so deep as to keep them from growing. Most of the time he hauled wood to the sawmill, he said. He would finish work about seven, eat dinner, watch TV, and sleep until it was time to work again. He had been on that schedule since he was twelve.

"Are there girls here?" I asked.

"Ugly ones, in Abuná."

"What do you like best living here?"

"Work," Claudionei said. He looked up from beneath the hat. We bumped along the rutted road, and I had to grip the back of the tractor.

"When you're poor, you work. I'm poor, I work."

I asked Claudionei if there was anything he wanted to ask me. I had been asking questions for half an hour. Maybe there was something he wanted to know.

"What's the price of beans in New York?" he said.

I didn't know.

"How much is rice?"

I didn't know. It was hot, and the heat soaked through my shirt. Miguel's neck was scarlet. We'd only been out thirty minutes. I said, "Anything else you want to know?" I figured he might ask about girls, or sports, or music.

"No," Claudionei said.

.   .   .

In 1964, when the Brazilian military government decided to launch its push into the Amazon, it created the agency SUDAM (Superintendency for the Development of the Amazon). SUDAM's job was to lure businessmen into the region by offering tax incentives. "If you had a plastics factory in São Paulo and you owned a million in taxes, you could take half and start a ranch. It wouldn't cost you anything," said Maritta Koch-Weser, senior sociologist in the environmental division of the World Bank.

It was a no-lose situation. Investors wouldn't be spending any extra money. If the ranch failed, they could sell the land, which was surging in value. They could borrow money from the Brazil Central Bank at interest rates so low that, considering inflation, they made a profit.

The program worked in terms of getting new ranchers into the Amazon, but it didn't keep them there. Often the new owners weren't as interested in ranching as they were in tax breaks. They took the incentives and burned down the forest. Burned land counted as "improved" land under Brazilian law. "Improved" land proved ownership. They overstocked pasture for quick profit. Then they sold the ranches. Or abandoned them.

"SUDAM-approved livestock projects . . . encompass a total of 8.4 million hectares in the Amazon and . . . have been the single most important source of deforestation in Southern Pará and Mato Grosso," said a study funded by the World Bank.

"Few (SUDAM) ranch owners were seriously interested in developing sustainable beef," concluded one Brazilian government report. "Many projects were exploited solely for fiscal benefits."

Virginia Tech economic anthropologist John Browder, after making a study of SUDAM ranches, concluded, "Beef cattle production in the Amazon is only financially sensible given the government subsidies that support it, and the possibility of cannibalizing ranch assets that those subsidies sought to develop."

But if the system caused environmental damage, that didn't mean it was a failure as far as its designers were concerned.

"Remember, these tax programs were designed to get the Amazon occupied, and SUDAM helped do that," said Brazilian Congressman Fabio Feldmann.

.   .   .

People didn't seem too happy on the Santa Carmen Ranch. Walking now, Claudionei led us through a field of cut trees to a water hole where John Evangelista built a mud dam with a small bulldozer. He was friendly but guarded.

"I'm not answering questions about the ranch," he said.

"How about if we talk about how you came here?"

"The government took my farm near a dam and never paid me. My brother told me life would be better here. I hate working for somebody else. I want my own land."

"How long will it take to build that dam?" I said.

John Evangelista drew himself up on the tractor. "Why are you really here?" he said.

Claudionei introduced his sister, the schoolteacher and nurse. We sat in her living room while her son and daughter watched a Los Angeles cop show dubbed in Portuguese. The detectives looked like millionaires. They wore new clothes and drove cars. They could afford to eat in restaurants.

"I hate it here," said Rita Luiza Ferraz, twenty-five. She was a slim, thoughtful brunette who considered each question before answering it. "My brother-in-law wrote us that it was paradise, but when we got here, there were rats in the houses, and spiders. No electricity. The funny thing is, my husband came here first and hated it so much he decided to go back. I never got his message. I came with the kids, and then we were broke and it was too late to go back."

"Last month a jaguar kept coming to the ranch," she said. "It ate a cow. We found its body without a head. One night we were in the house, and we heard it growling. The men rushed out and shot it. Now I don't let the children out at night anymore."

Rita Luiza showed off the school, a single room with desks and children's drawings of the Easter bunny on the walls. There are no rabbits in the Amazon. She showed us the infirmary where she administered malaria tests to ranch hands and their children. She had a microscope and slides. She would look at blood samples and find the easily recognizable U-shaped bacteria. She kept boxes of quinine pills. They were half-empty since everyone kept getting sick. She had two huge tarantulas preserved in bottles, and a dead snake.

"To me they symbolize Rondônia," she said.

She also kept a "rare deadly snake" that someone had killed on a clothesline. I stared into the glass bottle where it floated in water—a twisted green shape with translucent oblong wings. An insect, not a snake. Harmless.

"It's poisonous," she insisted. Then she said, "Do you mind if I ask you a question? What are you really doing here?"

I told her. "I believe you," she nodded. "But other people don't."

Everybody was too nervous. People in the Amazon were often suspicious when I met them, but that was only natural, considering the critical things foreign journalists wrote about them. But at the Santa Carmen Ranch the degree of uneasiness exceeded anything I had encountered.

Claudionei led the way back to the cluster of wooden shacks by the road to the highway. His parents lived in one. They offered sweet, hot coffee on the screened-in porch. His father sat in a rocking chair. His mother Helena leaned against the door.

"I made a mistake coming here," his father admitted. "I had a farm in Londrina, a nice place. Three bedrooms. A flower garden. Good neighbors. There was a church. Friends. But the land was getting bad, the crops weak. My son-in-law wrote that this place was wonderful. Tough, but it had a future. We could build something here. We talked about it, and we decided to come."

He seemed a gentle man smiling through pain, and then he said he'd gotten malaria after one month on the ranch. He'd never fully recovered three years later. He still couldn't work.

"I didn't know we would be so far from everything," he said wistfully.

Inside, the house was immaculate. Floors swept. Lace doily covering the propane tank by the stove. Plates and dishes clean and arranged on a steel hutch. Beds patted down and made in two bedrooms. Pictures of the Last Supper. Magazine photo of Rambo on Claudionei's wall.

"I sold the farm. We rented a truck to take us here," the father said.

The truck had cost a year's salary, but at the mention of "truck" everyone started to laugh. Oh, that trip, Claudionei's mother said. She wiped her eyes. That thousand-mile trip with everything they owned in the truck—Hammocks strung and pitching. Furniture crashing around. Everyone singing songs or listening to soccer games on the radio. Everyone bathing nude together in streams by the road. Hanging from the back of the truck while the pretty marriageable daughter called out to handsome men, "You! You! Handsome!"

Claudionei's mother doubled over, laughing. His father shook, chuckling. His sister giggled. Claudionei smiled.

"We laughed the whole way," his mother said.

"When did the laughter stop?"

"When we got here."

I asked them if they had been angry at the son-in-law. If they were still angry. "No," Claudionei's father said. "He was fair to us. He told us it would be rough."

"But the rats," I said.

"Fair," Claudionei's mother said.

The next day I asked again. They repeated the answer.

"Not even a little mad?" We'd been talking about snow in New York. What it looked like. How it felt.

"Well . . ." said Claudionei's mother. Her normally jolly face hardened. "I told him," she said. "I told him!"

Claudionei's father laughed. "She was mad."

.   .   .

I wanted to keep an open mind at the Santa Carmen Ranch, especially because of Leslie Hewitt and Friedrich Brugger. I'd met them at the Hotel Equatorial Bar in Belém. They worked for the Swiss company, Ciba-Geigy, growing passion fruit on a farm in Pará State. They had spent years on agricultural projects in the

Amazon. Tax breaks *could* help develop the Amazon, they said. And not all agriculture was bad.

Hewitt was an English engineer, an ex-military man from the Isle of Wight, who took me to the farm. In fields hewn from the jungle, rows of passion fruits grew fat on vines thanks to new grafting techniques. The fruit was reduced to concentrate at a new factory and shipped all over Brazil.

"Ten years ago this was jungle," Hewitt said. "The road. The farm. The factory. Don't believe you can't grow things in the Amazon. You can. This is what Acre will be like in twenty years. It's what the United States was like in 1850."

"Nature was never nice," Hewitt said. "It's only pretty perfumed flowers in books. But nature itself is a hard, hard business. I will admit that we lost a lot of animals, insects, and birds. It's a pity, yes, but what do you want? Humans or animals?"

Brugger was a tall, handsome Swiss who dressed in khaki and who had been a manager of the Volkswagen Cattle Ranch, a five hundred thousand-hectare spread in Pará that had been sold to a Japanese company.

"Ranching can be profitable in the Amazon," he said. "Volkswagen got incentives from the government, fifty percent directly out of taxes. And the ranch worked. We had the same climate as Brisbane. The same soil, the same acidity, the same specifics. We had the most advanced techniques in pastures. It took twelve years to get a profit, but we did. The problem wasn't cattle, it was people. The Greens in Germany gave Volkswagen problems, accusing us of taking slaves, of burning the Amazon. The satellites said we burned a million hectares, but they were detecting only the smoke. A little fire can create lots of smoke."

Brugger was angry at ecologists who said ranching was impossible in the Amazon. "They don't live here. You have to define what is good ecology. Is it against humans? What good is the forest? Humans can't survive there. Go in for a day and come out. If you're not sick, you're happy. Go in for a month and if you're alive, you're happy. What we need is a development program, not a protection program."

It wasn't just Hewitt and Brugger. Ecologically inclined scientists kept changing their statistics about just how much danger the jungle was in. When it came to the Amazon, everyone kept changing statistics. One night at the pool at the Hotel Villa Rica in Pôrto Velho, I sat with a Brazilian magazine reporter and an American anthropologist who had supposedly spent years studying cattle in the Amazon. The reporter mentioned a figure for the number of cattle she'd heard were there. The scientist said, "Wow! I can raise my statistics seventeen percent!"

Another time a scientist named Philip Fearnside gave me some papers he had written in his office in Manaus. Fearnside was widely quoted as one of the top environmental researchers in the Amazon. The first paper I looked at included comments like "factors *appear* reasonable" and "incorporation of indirect approximations of biomass . . . is *probably* justified." In another case part of the paper he corrected his own earlier approximations of how much biomass is in the Amazon.

Also, I remembered how in 1984 one of Brazil's leading environmentalists, Dr. José Lutzenberger, had predicted that Rondônia would be completely deforested by 1990. Now it was 1990, and the most dire analysis said twenty-five percent of the state was gone. And Rondônia was supposed to have suffered some of the worst deforestation in the Amazon.

·   ·   ·

"Ah," said Miguel, the Robert Frost scholar. "The road not taken."

At lunchtime everyone had disappeared into houses. We were alone and unsupervised on the ranch. Still wondering why the workers were so nervous, we walked up the road beyond the sawmill, the one that disappeared over a rise.

Gullies lined the side of the road—eight, nine feet deep. Deep enough to cover up a person. Someone had thrown wood planks from the sawmill into the crevice to slow the erosion, but no one had bothered to fill in the gullies.

We reached the crest of the hill and looked out from the other side.

"Oh my God," Miguel said.

It was like a desert. A long expanse of destruction. Hectare after hectare of nothing. No trees. No grass. Not even weeds. Just hard, bare earth. The size of dozens of football fields.

Garbage had been thrown in the small depression at the top of the hill. Bulldozers had moved some boulders. We looked back toward BR-364 and saw green grass, cows, little houses, trees. We turned back the other way to see a ghost landscape.

Without vegetation it seemed hotter here, the heat seeping up through the earth, through shoes.

We walked into the dead part of the Santa Carmen Ranch. The air was still, and we grew nervous about being discovered. Clumps of cow manure lay on the compacted earth, some of it deposited so recently that it smelled. There weren't even any Brazil nut trees, the national tree that had to be preserved even if dead. Webs of gullies fanned out from the road. We kept going, wondering when the dead area would end. It didn't. The bare field gave way to scraggy secondary vegetation, gravelly earth, weeds, more scooped-out areas looking like open pit mines.

"Miguel," I said. "I come from a city. Maybe I'm taking this wrong. You grew up on a farm. What are we looking at?"

"This is the worst thing I ever saw," Miguel said.

We had been gone too long. We turned and walked back quickly. We strolled to Claudionei's parents' house. They met us on the porch. They were smiling.

"Did you get the free lunch?" Claudionei's mother said.

"What free lunch?"

"Oh, when visitors come here they always get a free lunch in the main house. A really good lunch, and it's free."

"What visitors?" I said.

"Government people. Or rich farmers who come."

"Do you get free lunch?"

"Are you kidding?" Claudionei's mother said.

.   .   .

"The United States is fucking over Brazil!" José Evangelista shouted. He whipped his hips back and forth in mockery. He was a rugged, sunburned man with liver spots dotting the backs of his thick hands. His widow's peak and chiseled features gave him a resemblance to the actor Jack Palance. "Who pollutes the world the most?" he shouted. "Huh?"

We'd given up trying to phone him and gone to his house in Pôrto Velho, in a busy commercial and residential part of town. There was a beautiful freshly painted blue truck outside that said Santa Carmen Ranch. José Evangelista lived in a walled-in compound with glass shards topping the adobe-like outer walls. Inside there were three or four one-story buildings, a nicely laid out stone patio, lots of empty Coca-Cola and beer bottles piled in crates against a wall, and a guard who sucked at a toothpick and looked out at us through the locked steel gate.

The guard had regarded us blandly when we introduced ourselves, clicked off with his cowboy boots echoing on the patio, returned, and nodded us onto the grounds. He'd locked the gate behind us.

José Evangelista had been eating a lunch of steak and onions at a small round table in an extension of the patio behind the main house. We'd declined the offer of food, and he'd asked us to wait in his office. It was cold from the air conditioner. He looked tense across the desk.

"Amazon farmers should go to the United States," he said bitterly while his son, who looked about twenty, looked on. They sat side by side. The clenched muscles in their jaws looked identical. "In the Amazon it's not possible to work anymore. Try to cut wood, and the government stops you. SUDAM doesn't give incentives anymore. My three partners and I are losing money. Our aim was to cut six thousand hectares of the twenty-five thousand for pasture. We stopped at fifteen hundred. I want the pressure to stop!"

"Did the ranch ever make a profit?" I asked.

"No, not in seven years."

"Where did the money come from to keep it running?"

"I told you. But SUDAM incentives stopped."

"How will you keep the ranch running now?"

"Every year two hundred calves will be born. I'll sell them. I'll cut the wood in the areas where I'm still permitted."

He erupted again. "Maybe we should kill our Indians like in the United States! Maybe we should destroy the whole Amazon, and then we can join together with the United States and oppress another country!"

Both Evangelistas leaned forward angrily over the desk. I told a story. On the day I sold the idea for this book, I had gone to my shoemaker in Brooklyn to get heels replaced. In the hole-in-the-wall shop I'd noticed a beautiful drawing on the wall. An artist's conception of a map, a lush green, depiction of a forest from the air, dotted with quaint towns and a few houses. I told them that, fascinated by the pastoral drawing, I had leaned toward it in the shop to read the caption. "Do you know what that drawing was?" I said.

"The Amazon," José Evangelista said sourly.

"No," I said. "Brooklyn. In 1775."

José Evangelista started laughing. He told his son to bring us beer. The air conditioner was roaring, and every time we took a sip the son poured more. "What's the matter?" José Evangelista said. "Don't you like beer? Drink?"

José Evangelista's son was smiling now. "Dad, tell him about the trouble with the Indians," he said.

"There isn't any trouble with any Indians," José Evangelista said.

"And the *posseiros* (invaders)," the son said five minutes later. "The trouble with them."

"There aren't any *posseiros*," José Evangelista said. "Drink!"

The conversation moved on. There were "no plans" to build another sawmill. Before coming to Rondônia, José Evangelista had been "sort of" a rancher. Now he owned other businesses too. He owned a company that sold telephones. He bought and sold land in the state of Paraná.

"If you include the wood that you sell with the cattle, do you make a profit at the ranch?" I asked.

José Evangelista shouted again. "Who pollutes the world!"

It was clear that a calm moment would never arrive to bring up the destroyed area of the ranch. "I'm wondering if you can help me," I said. "I like to describe areas I write about, but there's a part of your ranch I never saw. The part behind the sawmill, over the hill. I saw the other road, but not that one. What does it look like back there?"

"It's pasture," José Evangelista said.

"Pasture? You mean grass?"

"Beautiful grass," José Evangelista said.

"Just grass and cows, green grass," I said.

José Evangelista nodded. He pulled out a photocopy of a drawing of the ranch, divided into squares, each square labelled.

"See? It's pasture," he said.

On the map, a lot more than fifteen hundred hectares seemed to be pasture.

"Can I have a copy of this?" I asked.

José Evangelista pulled it away and put it in a drawer.

"This is the office copy," he said.

There was only one more topic to talk about, and that was the family. They had suffered a bit of a rough time on the ranch, José Evangelista said sympathetically, while his son poured more beer. It would probably be better for them if they moved to town.

"Why don't they move to town?"

José Evangelista said, "I need them on the ranch."

.   .   .

On Sundays, Claudionei didn't work. It was sunny today, and he decided to go hunting. He had come a long way since first arriving at the Santa Carmen Ranch. The jungle had scared him then. He'd never seen jungle before Rondônia, but now he liked to go off by himself.

Claudionei hoped to shoot a paca today, an edible rodent. But even if he didn't, the forest was beautiful and green, and sometimes while there he was reminded of his hero, Rambo. *Rambo* had been shown on TV, and there were lots of jungle scenes. There was one really terrific shot where Rambo blended into the forest so well, nobody realized he'd embedded himself in a mud wall, "become" part of nature, until he started to move. That's a hunter.

Sometimes on Sundays Claudionei left the ranch and worked on other land, the family's land, given to them by INCRA, another Brazilian government agency. Like SUDAM, INCRA was set up to draw people to the rural Amazon. It was established to help alleviate overcrowding and joblessness in the East, but unlike SUDAM, INCRA worked with poor people. INCRA got Amazon land, sometimes buying or seizing it from people who didn't use it, and divided it into fifty- or seventy-hectare parcels to distribute to newcomers. The problem with lots of INCRA land, critics said, was that settlers couldn't grow things on it. It had poor soil, jungle soil where all the nutrients were in the vegetation, not the ground. The settlers would burn the jungle, and the rains would wash the nutrients away. Then the settlers would grow crops for a few years, each year's yield getting scrawnier, until they'd have to burn more forest and start again. They would keep going deeper into the forest, burning more land.

Claudionei and his brothers had burned forest on the family's land. "We cut it, let it dry, and then I put a match to it. The fire cleared the area fast," he said. "The fire was beautiful."

The family land was their only hope of getting off the ranch, Claudionei's father said. He wished Claudionei could work on that land full-time. "But my son-in-law needs him on the tractor."

Claudionei didn't shoot any pacas this morning and came home for lunch. Nobody was working, and the day was hot. In the stream near the house, at least a dozen boys and girls in bathing suits screamed with delight, jumping off tree trunks into the water. John Evangelista sat in the shade on the bank, relaxing. Claudionei was too old to splash with the kids. His friends on the ranch were the older single men. He remembered that when he was twelve in Londrina he had had a friend named Miguel. They'd gone to school together, ridden bikes together. Each day they would meet up on the way to school. He was sad to leave Miguel and to have to stop attending school. At one time he had hoped Miguel would come and visit. They'd written to each other, but Rondônia was too far. That was in the past now anyway.

I knew that SUDAM had first stopped incentives to Amazon ranchers in 1979. But the ban was difficult to enforce and the loans started again. In 1989, under Brazil's Our Nature program, SUDAM again halted loans for new ranches in the Amazon. The question was, would the ban remain?

"We have laws on the books to protect the environment," Randau Marques, Brazil's most famous environmental writer told a symposium in São Paulo. "If they were enforced, we would be the most civilized country in the world. But they aren't."

Meanwhile, Claudionei was the new Rondônian. From Claudionei's standpoint, the SUDAM and INCRA programs were a success. They'd been designed to bring settlers here, and here was Claudionei. He didn't remember Londrina so well anymore, and unlike the others of the Santa Carmen Ranch, he'd come of age in the new land. Claudionei sat on the log and fanned himself and watched the children play.

"There's food here and work, and my brother-in-law is thinking of buying a gold dredge. Maybe I could work on that in the river. If not, I'll stay on the ranch."

"I love this place," Claudionei said, looking out beyond the stream to the green pasture. With so much land back there, there were still plenty of trees to cut. "I never want to leave."

The Banker and the Rain Forest

In the last twenty years, as Brazil's forest cover shrank fifteen percent, banks far away in New York, Washington, Tokyo, and Europe played a major role in funding the damage. During the 1970s private and multilateral banks lent billions to Third World countries for dams, roads, and other "development projects." Many of these, like BR-364, were built despite warnings that they would cause massive environmental destruction and not even provide profit in the end.

Bank loans paid for the Samuel Dam, Highway BR-364, the whole Polonoreste project, the big pig iron plants using the forest for fuel in Pará State.

By the 1980s the Third World was $1.2 trillion in debt, one-quarter of that owed by rain forest countries, including Brazil, Indonesia, Madagascar, and Costa Rica. Brazil alone owed $150 billion, and the government was still trying to borrow more.

And banks were under fire from conservationists. The World Bank and Inter-American Development Bank grudgingly announced changes in environmental policy after a concerted attack by environmentalists and a U.S. senator. They had a long way to go, critics said. Private banks, less accountable to the general public, considered restructuring the debt and in a few cases gaining some public relations benefits from helping to save forests.

When I met Randy Curtis and Lamond Godwin, they were trying to form a partnership never before realized between conservationists and bankers, to use foreign debt to conserve endangered forests. They were among a handful of people exploring a new kind of deal called a debt-for-nature swap. They were starting out small, in another rain forest in Costa Rica. But they hoped the process would carry over and help preserve the biggest remaining rain forest on earth, the Amazon.

.   .   .

Randy Curtis slid from the taxi and hurried into the World Financial Center. He was in the heart of New York's Wall Street area. If his meeting went well this morning, "it would take conservation to new heights." Would funnel millions of dollars to protect jungles in Central and South America. It was all up to the man upstairs. All up to Lamond Godwin.

A partnership. An unprecedented arrangement between a conservation group and a bank. That's what Randy had dreamed of for years. But now the very wealth of the American Express Tower, the sunken marble atrium, rows of palm trees, well dressed bankers flooding elevators to electronic flute music—filled him with as much disquiet as hope.

"I didn't want to be overwhelmed," he said.

For a year and a half Curtis had been cold-calling bankers around the country from his office at The Nature Conservancy near Washington, D.C., pitching a new idea. A notion to turn foreign debt—money poor countries owed U.S. banks—into rain forest protection. Hundreds of calls. And rejections. Meetings in Cleveland and Indianapolis that hadn't worked out. "I would do it if I could," dozens of mid-level bankers had told him. "My boss will never go for it."

But the lanky, slow-talking Curtis had not given up. The potential was too exciting, too lucrative. And now, after a series of phone calls and letters and even an on-the-run meeting at National Airport between Godwin's appointments, it looked as though the deal might go through.

Randy got a pass from a guard and squeezed into an elevator. The people around him smelled of Joy perfume and Paco Rabanne cologne. Every dollar from us, he thought, turned into up to eight dollars in the jungle. For park guards. Boundaries. Helicopters. Jeeps. For education programs to keep squatters out of the forest.

With Geoff Barnard, Nature Conservancy Vice president, he fidgeted in a reception room that looked like part of an English manor home, with its panelled walls and winding staircase. Their organization was thirty-seven years old in 1988 and worked with corporations and private donors, buying wild areas for preservation. It had acquired six million acres of reserves in the U.S. and ran programs in Latin America with local conservation groups.

American Express Bank, Barnard and Curtis's targeted partner, had earned profits of $149 million in 1988 after losing $625 million in bad loans to the Third World. As first vice president of the bank's International Capital Corp., Lamond Godwin's job was to come up with creative ways to get rid of bad debt.

The banker personally came out to escort them inside. He was a big, handsome man in a charcoal-black double-breasted suit. A contrast in appearance: There was Randy with his boxy brown jacket. Lamond with a red silk handkerchief in his breast pocket. Randy with his sensible wire-rimmed glasses. Lamond with his little leather briefcase. Walking past secretaries into a conference room overlooking the Hudson River. With their different backgrounds. Randy the ex-VISTA volunteer. The scoutmaster. The man who had founded a company to ship food aid to Nigeria. Lamond the economics major who applied financial theory to social problems. Who'd written papers on rural poverty and racial discrimination in the construction industry. Who'd run job-training programs as a special assistant in the United States Labor Department. Who'd worked as a chief strategist in Jesse Jackson's 1984 presidential campaign.

To many bankers, conservationists were dreamers with no understanding of the financial realities of life. And to ecologists, bankers were moneygrubbers like the man in the cartoon posted outside Randy's office back home. A banker at a podium addressing other bankers. Pushing the idea of replacing food crops with luxury crops in poor countries. "Before long the population has forgotten how to feed itself and must import foodstuffs," reveled the banker. "With any luck we can sustain this vicious cycle forever!"

Now the three men sat around a table of polished mahogany. The muted sounds of bankers on speakerphones blended into a mélange of financial talk and evening plans. Steam rose from the Hudson below. Helicopters whizzed by outside at eye level.

It's going to happen, Randy Curtis thought ecstatically. It's really going to happen.

Lamond Godwin smiled.

We'll do it, he said.

.   .   .

Debt-for-nature swap was what the newspapers called it. Financial magic to leverage a little money into much more. Its roots lay in the Third World debt crisis. Back in the 1970s, banks had lent billions to poor countries during an oil boom to fund highways, factories, dams, and roads.

At the time lenders predicted big profits. But Lamond Godwin had a more cynical view. "Lots of bankers knew they'd never be repaid," he said. "They lent money anyway because they got big bonuses for getting business. By the time there were problems, they were working somewhere else. How do you think all these banks got so many bad loans on their books? You think everybody was that dumb?"

In 1982, Mexico announced it couldn't pay its debt. Forty countries followed. The crisis had begun.

But bad news for banks held hope for environmentalists. As the crisis worsened, Tom Lovejoy, then a World Wildlife Fund vice president, had the idea for swaps.

"I was sitting in a Congressional hearing, listening to a Brazilian ecologist rant about connections between debt and rain forest destruction," said Lovejoy. "He explained that to pay back debt, poor countries needed dollars. And to earn dollars they had to sell products overseas. Like timber, or soybeans." Crops that replaced rain forests. That caused big agricultural concerns to displace rural poor.

"They go to Rondônia and cut down forests," the Brazilian told the congressmen.

"As I sat there," Lovejoy said, "I remembered another connection. I'd returned from Brazil a few weeks before. There had been no money to pay park guards. Another casualty of the crushing debt burden."

Lovejoy wrote up his idea in the *New York Times.* "I wondered if there was a way to reduce foreign debt in exchange for environmental protection," he said.

Lovejoy's hope was that banks would simply donate bad debt. Few people took him seriously. Banks were interested in making money, not giving it away, critics said. Bankers who gave away debt would be in trouble with stockholders. Loans were held by many banks, which had signed agreements with each other, preventing any one of them from acting alone. And conservation groups were too undermanned to waste time on such an untested idea.

"It took me a while to realize the reason we put money in banks is because they don't give it away," Lovejoy laughed. "Anyway, a lot of people thought I was off my onion."

But by the time Randy Curtis called Lamond Godwin, the situation had changed.

A multimillion-dollar debt market—a great big gambling casino for foreign debt—had formed among banks. These banks held papers, legal obligations naming the amount of debt to be repaid. But with no one certain of how much of it would be repaid, the banks began buying, selling, and trading one another's debt, gambling on its ultimate value. A million dollars of paper might sell for as low as $100,000 in New York.

The second step occurred when American corporations began *using* the discounted debt to get good deals overseas. This was called debt-for-equity swaps. "Say one of our clients wanted to build a factory in Chile," Lamond Godwin explained. "The factory would normally cost $6 million dollars. But using a swap, instead of paying $6 million, the client could buy $6 million *worth* of Chilean debt for $1 million. The Chilean Central Bank would redeem the full value in Chilean currency, which of course is useful only in Chile. Our client would use the currency to build its factory. In the end the client would get the factory for $1 million. Chile would get reduced debt. American Express might make a loan, get some equity, take a tax loss on the bad debt, find investors, get a commission. It would come out even or a little ahead. A win-win situation."

"If companies could do swaps, why couldn't we?" said Randy Curtis.

In 1987, Conservation International announced the first debt-for-nature agreement. Not a safeguarded financial deal as far as Lamond Godwin was concerned. More like a promise. The organization bought $1 million of Bolivian debt for $650,000. It ripped up the debt. Bolivia promised to increase protection for its Amazon area.

Immediately, rumors began trickling out of Bolivia that the area wasn't being protected enough. Debt swaps were new, and techniques would be refined.

"Bad deal. Dumb deal," said Lamond Godwin.

.   .   .

Randy, Geoff and Lamond went over the Costa Rica deal again. Costa Rica was small, only twice the size of New Jersey, but it was the future, they hoped. A blueprint for larger deals they would do in Brazil. Within Costa Rica's varied terrain; mountain forests, lowland forests, and coral reefs, it had four percent of all biodiversity on earth. Eleven percent of the country was in parkland, Randy said, but hunters, loggers, and developers pushed into protected areas.

"Fourteen percent of the budget just goes to pay interest on the debt," Randy said. The Costa Rican government had come to him because he ran The Nature Conservancy's Costa Rica program when he wasn't doing swaps. If the Conservancy could raise $784,000 to buy $5.6 million worth of debt, Costa Rica would repay the whole sum in local currency and use the local money for the National Park program.

"Corcovado Park," Randy said, "has squatters, gold miners, poaching, timber. Its wildlife is in danger."

At the moment a dollar of Costa Rican debt was selling for fourteen cents in New York. American Express traders would be able to buy debt over the phone in minutes. The bank charged the Conservancy nothing. The cash for the transaction came from donors, including the Frank Weeden Foundation of Connecticut. The Costa Rican Central Bank took seventy percent off the top. It issued monetary stabilization bonds for thirty percent of the debt's face value, $1.7 million. The bonds would eventually generate $3 million in income. In the end, for every dollar the Nature Conservancy spent, Costa Rica would get $6 of protection.

Magic, Randy thought.

But Lamond Godwin thought Costa Rica had gotten off too easy with the seventy percent discount business. *Next time* The Nature Conservancy shouldn't have to give seventy percent away. *Next time* The Nature Conservancy might try to index proceeds to inflation in the country. And if there was going to be a next time, Lamond said, The Nature Conservancy ought to become a regular client.

The Conservancy transferred a $1 million certificate of deposit to the bank. The partnership was in place.

"But the *big* deal I was dreaming about," Randy Curtis said, "was Brazil." He had the sort of half-smile, faraway look that usually came into conservationists' faces when they talked of a swap in that huge country.

Brazil owed the world $150 billion. It had forty percent of all remaining tropical forests on earth.

"Brazil would be the big kahuna of swaps," Lamond Godwin said.

.   .   .

"The financial strategies used in swaps aren't new," Lamond Godwin said. "What is new is using them with a conservation group."

Lamond and I sat in a twenty-second-story conference room at the bank, Godwin sipping tea from a china cup. He was a cordial, direct man who broke banking terms into commonsense descriptions, so they were easy to understand. He exuded a candid, patient quality, never looking at his watch during our first two-hour meeting.

"Some guys are lenders. That's not my forte," he said. "I like to find creative ways to add value to a deal."

Over the years, Godwin had straddled a line between economics and social programs. Growing up in Mobile, Alabama, he'd worked as a graduate student researching racial discrimination in the construction industry, at the University of Texas. Later he'd written papers with his mentor, Ray Marshall, on rural poverty in the South.

Presidential candidate Jimmy Carter used their studies in his position papers. When Carter was elected, and named Marshall Secretary of Labor, Godwin moved to Washington too, as special assistant to the Secretary and Director of National Programs. After working on Jesse Jackson's 1984 Presidential campaign, he was a Harvard Kennedy School Fellow in economics, and professor at Rutgers.

"Every time I did something new, people would say, "You're not an agricultural economist! You're not a politician!" Godwin laughed.

Now he spent time traveling to Poland to negotiate a license for American Express Bank. To Mexico to do debt-for-equity swaps to repair storm damaged hotels. To Peru to try to get a "Supreme Decree" authorizing a whole swap program.

"Anybody can do anything," he said.

Before meeting Randy and Geoff, Godwin had familiarized himself with The Nature Conservancy. *National Geographic* had described the group as "At home in the boardroom as well as the wild, The Nature Conservancy is striking deals to preserve the earth's biological diversity. . . . The Nature Conservancy uses a business rather than a confrontational approach."

"I liked that," said Godwin, who could be critical of more strident environmentalists. "These guys, sitting in their offices, saying what's good for the Third World, looking out their windows and thinking the smog in L.A. is because some poor devil in the jungle is trying to clear land, to grow some beans—that's what George Wallace, with whom I disagree on everything else, called fuzzy-headed liberal thinking. When the environmentalist is doing more damage driving his car to meetings.

"The Nature Conservancy had a track record," Godwin said. "And I never knew Costa Rica was that important. Do you know one acre of forest in Costa Rica can have four hundred species of trees? I had no idea. To me, Costa Rica was a place with bad debt."

Still, Godwin found the conservationists "naive." "I could tell they knew a lot about conservation, but they wanted us to donate the money." Godwin chuckled. "Then they wanted to buy the debt at ten cents a dollar when it was selling at fourteen cents. I told them that nobody was going to sell debt to you at ten cents when they can get fourteen. But they had only so much money, and they knew how much debt they had to buy. They figured people would give them a break."

But Godwin didn't see eye to eye with everyone at the bank, either, although it helped that The Nature Conservancy and American Express shared a board member.

"The attitude here often was, you can't do business with a conservation group. That's not really business, with those tree huggers. Who gives a shit about Costa Rica? A debt-for-nature swap? Who ever heard of that? In the minds of people who like to think of themselves as right-wing Republicans, it was like, that's not a financial transaction, that's a social cause."

Once the swap was complete, though, the bank got a wave of good publicity. The deal was written up in *The New York Times*, *The Wall Street Journal*, and all over Latin America. American Express bragged about the swap in their annual report. "Costa Rica's tropical forest will benefit from an innovative debt-for-nature swap set up by the bank," the report said.

"That much publicity would have cost the bank a hundred thousand dollars, and we got it for free," Godwin said. "Our Latin American division loved it. And in the end the bank made as much as we would have earned selling debt on the market. We took a little loss, sure, but that's the price of a bad loan."

"And the guys who made fun of you beforehand?" I said.

Godwin leaned back. "They said, 'Pretty smart to achieve your aims in business and create a new product.' "

"Product?" I said. "That made the swap legitimate to them?"

"Yeah. Legitimate. A way of wrapping it in language acceptable to bankers," Godwin said. "I was creating a market for low-value debt." He smiled. "Product," he repeated. "Market."

. . .

By 1990 the role of another type of bank in rain forests was under fire by environmentalists. The World Bank and Inter-

American Development Bank, *multilateral* banks, were funded by national treasuries of member nations, including the United States, France, West Germany, and Japan.

Multilateral banks lent money based on votes from their boards of directors, each director from a funding country, each country's vote equal to the contribution it made. That gave the United States twenty percent of the power at the World Bank and thirty-five percent at the Inter-American Development Bank.

"The single gravest environmental impact of the multilateral development banks in Latin America may be their contribution to the accelerating deforestation of more than half the Earth's remaining forests," wrote Bruce Rich, an attorney with the Environmental Defense Fund in the mid-1980s.

"Multilateral development bank money is the motor behind big Third World development," Rich wrote.

In just 1983 the two banks lent $6.46 billion to Latin America. For each dollar that came from them, commercial banks often chipped in as much as three more. "Without the stamp of approval from the World Bank, countries can't get money for projects from private banks," Rich wrote.

BR-364 was a case in point. Brazil had planned to build it for years but couldn't do so until the World Bank approved loans in 1981.

In fact, for Bruce Rich and other environmentalists, BR-364 became the last straw, driving them into an unprecedented alliance with a conservative Republican senator, changing the way the banks do business.

It started in 1984. Horrified at the destruction along BR-364, Rich and other conservationists wrote World Bank President A. W. Clausen, begging him to change policy. Groups who signed included the Environmental Defense Fund, the National Wildlife Federation, the Audubon Society, and the World Wildlife Fund. Members of the West German Bundestag signed. So did the French office of Survival International, the Brazilian Bar Association. The Brazilian National Indian Support Organization. The Brazilian Anthropological Association. The Rio de Janeiro Environmental Policy Institute.

"The bank's $443.4 million investment so far," the letter

charged, "has contributed to uncontrolled migration, accelerated deforestation, conversion of land to unsustainable cattle ranching, land speculation, and encroachment on Indian lands."

Instead of stopping the excesses, the government was promoting *more* migration to the region, the letter complained.

"We urge the bank to undertake effective measures to regain control over its enormous investment," the letter urged.

The reply enraged Rich. Roberto Gonzelez Cofino, chief of the bank's Brazil division, wrote, "Polonoroeste is a carefully planned regional program. . . . We share your concerns. . . . We have discussed them in detail with Brazilian authorities and are encouraged by the discussions. Your concern will be considered as Polonoroeste continues."

Up until now the scenario had been typical. Environmentalists had been brushed off. But Rich did something different. He brought the letter to Senator Robert Kasten of Wisconsin, a conservative Republican who headed the Senate subcommittee overseeing U.S. contributions to multilateral development banks.

Kasten went through the roof. "As you know better than anyone else," he wrote Clausen, "securing support for the U.S. contribution to multilateral institutions is difficult at best. That the World Bank would respond in so cavalier a fashion to groups who would otherwise support their projects is difficult to understand."

The bank's letter was "an insult," Kasten said.

He didn't stop there. He shot off a note to Treasury Secretary Donald Regan. The World Bank is "arrogant and totally unwilling to receive constructive criticism which in the long run would help these institutions," he wrote. He began holding Senate hearings on the multilateral banks.

Clausen backpeddled; he set up conciliatory meetings with environmentalists and Kasten's staff. Too late. One of the oddest alliances in Washington had been formed. And it was so effective, both big banks started altering policy. In January 1985 the U.S. executive director of the Inter-American Development Bank blocked part of a $72 million loan for a continuation of BR-364 and the Polonoroeste colonization project into Acre until Brazil redesigned the plan to include comprehensive environmental and Indian lands protection. Two months later the World Bank halted Polonoroeste disbursements until the same conditions were met.

"If environmental groups had acted alone, the Brazilian government would have ignored them," said Steve Schwartzmann of the Environmental Defense Fund.

By 1987, Kasten was still charging the bank with "dragging its feet," the environmentalists still complained that Polonoroeste was out of control. The Inter-American Development Bank suspended some loans on the project when, once again, settlers and miners flooded the region and Indian areas weren't demarcated.

Brazilian politicians complained of foreign interference. "Environmental groups are too powerful," lamented Foreign Ministry Secretary General Flecha Tarso de Lima when I met him in Brasília. The politicians announced the road would be paved anyway, with Brazilian money, but the bulldozers fell idle. Without bank participation, stretches of BR-364 remained mud seas in rainy season, impassable. Completed new overpasses lay like islands off the road, not even linked to the path that was there. Trucks carrying goods along the rutted highway outside Rio Branco passed armies of parked earth-moving machinery—bulldozers, steamrollers, pavers, tractors—row after row ready to fire up, cut, clear, and lay asphalt when the loans started up again.

"There aren't any technical problems to paving the road," said one official from the Mendes, Jr. Company, which owned the machinery. "We could do a mile a day if we had money. The money just ran out."

All forces seemed posed for destruction or preservation. "BR-364 has become a line in the Amazon, a test case," said Mark Plotkin, vice president of Conservation International. "It's where we'll see how the whole region goes."

By 1989 the World Bank had added special environmental staff—sixty people—in Washington. "No loan of any kind can go through without environmental approval," said Marc Dourojeanni, senior environmental officer.

Even watchdog Bruce Rich wrote that the bank "tried to take decisive action to stem the rising tide of criticism."

"Many of the changes in the World Bank over the past year could bring lasting benefit with official encouragement," he said.

But the big word was *could*. There was always the gap between what bank officials announced in the office and what really happened on the ground far away.

For instance, one day I spent a few hours in Brasília with Bill Ellis, an Inter-American Development Bank representative in Brazil. He was a tall, rangy native of Seattle who had married a Brazilian and lived there for many years. He said the suspended IDB loan for the road was about to be renewed. Brazil had submitted a revised environmental protection plan. "A great plan," he said.

"Do you think it will be followed?"

Ellis looked sad. "No."

"Then why release the funds?"

Ellis pursed his lips. We were driving around Brasília, and he was showing me sights; a lake outside town. A suburban area with beautiful homes. The presidential palace. "What can we do?" he asked. "They rewrote the proposal. On paper everything looks good. We tried to get them to take the money for some other project, a road near São Paulo. They wanted this."

He had the same mix of hope and wariness that World Bank environment officer Maritta Koch-Weser exhibited when I met her in the bank offices near the White House in Washington. Koch-Weser, a senior sociologist in the bank's environmental division, was a slim, direct Swiss who was one of the few personnel at the bank praised by Bruce Rich and Senator Kasten's office. Fluent in Portuguese, she traveled to Brazil regularly for conferences or trips along BR-364. She said over lunch that the bank was considering a new loan in Rondônia, "Planaflora" for demarcating Indian lands, protecting parks, and environmental zoning.

Polonoroeste had been "horrible," she admitted. "It went out of control. What happened was not what we anticipated. Our original thinking was, small farmer development was better than large development. That areas could be protected. The agreement was, unsuitable areas would not be opened for agriculture.

"It didn't work. Part of the problem was land speculation. You could drive along the highway and see people burning forest. You'd ask them, 'What are you going to grow here?' They'd say, 'I don't know.' Speculation. The other problem was, how do you sequence development on a frontier? We thought you could do it simultaneously, protect and develop at the same time." She shook her head. "Next time we'd like to see consolidation of natural resource planning first."

Koch-Weser said Planaflora represented "the most progress the bank has made so far in the environment. The bank wouldn't have gone in with environmental financing if there hadn't been real progress in Brazil. Institutional reform. I admit they don't have a marvelous environmental agency, but at least they have an agency. They've cut incentives for livestock. They're ending the rules allowing farmers to get land by clearing it. They're creating legislation for extractive reserves, and zoning."

She gave a quick, knowing smile. "And we won't be working with government officials," she said, as if that was a plus. "Instead of working with government officials, badly paid, we'll contract for services. We want to get away from a situation where we have a very sluggish public sector, and a private sector trying to steal as much as possible."

She laughed.

"It took some convincing to get the Brazilians to do this," she added more seriously. "This $166 million is a real step for the environment. Just the repair of a landslide in Rio de Janeiro two years ago cost $200 million, more than this whole project, and if they had had an environmental program in the first place and not deforested where they shouldn't have, the landslide wouldn't have taken place."

Upstairs I met Marc Dourojeanni, Senior Environmental Officer at the bank, who would soon be leaving to head up the environment office at the Inter-American Development Bank across town. Dourojeanni was a courtly, animated Peruvian, former professor of natural history in Lima, ex-director of Peru's Forestry and Wildlife Department. His tie featured pandas down the front.

"Planaflora," Marc Dourojeanni said, "will delineate what is suitable for agriculture in Rondônia, and what is suitable for forestry."

He chuckled.

"It will be initiated by the government, and then it will not be enforced," he said. "But that is another story."

One by one rain-forest countries began completing debt for nature swaps. Bolivia with Conservation International. Madagascar with the World Wildlife Fund. Ecuador and Zaire and the Philippines. Always for a small amount of money. A million. A few million. Always Brazil lay on the horizon.

Debt swap proposals were on the table in Jamaica and Argentina. In Panama, as U.S. troops mopped up after the invasion toppling dictator Manuel Noriega, Nature Conservancy Vice President Geoffrey Barnard flew into battle-ravaged Panama City and drove past GIs with darkened faces, and roadblocks and sandbags, to the Presidential palace.

With gunfire echoing in the room, he met with the new President, Guillermo Endara, to propose ways of protecting Panama's biggest money-maker, the Panama Canal, from tons of silt washing into it from deforested hills. The meeting eventually led to Congress allocating $10 million of war aid to Panama for debt for nature swaps.

"It was scary," said Barnard.

But Brazil, with the biggest remaining chunk of rain forest on earth, remained elusive. Brazilian politicians always seemed to equate debt for nature swaps with foreign control. "We don't want the Amazon to become a green Persian Gulf," said Brazilian President José Sarney. Foreigners had long accused Brazilians with being "paranoid" about sovereignty questions. But a glance at Brazilian history showed the worry was justified sometimes.

Minister of Interior Joao Alves Filho listed a timeline of "international threats to the Amazon" in a fiery speech in 1989. First there was the original fight between Portugal and Spain for dominion of the Amazon, in the 1600s and 1700s. By the 1800s British explorers traveled the Amazon without Brazilian government permission, he said. British politicians proposed that the Amazon separate itself from the rest of Brazil in 1836, when British mining and ranching companies were starting up in the north of the country. The French actually occupied the Brazilian territory of Amapa in 1835, stayed until an international arbitration commission gave it back to Brazil in 1900, and in the interim offered to sell it to the United States, the way France had sold Louisiana.

After the Civil War the U.S. Ambassador to Brazil proposed sending American blacks to colonize the Amazon. In the 1890s Bolivia awarded a group of American businessmen, called "The Bolivian Syndicate," control of part of Bolivia's eastern Amazon. Residents rebelled at the news, and were annexed by Brazil.

And then there were the corporations, charged Filho. The American "Amazon Development Company." "The Canadian Amazon Company Limited." "The American Brazilian Exploration Corporation." The Japanese "Gensabure Yamanishi Kinraku." Brazilians often invited the companies in and provided excellent business incentives, then turned around and started complaining they were trying to take over. But Filho didn't mention that part.

He did dwell on a proposal by American futurist Herman Kahn, in the early 1970s, that the Amazon be converted into a gigantic internationalized lake, for hydroelectric power.

If these stories seem laughable to North Americans, they are taken more seriously in the South. "When I was working in Wildlife Management in Lima, in 1965," said Marc Dourojeanni at the World Bank, "a U.S. Colonel visited us asking us to do research in the Amazon. Anywhere. They'd provide the money. He said surveys were being conducted by the U.S. on having the Amazon occupied in case of nuclear war. If that was *my* experience as a professor, think what the military knows."

Now environmentalists like Randy Curtis kept trying to stir up Brazilian government interest in a swap. They said they wanted to work with local groups. They stressed that when they did swaps in other countries, local groups managed the funds, not the foreigners. *The New York Times* editorialized that an $8 billion debt-for-nature swap in Brazil would "ease Brazil's burden of foreign borrowing and preserve the Amazon forest." Time after time waves of excitement swept the environmental community at rumors that the deal they all dreamed of, the big Brazil swap, was imminent. The Nature Conservancy even sent out letters to donors predicting a swap would happen "within the next thirty to sixty days." "Several banks have agreed to cooperate," the letter said. "The President's son is interested."

Nothing happened.

"Things always seem to be on the verge," Randy Curtis complained.

In Washington I asked Brazilian ambassador to the United States Marcilio Marques Moreira if he thought debt swaps were just a way for foreigners to buy up control of a region. "That is a crude but accurate description," he said dryly. He added, "We don't ask for Yosemite."

Foreign Ministry General Secretary Paulo Flecha de Lima told me that swaps wouldn't solve the problems anyway. The Amazon was too big, the proposed swaps tiny. "Does that mean you would consider a big swap?" I asked. De Lima changed the subject.

Brazilian conservation groups held meetings in the summer of 1990, trying to put together a series of debt-for-nature proposals, specific programs, for submission to the Central bank.

Nothing happened.

Brazilian groups held a second round of meetings in the fall of 1990. They sent proposals to the Central Bank.

Newly elected president Fernando Collor de Mello announced he was in favor of swaps.

Randy Curtis sighed. "Brazil is a conundrum," he said.

·   ·   ·

The evening was cool and beautiful, and the setting sun glowed above the Hudson River and New Jersey palisades. Lamond Godwin relaxed at an outdoor cafe on the promenade, ordered a glass of rosé wine with his dinner, and sipped at it so sparingly that half was left when he was through.

"This isn't like New York here," he said, glorying in the evening. Leafy trees shaded the patio. The smell of spicy pesto sauce mixed with the pleasant odors of trees and river. Godwin lived within walking distance of the bank, and strolled along the promenade to work each day. When he talked of going into the rest of Manhattan, he called it "the interior."

Three years had passed since Randy Curtis's first call to Godwin, two years since the Costa Rica deal. Since then he'd helped The Nature Conservancy with swaps in Ecuador and Argentina. The U.S. Congress had authorized the use of vast portions of bilateral debt—money that foreign countries directly owed the U.S. government—for swaps too. Godwin was working with Curtis on more swaps in Honduras and Jamaica. Curtis was due in New York in a few weeks to introduce Lamond to the head of the Dominican Republic's largest conservation group. The government there had just authorized a $80 million quota to be redeemed in swaps.

Godwin said the original ad hoc Costa Rica deal had become a "partnership."

"We have a strategy now, an agenda. We know which countries we want to do and which projects. American Express wants to do something that will enhance our reputation as a corporate citizen. These swaps turned a mistake, bad loans, into something positive."

Curtis had come a long way in terms of his knowledge of finance, Godwin said. That first deal with Costa Rica hadn't been as beneficial as it could have been, but American Express had gotten better terms in other deals later.

It was funny because the week before I'd asked Randy if he'd felt naive when he first met Godwin. "Sure," he said. I'd asked if the Costa Rica deal had been bad.

"No," he'd said. We'd been in another cafe, this one in Washington. "Costa Rica had already set the terms when they came to us," he said. "And we still got $2 to one. But more than that," he said, smiling, "there was the good will. I'll tell you a story. Two boys grew up as friends in Costa Rica. One became the head of the Central Bank. The other an adviser to the president. But they'd lost contact until these debt swaps started. The friendship started up again. And before the adviser left office, it was the *banker* who said, Hey, let's do one more swap before you leave. And they did.

"How do you put a dollar value on the relationships that come out of swaps," Randy said. "Swaps won't go on forever. The debt crisis will be resolved one day. But these relationships will continue. They're a fundamental change."

In a good partnership, both partners are satisfied. Now Lamond told me it would be a mistake for me to regard American Express's interest in swaps as typical of banks. "American Express Bank works for American Express Company," he said. "And the company has a big stake in tourism. When the beaches were destroyed in Cancun a few years ago in a hurricane, we had a stake in getting them rebuilt. Eighty percent of our income comes from people using credit cards and traveler's checks and booking tours through our travel offices. Concern about the environment is a mainstream issue here."

Still, other banks had at least made token contributions in the debt for nature effort. Morgan Bank had sourced debt for the World Wildlife Fund, as had Citibank. Fleet National Bank of Rhode Island had donated $250,000 to the Nature Conservancy in one Costa Rica deal. Lawyers at Sherman & Stearling in New York had given the World Wildlife Fund free legal counsel on swaps. Swaps involved financial types who had not previously been able to use their skills to help conservation.

"Swaps are fun," Godwin said, eating the chicken out of his green salad, leaving the vegetables. "We've been able to take a little acorn, that first Costa Rica deal, and grow it into an oak tree. A company-wide initiative on the environment. At American Express the environment has gone from the bottom of the agenda to the top. We don't view this as philanthropic. We view it as marketing. The same reason you want to advertise at the Olympics, or give to the United Way."

The change in corporate attitude had not come about solely because of swaps, he said. There was a whole range of reasons. "The environment itself," he said. "Global warming. *Fortune* magazine did a spread on it. Bankers read *Fortune*." The *Exxon Valdez* going aground had subjected corporations to pressure from environmental groups, he said. Shareholders, church groups holding blocks of stock, began showing up at meetings demanding we sign an environmental policy statement called the *Valdez* principles. The publicity after the swaps had helped. So had Godwin's love of creative deals and CEO James Robinson's support and desire to unload debt.

In fact, Godwin was working on a new initiative now. "Cause-related marketing," he said. "Like what we did with the Statue of Liberty. Every time you use your credit card, we make a donation to the Nature Conservancy. It looks like it's going to go through in North America. And it might go through in South America too. Brazil has the most holders of American Express credit cards in South America.

"We've done research convincing us that a significant number of our card members would respond positively to this initiative," he said. "People who fit our profiles support conservation. They're highly educated with high incomes. People who travel a lot."

Lamond said Brazil's President Collor had been in New York the week before. He had eaten dinner at the home of American Express chairman James Robinson and told him he was interested in swaps.

"Nothing new about that," I said.

"I also think Latins are at the point where they see environment as their major asset. They're trying to figure out ways to play that trump card as leverage," Godwin said. He leaned back. He was late for his next meeting, with the ambassador from Niger, to advise him on a real estate deal. It had been a slow, pleasant, easy dinner. With night, a cool breeze came off the river.

Godwin knew that a consortium of Brazilian groups had submitted a swap proposal to the Central Bank. He knew the Nature Conservancy and other U.S. groups were holding their breaths, waiting to see what happened.

But in some ways what happened with nonprofit groups wasn't even the point anymore. In some ways the new partnership between the Nature Conservancy and the bank was moving again, changing into a new phase.

Godwin wanted to do cause-related marketing in Brazil, whether or not the Nature Conservancy was involved.

"We wouldn't even consider a deal unless it was something Brazil wanted," Godwin said. "You gotta find the formula, the right formula. We could just as easily give the money to a Brazilian group. The Nature Conservancy would like that. I mean, I would still try to lock them into the deal if I could.

"I don't want to blow these guys out of the water," he said, meaning the Nature Conservancy, "and nothing's going to happen this year anyway. Our budget for that kind of thing is used up. But I think something's going to happen next year. One way or the other. I'll give them a chance to put something in place, but," Lamond said, standing to go to the next meeting, "if my people decide they're ready to move and the conservation groups have made no progress, I'll do it myself."

The Forest Police

The bus jolted to a halt, and up and down the dark aisle shadowy figures groped for luggage in the overhead rack. "Extrema!" the driver said. Groggily I sat up, shuffled to the front, and stepped down onto a dirt road. It was 5 A.M. As the bus pulled away, lights receding, passengers fanned out around me, sure-footed in the dark. After two or three minutes I couldn't see them anymore.

In the fifty kilometers between the Santa Carmen Ranch and Extrema, the bus had passed ranches, gold mining camps, and bumped over turn-of-the-century bridges on wooden slats laid over rotting railroad ties. We'd been ferried on a barge across the Madeira River, had passed beyond the paved part of the highway. From now on the road would alternate surfaces—dirt to asphalt and back to dirt.

Extrema was a frontier town of colonists and sawmills, a town building itself out of the jungle, a town where I hoped to find the famed forest police.

Everywhere in Brazil I had heard boasts about the forest police, both the state and federal kind, who would be enforcing the country's new environmental laws. "Our state agents will help stop illegal burnings in the forest," the governor of Rondônia, Jerônimo Santana, had told me in his Pôrto Velho office. "The federal forest police have received new men, better equipment," said João Alves Filho, in Brasília, poking a floor-to-ceiling map of the country.

I had never met a forest policeman, but they seemed to me, as I listened, to be the Texas Rangers, the Eliot Nesses of the frontier. On one side, the rampaging forces of illegal destruction, powerful ranchers, and sawmill owners accustomed to having their way. On the other, a handful of brave officers. *Hold it, buddy! Forest police!* Would they really turn out to be that way?

Extrema, which I could barely make out in the dark, seemed the perfect setting for the sort of confrontation I envisioned. Groping toward what I hoped would be the center of town, I passed two-story, squarish shadows of houses and stores. Dogs barked, and the barking got closer. I slipped between buildings and on a smaller street caught sight of a glow ahead and moved toward it. But when I reached it, I saw it was a dying sawdust fire in a mill. Unattended, it must have burned all night. The glow lit the bandsaw, the open-air shed, the neatly stacked beams for export or construction. I felt as if the saw had been working through the night on its own, a tropism of commerce and destruction, slicing trees. I remembered that the international tropical hardwood trade is a $7 billion-a-year business. The number of sawmills in Rondônia rose from 4 in 1959 to 330 in 1982. And in the tropics in general, logging—much of it illegal—accounts for 12.5 million deforested acres a year, report researchers at the National Institute for Research in the Amazon. Over half of the hardwood exports come from Indonesia, the Philippines, and Malaysia, but as those forests get logged out, the Amazon will come under more pressure. And the forest police will have to be the ones to protect it.

I stepped into a ditch, almost losing balance, and onto another road. I caught sight of the bus a hundred yards ahead and realized I must have gotten off at the wrong end of town. There was an official bus depot which I walked toward more briskly. At 5:30 A.M. the mosquitos came out. Dawn and dusk are the most dangerous times for contracting malaria, and since most people in Extrema get malaria, I preferred to be inside. I drew my collar around my neck and quickened my pace.

"You want to visit the forest police?" Governor Santana had said, smile broadening. "Absolutely! Arrange it with the secretary of the state institute of forests." My meeting with the secretary, Chico Araujo, had been easily set up. We'd sat in his office during a power failure, leaning toward each other and squinting in the candlelight as I tried to take notes. A brand-new building for a brand-new government agency. And no electricity to run it.

Araujo, a fortyish man with a thick black mustache, lamented that he had funding problems. He wanted more money from the World Bank. He said that in the Amazon burning is the only way, the historic way to clear land. And that his job was more to persuade people not to burn than to punish them for doing it. He was happy I wanted to visit the forest police and wrote me a note guaranteeing total access.

The bus depot was a small restaurant with a few wooden tables, lit by flickering candles in glass holders. The proprietor introduced himself as Roberto and reminded me of a jolly German publican. Blond and thirtyish, he had arrived in Extrema eight years ago as a colonist. He poured cups of hot, sweet coffee as the bus pulled onto the unpaved highway and headed west. "In the beginning here," he said, "the government gave away land. We heard about it on TV. Settlers came from south of Brazil, pushed out by big soybean farms. We arrived on buses with nothing. No tools. No food. We lived in tents. Many people got malaria, and others left. I don't have my farm here anymore, I have the restaurant. But the ones who stuck it out are happy now. And we have big plans. We're forming an association. We want to plant palm oil trees, rubber trees, coffee. The bishop of Acre helped us get funding from Holland."

The sun was coming up slowly. The town glowed orange. The first car drove up to the restaurant, and men got out and ordered coffee. Eight hundred people lived in Extrema. I saw neatly laid out red dirt streets lined with tin-roofed homes. And ahead, an out-of-place ski chalet, a Swiss dream in the jungle. I told Roberto I had come to interview the forest police. I hoped the forest police would really be here. Back in Pôrto Velho, Chico Araujo had pointed out on his map another town, Abuná, and told me to go there if I wanted to meet forest police. On a Saturday I'd made the three-hour drive along BR-364 and asked directions to headquarters.

"Forest police?" a man with a fishing rod over his shoulder had said, scratching his head. "There aren't any forest police here."

"Forest police?" the local police sergeant had said. "Nope."

Now Roberto pointed down a narrow road leading from the restaurant past wooden houses. "Fifty meters that way. They open at seven. The forest police," he added, "have a tough job."

.   .   .

Extrema was in a big mess. Nobody knew what state the town belonged to or even the official name of the place. The argument over who owned the colony—Rondônia or Acre—had heated up recently with the discovery of gold nearby. As I walked through the streets, smearing on insecticide, I saw evidence of the public relations battle everywhere: THIS IS TANCREDO NEVES screamed immense yellow, blue, and green banners hung from Rondônia government buildings. Tancredo Neves was the Rondônian name for the town, as well as the section of Pôrto Velho Bimarzio Fabio Filho had lived in. WELCOME TO ACRE proclaimed more modest announcements in white. Half of the vehicles were the heavy, copper-colored Jeeps and Toyota Bandeirantes favored by the Rondônian government, with RONDÔNIA stenciled in black on the sides. The other half were smaller white Chevrolet sedans with attractive green ACRE GOVERNMENT painted in more humble letters. I asked directions from a man carrying a machete, and he sent me to a building where two men stood with their boots on the bumper of an Acre car.

"Oh, you want the Rondônia police. We're the Acre police," they said when I showed them Chico Araujo's card. "The Rondônia police are a two-minute walk."

I asked them if they knew the time. "Acre time or Rondônia time?" they said. "There's an hour difference."

I remembered how three weeks before, when I arrived in Brazil, headlines had screamed that Rondônia had sent troops to seize Extrema and New California, a sister town down BR-364. A day later the papers had announced Acre was sending troops too. In Brasília, a general named Rubem Bayma Denys assured me there was no danger in traveling to Extrema because federal troops had been dispatched to keep the states from fighting each other. Terrific, I'd figured. *Three* armies.

"The troops went home," one of the Acre policemen said now. "They kept to themselves anyway. There was never any fighting. In fact, this dispute is the greatest thing that ever happened to Extrema. Neither state used to pay us any attention, but now we have three medical centers, two police stations. The governor of Rondônia was here last week, and the governor of Acre is coming this afternoon."

"Nobody pays taxes to either state," said the other policeman. "Suppose they choose wrong?"

"I hope," said the first policeman, an Extrema patriot, "this fight never ends."

With the sun higher, I could see a quarter mile to the edge of town. A truck rumbled by on 364, throwing up dust, heading for Rio Branco. The jungle rose on all sides, and the canopy, this close, broke into different trees. A macaw flew over the THIS IS TAN-CREDO NEVES sign on the newly constructed Rondônia civic center and winged into the forest.

"The forest police must have a hard time keeping tabs on ranchers," I said to the policemen. They shifted their boots on the bumper of the car. I remembered words I had read in a report published by the National Institute for Research in the Amazon: "Establishment of rational forest land-use policy and adequate forest management techniques has become *the* priority for governments in the region if the Amazon is to be developed for greater human use without incurring severe ecological and economic consequences in the near future." Easier said than done, I gathered from the look on the policemen's faces. They had compassion for any law enforcement officer, no matter which state he worked for.

"The forest police," said the first policeman, nodding, "have a tough job."

. . .

He carried an attaché case instead of a gun. I'd expected a uniform, but twenty-six-year-old Robson Vitali wore a red basketball shirt, jeans, and pointy-toed cowboy boots the color of faded earth. His sunburned face and blond curls gave him the look of a California beachboy. I didn't show him Chico Araujo's card. I was curious to see whether he would be reluctant to talk, whether he would need official prodding. I was curious about whether or not he was crooked. But Robson smiled broadly and invited me into his office. Already a line of supplicants had formed, waiting to see him.

Robson and his attractive, dark-haired secretary sat at side-by-side desks in front of the colonists. There was a refrigerator behind them, but it wasn't plugged in; they stored government forms in it. A photograph of Governor Santana leaned against the wall on the floor. The governor was smiling, wearing his green sash and holding his cane, his trademark, though when I had met him in his office he'd rushed around without it.

There was a pile of small wooden blocks in a corner, samples of different kinds of timber from the jungle. I picked one up. A tarantula crawled around underneath. "Don't step on it," Robson called over. "They kill insects."

I leaned against an olive-colored file cabinet, as bored as I would be waiting for any government employee to fill out forms. The people here today wanted permission to burn rain forest, to expand their farms. Under new laws apparently being honored at the moment, forest police had to approve any cutting. Robson met with a widow from São Paulo who had moved here two years ago. A farmer in his best white shirt who carefully unfolded the deed to his land. A fourteen-year-old girl who had hitchhiked into town to get Robson's permission to burn, and to bring her little brother to the malaria clinic.

Each time a colonist presented a deed, Robson checked it against an immense blueprint tacked to a wall, carved into rectangular lots. It might have been a California subdivison, but it was the Amazon jungle. "Where is the northern boundary of your lot?" Robson would ask. "Who is your neighbor? How did you get this land?"

"Remember," Robson told the man in the white shirt after granting him permission to cut, "don't burn Brazil nut trees. It's illegal."

"I'm sorry but I'm going to have to keep your papers," he told a man in a black cowboy hat. "Your deed isn't signed. You have to go back to Pôrto Velho and bring the man who sold you the land here. I have to talk to him."

Robson went out to the Toyota and came back to distribute a stack of save-the-forest pamphlets, sent to Rondônia by the Ministry of Interior. The booklets contained a cartoon story of the old farmer who burns the forest and has to abandon his farm, and a young man who preserves the forest and grows healthy crops.

A knot of colonists standing by leafed through the pamphlets. I noticed the widow staring at a caption.

"I can't read," she said.

Wait a minute, I thought. What about the new equipment? Midnight police raids? This was more like jungle bureaucrat. As the time ticked by, the self-contained aspect of the whole process began to bother me. Tucked away here, away from the vast jungle outside, could a single man really monitor five hundred thousand hectares of forest, Robson's responsibility? Were the neat blueprints, the detailed questions, the sense of order deceptively incomplete? Robson, cool, kind, and unflappable, patiently repeated instructions to each person in line.

Finally, he asked me if I wanted to go into the forest.

.   .   .

Dodging potholes, the Toyota Bandeirante shot east along BR-364. Outside of town I counted sawmills, all smoking, gray funnels rising into the Amazon sky. Four in half a mile. Five. "Where do you want to go?" Robson asked.

"A big ranch," I replied. "I want to visit a big rancher who applied to burn forest."

Robson had his machete, water bottle, and attaché case on the front seat. After a while we left the main road, drove into a ditch, and cut across a field of pasture. We stopped to unhook the latch on a barbed-wire gate and rolled up to a modest one-story ranch house made of timber. Three women were gathered on the front steps watching us. They were better dressed than the colonists at the office. Two of them wore designer jeans.

The owner, it seemed, was across the highway at work in his rain forest. We thanked the women and followed their directions, parking at another fence and slipping through the strands of barbed wire. Robson led the way across another field, toward a wall of jungle, past a muddy waterhole, four white Brahman cows staring at us, and across a log that spanned a stream. Already I was sweating, and insects bit my neck. As we reached the shadow line of forest, two men seemed to detach themselves from the trees and approach. The shorter, stockier man, dressed in grimy khaki shorts and a shirt, turned out to be a sawmill owner here to appraise the property. He greeted Robson, shook hands, and quickly left. The owner reminded me of the Marlboro man. Black cowboy hat. Sideburns neatly trimmed, all the way down near his chin. Cigarette. Pointy boots. Rolled sleeves on a twin-buttoned shirt. He seemed glad to see Robson, and he led us along a trail into the forest. Ahead of me, Robson looked funny with the machete and the attaché case.

Suddenly there was a crashing in the underbrush. A man burst into view, wielding a scythe. Sweat drenched his face, undershirt, and running pants. "Ants! Ants! I'm fever," he cried. He worked for the rancher and had been attacked while cutting. Already he was catching a fever from the bites. He sat on a log, lit a cigarette, gasped for breath.

We reached the area that the rancher had applied for permission to cut, but the trees were down already. Trunks lay drying, readying for fire. Foot-high masses of brush turned brown. In the new man-made clearing, the sun seemed very hot.

"You're not supposed to cut *before* you get permission," Robson said.

The rancher nodded, eased closer. "I know it," he said "and I want to tell you something." He touched his heart. "*I* did not cut this. It was my worker who cut it. I told him not to cut it, I told him, 'Don't cut it.' Can you imagine that? He didn't listen!"

We stood in a field of dead, slashed-away wood. The rancher lit another cigarette, and we started off again. After awhile we saw a Brazil nut tree on the ground, dead.

"You're not supposed to cut those," Robson said.

The cowboy hat went up and down. "Don't you think I know that? But you know what? *I* did not do that. *I* would never cut a Brazil nut tree. I like Brazil nut trees. The former owner did it."

And again, at a waterhole, Robson pointed to trunks on the ground. It was illegal to cut trees beside the water. Bad for the cattle. They could get stuck in the mud and die.

"The former owner," the rancher said.

The rancher asked if we wanted to come back to the house for coffee, but Robson demurred. We had to go. In the truck, as Robson drove, I asked him if the rancher would be fined.

"Probably," Robson said.

"What do you mean, probably? Will you fine him?"

In the same calm tones, Robson said, "I'll write it up in my report and give it to the man from the federal government." The federal agent for the Brasília-based agency called IBAMA (the Brazilian Institute for Forest Development) had a job similar to Robson's except that he enforced federal, not state, environmental laws. Both agencies had to approve certain types of cutting and burning, but only IBAMA could issue licenses to sawmills to cut trees. And IBAMA agents could theoretically call in federal troops or federal police if their edicts were thwarted.

"Well, may I ask a question? Do you have the power to fine him?"

"Oh, sure," Robson said.

"And didn't you tell me the federal inspector has a few hundred hectares to patrol? What if he never gets around to visiting this ranch?"

Robson nodded sadly. "That is a problem," he said. In parts of Pará, I'd heard, officers responsible for monitoring forest had as many as one hundred thousand square kilometers—close to 30 million acres—to watch over.

"And besides," I pushed, "how come, if there are only two of you for such a big area, you and the federal agent, you have to do the same work twice?"

Robson glanced into my eyes. "I'd rather lose my job than my life," he said.

"That's what this is about? That rancher would kill you?"

The forest policeman shrugged. "Someone would."

Neither of us spoke for a few minutes. The gray smoke from the sawmills came into view. Robson said eagerly, "You want to see the illegal things they're doing at the mills?"

I was confused. Robson didn't seem embarrassed. He didn't seem to be hiding things. Why did he want to show me crimes he was supposed to solve but did nothing about?

·   ·   ·

The mill occupied the base of a stadium-shaped depression in the earth the size of half a football field. It smelled of burning wood and sap and gasoline. A controlled sawdust fire raged twenty feet from the mill, and I felt the heat and saw, through the convoluted air, the flickering forms of shirtless, grime-smeared workers, the fat logs propelled on mechanical trolleys toward the screaming blade. A long semitrailer with license plates from Rio, fifteen hundred miles to the east, was loaded with freshly cut timber. Logs lay in piles around the hillside, waiting to be cut.

All work stopped as the men caught sight of Robson.

Everything here is illegal," Robson told me, still in the cab, as the workers began drifting toward us like creatures out of *The Night of the Living Dead*. "See the truck? That's illegal wood in there, under the top layer. Plus they have Brazil nut trees hidden around here somewhere, probably in back. They cut them and ship them at night. They're supposed to have a license to do *any* cutting, but IBAMA, which issues the licenses, is on strike. The mill doesn't have a license to cut any of this."

We were surrounded the second we left the truck. The mill owner, a surly-looking, curly-haired man with a clipboard, stepped nose to nose with Robson. "What do you want?" he demanded.

"Just to look around," replied the jungle policeman. "Is the wood in the truck legal?"

"Oh, absolutely," the owner said.

"Do you have a license for it?"

The owner smiled and held out a piece of paper. Lots of times, Robson had told me, mill owners use the same license over and over, just changing the dates.

"Where are you hiding the Brazil nut trees?" Robson asked, and everybody laughed. Big joke. "Ha ha," the owner said. "Brazil nut trees? What Brazil nut trees?"

Robson appeared to be defusing the tension. He climbed up the side of the semi and looked down at the wood inside. He didn't touch anything. He walked thirty feet up the hillside and glanced at a pile of logs. The workers returned to their jobs. At the screaming bandsaw, steel pincers rotated a four-foot-wide log, positioning it for cutting. Water sprayed over the saw as it worked, cooling it.

"Let's go," Robson told me.

"I don't get it," I said, back in the Toyota. "Why didn't you look under the top layer of wood in the semi?"

"Are you kidding? There are twenty of them and one of me."
"Why didn't you give a summons for sawing without a license?"
"The owner would just rip it up."
"Why didn't you check for hidden Brazil nut trees?"
"Listen," Robson said. "Until Acre and Rondônia figure out who owns this place, the states have agreed to stop enforcement. I'm under orders."

. . .

Robson and I went to the Rondônia restaurant in town. I knew it was the Rondônia restaurant because every vehicle parked in front was owned by the Rondônia government, and every car across the street in front of another restaurant was white and green, Acre colors.

THIS IS RONDÔNIA proclaimed one of those big banners near our outdoor table.

The waitress brought heaping plates of steak, rice, beans, potato salad, and extra-large, iced bottles of Antarctica beer. The flies liked the steak and potato salad equally. I liked the potato salad better.

"I noticed that all the applications you worked on in your office came from colonists," I said. "Do you ever have time to check the property of people who don't apply for permits to burn? Squatters? Big ranchers?"

"No," Robson said, chewing.

"Do you ever get to check the property of rich people?"

"No," Robson said matter-of-factly, unflappable.

"What happens if a rich man gets fined?" I asked.

Robson took a second helping of beans. "We have to take it back," he said. "Once I fined a Rondônia State senator, and it didn't work. Last year I fined a rich rancher. My boss ordered me to cancel the fine."

Robson poured more beer. "Look," he said. "The Amazon has been populated by people without hope, desperate people. It's very easy for strong people to dominate the population. You want to know how Brazil exploits people? The man with nine hundred thousand hectares of land doesn't farm it, doesn't even use it. He sells the wood and gets rich. After he takes all the richness from the land, it is occupied by poor people. What happens when poor people occupy poor land? They get poorer."

I stared at Robson. He relaxed, lapsing back into his calm, even-handed demeanor.

"Want more potato salad?" he asked

.   .   .

Talking to Robson about enforcement difficulties reminded me of Paulo Benincá De Salles, a top IBAMA official I'd met in Brasília. There the government had seemed so much more powerful, at least on the surface. Finer, richer. Brasília was a perfectly planned city, a monument of human order over nature. The ministry buildings all lined up in rows, all of green glass and marble, in the center of town. The hotels in the "hotel sector." The students attending classes in the "school sector." The Waldenlike perspective of the political pollster who had given me directions to his office by saying, "It's in commercial sector three, block two."

Amid this splendid planning, which had launched Brazil into its interior in the 1960s, the spanking new IBAMA building had occupied a beautifully landscaped property, with flowers and gardens all around. Classical music, Ravel, pumped softly into the reception area as jacketed waiters brought tiny cups of coffee on silver trays. IBAMA vice president José Carlos Carvalho lounged in his office with me and described how his department would combat illegal fires in the Amazon. "They are decreasing even now," he said. "We're establishing ecological stations to protect the region. Our goal is to work on prevention."

But afterward, in a small meeting room, Benincá, IBAMA's head for Acre, told me how thugs had almost killed him when he tried to enforce the law. The attack had taken place at 10 P.M. in downtown Rio Branco, a hundred miles west of Extrema. It had resulted in the hospitalization of Benincá's boss, Rente Nascimento, who was in charge of IBAMA enforcement for all of Brazil.

"We had confiscated illegally cut wood at a sawmill that day. Then Rente and I went to dinner in town," Paulo said. He was a lean man with prematurely gray hair, brushed back so that he faintly resembled Italian actor Marcello Mastroianni. "We were driving back to the IBAMA compound where we sleep. A white

Fiat came alongside us. The passenger pointed two guns out the window. He ordered us to pull over.

"When we got out I saw there were two men. A short one, with the guns. Dark. Heavy. With cowboy boots and a black shirt. And a taller man, who carried a stick. He was better dressed and seemed to be in charge. The one with the guns pointed them at me. Then the other man began hitting Rente with the stick, on the head, the shoulders. He kept saying, 'Don't do it again.' Rente went down, but the man kept hitting him. I grabbed the stick and fought with the tall man. The other one yelled, 'Do you want to die?' and fired near my foot. But Rente got up during this and ran into a construction site. Then the men drove away."

Paulo still lived in the compound in Rio Branco, but he didn't go out at night anymore. His men were on strike for better police protection and higher salaries. When I asked him if he could take a drive with me and point out the worst sawmills, he refused. "They have guns," he said.

Rente confirmed the story on the phone. "Police found the Fiat at the sawmill," he said. "The bloody stick was still inside. I used to believe if I did my job, the situation would improve, but it's bad. In south Pará State, in Mato Grosso, Amazonas, people have no security. Professional killers walk the streets. The owners have gotten rich based on no law. I'm quitting my job and moving away."

A few months later Rente went to work for the Inter-American Development Bank in Washington, D.C.

.   .   .

Then there was Miguel Ferrara, the Acre equivalent of Robson. I met him in Rio Branco. "You'll change my name if I talk to you, right?" Miguel said. I agreed. Miguel isn't his real name. "You won't say if I'm a man or a woman too, okay?" Since Acre's state environmental enforcement branch, called IMAC, has both men and women inspectors, I said I would do that as well.

The restaurant where we met was noisy, but Miguel leaned forward and lowered his voice. Pork chops and cold Fanta sat on the picnic-style tables in front of us.

"I used to inspect ranches with the IBAMA agents," he said.

"We'd go to a ranch where the owner applied to cut one hundred hectares, except he'd cut three hundred. 'That's illegal,' we'd say. 'You're wrong.' He'd say, 'Okay, I'm wrong, but what should I do? I don't want to get in trouble. Let's have lunch.'

"So we'd all go to lunch at his house. And the rancher would say at the table, 'Look, how much would the fine be?' We'd say maybe fifteen thousand cruzados [about $3,000 at the time]. He'd say, 'I'll give you three thousand if you forget it.' So we'd take it."

Miguel leaned closer. "No name, right? We used to have a little stand we'd work from, at the side of the highway, near a Coca-Cola factory. Lots of times we would see Brazil nut trees that had been cut going by on the logging trucks. And we'd smile. We'd know we were going to make money. We'd trail the truck to the sawmill. 'It's illegal to cut Brazil Nut trees,' we'd tell the owner. He'd shrug. 'What's done is done. What do you want?' he'd say.

"Look. You know those federal inspectors who are striking at IBAMA? Look at their clothes. They get paid what amounts to about $90 a month on the black market. They have wives, kids. How do you think they can afford to live?

"I was young when I started," the inspector said. "I considered trying to stop them, but they just would have found a way to shut me up. They would have said, 'I've worked for the government for thirty years! Miguel just started!' "

The inspector looked around again. "No names, right?"

．　　．　　．

So these were the Texas Rangers. These were the forest police. After a while I began to see Robson differently. He wasn't a coward. He cared about what he did. He showed me things he thought were wrong, and practically speaking, he had decided he could do nothing to change them. His matter-of-factness seemed more gentle now. He liked to talk about his philosophy of his job.

"I am a teacher. That's what I can do. I don't want to confront people. Jesus said, 'Don't give a starving man a fish. Teach him to fish.' "

Robson invented laws as teaching aids. When we went to ranches, he would tell white lies to protect the environment. "You have to keep Brazil nut trees standing," he would say. That much was true. "And you have to keep fifteen meters of vegetation untouched around the trunk."

"That's not a law, is it?" I asked him.

"No. I made it up," he said in his soft-spoken voice. "But when people leave Brazil nut trees standing but burn the rest of the pasture, the trees die too. They're roasted. Keep a buffer around them, and they live."

It made sense to me. I'd seen dozens of dead, charred Brazil nut trees still standing in pasture.

"You have to keep copaiba trees standing," I heard him tell one rancher. Copaiba trees provide oils that are prized for medicinal value and against insects. In fact, the Body Shop, a London-based organic cosmetics chain, ordered eighty tons of copaiba oil in 1990 to be used in natural shampoos, soaps, face cream, and massage cream. But there is no law protecting copaiba trees.

One of Robson's jobs was to stop illegal hunting. "I don't want to fine people," Robson said. "I suppose I could take them to jail, but I'd be in serious trouble when they got out. They could shoot me."

"Do you have a gun?" I asked Robson.

"No," said the forest policeman.

"Do you want one?"

"No. I want to keep people from hunting another way. For instance, there was a man who would always shoot pacas [edible rodents with a delicious flavor], so I gave him a paca as a pet. I thought, if you give a man a pet, he won't shoot animals anymore."

"Did he stop shooting animals?"

"Well, he stopped shooting pacas."

Robson loved the jungle. He liked to camp in the forest on weekends and sleep under the stars. He liked to fish. He had never formally studied rain forest ecology, and had a high school education, but he read every magazine he could find about endangered forests. He asked me, "Why does the World Bank give money to Brazil? It's bad for the forest."

He shared an apartment upstairs from a malaria clinic with a federal employee responsible for distributing land to new colonists. Holes in the walls provided an excellent view of the street outside, and the bathroom sink was smeared with the blood of squashed mosquitos. There was a lone table with a *Playboy* magazine on it, a refrigerator, a single bed protected by a mosquito net. Social life in Extrema stank, Robson said. "The only pretty girl is my secretary, and she has a boyfriend."

"He's probably a jerk," I said, trying to be sympathetic.

"I don't know," Robson replied, not wanting to speak ill of anyone. "I never met him."

After dinner Robson had to address a colonists' meeting. We drove to a small wooden shack where nine adults were squeezed into the living room. The house seemed to be rotting from the inside out. Its wooden planking had warped so much that gaps were visible in the walls. No mosquito net or glass pane covered the window, only shutters. Like all colonists' homes I visited, it was swept immaculately clean. I saw a cheap decorative banner of white terry cloth, a red-and-green toucan on it, strung in the living room. There was also a series of very old photographs, daguerreotypes almost, of men in starched collars and women with their hair in buns. Suddenly I realized two of the people were owners of the house, both under thirty years old. Somehow the pictures had been created to look old.

Two blond girls watched television in the bedroom in back.

The colonists leaned forward, intent, hopeful. They were the group the restaurant owner, Roberto, had described to me that first morning, the ones who dreamed of growing palm oil, rubber, and cocoa, and who had gotten funding from Holland. They had bet everything on the move to Extrema, and Robson was to be their agricultural adviser. He regarded this as the most important part of his job.

"Brazil nut trees. Plant Brazil nut trees," he said. There was an increasing market for the nuts, and the Extrema area was well suited for growing them.

At 11 P.M. the meeting broke up. Robson, Roberto, and I sat in the bus station restaurant, eating more chicken, beans, and rice, for which Roberto refused to accept any money.

"You're a guest here," he said. "I would never take money from a guest."

We did magic tricks for Roberto's seven-year-old daughter. I pretended to take off my thumb, and she gasped. I pretended the Coca-Cola bottle was telling me secrets about her, which Roberto had already whispered to me, and she stared at the bottle, laughed, and tried to get it to talk. The bus back to Pôrto Velho was due at 3 A.M., but the ticket agent didn't know if that was according to Acre or Rondônia time. Electricity goes off at midnight in Extrema, so Roberto had his candles ready. As Roberto and Robson chatted, I took a short walk down the street, along a darkened lane. I stopped beside the ski chalet and looked back at the bus station.

In the lone glow of a lamppost, the station took on the look of an Edward Hopper painting. The long, lonely one-story building. The harsh glow from the streetlight. The lounging figures on the front porch, some wrapped in blankets, asleep, waiting for the bus. The ticket seller in the glassed-in booth, head bent, maybe reading, maybe asleep.

The United States had grown great because of people like these, colonists who left their homes, or farms, or countries, and forged into a land they considered hostile. They'd built new homes, died of disease, harvested crops where forest had been. I walked back to the station where Robson was getting into the Toyota. He wanted me to come back to Extrema again so he could take me fishing. He said that if I were ever in Brazil, I should come back, and he would show me a really beautiful, special place in the Amazon that he loved. There were lots of places that he wanted to show me. "So come back," he said. "Come back."

Robson climbed into the Toyota and started the engine. Then he seemed to think of something. He leaned toward me over the front seat, his face framed in the half-open window. He didn't seem sure how to phrase it at first, and he frowned slightly. Then he said, so softly that I had to ask him to repeat it, "I'm going to get them some day." I knew who he meant. So did Roberto. "You have patience," Robson said, "And you wait. And then, when the time is right, you get them."

He rolled up the window, put the truck in gear, and the forest policeman was swallowed by the Amazon night.

The Ad Man and the Rain Forest

Rain forests burn, and high above the earth the balance of chemicals in the atmosphere changes. Air currents shift, temperatures rise, and some scientists wonder if the burnings accelerate the destruction of the ozone layer, the protective shield around the planet that keeps out ultraviolet rays of the sun.

Without the ozone layer, scientists predict skin cancers will rise, human immune systems will be suppressed, crops will die off, and so will plankton, the base of the ocean food chain.

And the ozone layer is deteriorating. In Antarctica, a section of the layer the size of the United States showed a fifty percent depletion between 1979 and 1985. In New York there has been a five percent loss during winters over the last fifteen years, NASA scientists found.

"Nothing in summer yet," said Dr. Michael Prather at the Goddard Research Institute, "but if it happens then, when people are outside more, it will be bad."

Although there are no confirmed links between rain forest destruction and ozone depletion, Prather said, forest destruction may be worsening ozone loss. The theory is this. Decimated rain forests release carbon dioxide that contributes to the greenhouse effect. The greenhouse effect heats up the lower atmosphere and cools the upper one, the stratosphere. The ozone layer is in the stratosphere. And the colder the stratosphere gets, Prather said, the faster the loss.

Some researchers believe that ozone loss from the greenhouse effect could be enhanced by as much as ten percent.

It's a Rube Goldbergesque theory. We sat in Prather's office down the hall from James Hansen's, on a muggy February day. Prather was a youngish man with a direct, authoritative delivery that was not too technical for a layman to understand. He had just returned from the Arctic, where he'd flown around measuring ozone loss with scientists from Norway, England, and the Soviet Union.

"The ozone layer over the Arctic is primed for destruction," the scientists' report read.

I told Prather I was researching ways the fashion and cosmetic industries were changing with the climate, altering styles, products, and notions of beauty as the public grew fearful of the sun.

Prather stressed that the rain forest–ozone destruction connection was only one of several scenarios that could occur if forests kept going down. It was possible, he said, that rain forest destruction could have no effect at all on the ozone layer. Or even that destroying rain forests could *benefit* the ozone layer. Standing rain forests release nitrogen oxide into the atmosphere, and nitrogen oxide is a chemical that contributes to ozone loss. Cut down forests, diminish nitrogen oxide emissions, and it's possible you could slow the destruction of the ozone layer, Prather said.

Then maybe I should keep the ozone–rain forest connection out of my book, I said. "And wait for more studies before I write anything. Maybe it's premature to even mention the theories now."

"No," Prather said. "The point is, it's a frightening issue. Burn down rain forests, and you add uncertainty to the atmosphere. You have a major effect on the atmosphere and, in a secondary way, on the ozone layer. Remember, we only go down one of these paths in the end. What if it's the worst-case scenario? We'd better be careful with forests because we don't know."

.   .   .

The creature in the doorway stood over six feet tall. It had furry green hair and wore a sombrero. Gigantic sunglasses hid its eyes. "Hi, I'm Joel Mole. Hee hee hee," it said.

All the luncheon guests turned to stare. The waiters cleared away salmon and green salad. I was downtown from Prather's office on the sixty-fourth floor of Rockefeller Center, and Joel Mole was the

American Academy of Dermatology's new "spokescritter." His high-pitched voice was supposed to be cute, but he sounded more like an Irishman who had inhaled helium. He warned guests—marketing executives from Ruder & Finn, Westwood Pharmaceuticals, and the Academy, about skyrocketing skin cancer rates.

"Stay out of the sun from ten until two, hee hee hee," he said.

Big changes are made up of a thousand little ones. Added up, they make something unthinkable one year normal the next. Like tans suddenly being unattractive. The room was filled with all the silly, quirky aspects of advertising comics have poked fun at for years, but the talents of all present were being applied to reversing the way the public perceived the outdoors, to acclimating consumers to climate change.

The goofy-looking mole began spouting medical statistics. One in seven Americans will develop skin cancer in his lifetime. One in three new cancers is skin cancer. Skin cancer has increased fifteen hundred percent since 1935.

In fact, Joel Mole had been created to announce these facts on TV during National Skin Cancer Month.

"I'm on patrol! Mole patrol!" he cried.

Nobody was *saying* atmospheric change. Nobody was holding up signs saying *ozone* depletion. But a multimillion-dollar industry—sun protection—had sprung up because of medical warnings, in direct opposition to everything Madison Avenue had been selling for decades. Namely tans.

The very normalcy of the room marked transition. That the huge market had risen in the first place. That the world of advertising was applying its everyday selling strategies to it without a second thought, meant climate change had become as normal as zit medicine to the cosmetic and drug industries.

It was so normal, businesses weren't arguing over *whether* it was happening anymore. They were vying for the most profitable way to sell it.

In the Academy's press kit, I looked over hideous pictures of cancer growths. Of sores erupting like red craters. I read, "Facts about Malignant Melanoma": "In later stages, malignant melanoma spreads to other organs and may result in death. . . . In the 1930s the lifetime possibility of an individual developing malignant melanoma was about one in fifteen hundred. By the year 2000, one in ninety could develop malignant melanoma."

The PR people at my table scornfully brought up a rival company's sunblock ad. It was for a product called Skin Cancer Garde. The ad, which had run in *Spy* magazine, showed a group of black-clad mourners standing around a coffin. "Here's How You Can Look with a Healthy Tan," the caption said. "How did Irwin Goldberg dream up that ad anyway?" retorted one Westwood executive.

The ad had created a furor when it came out, been written up in the *Wall Street Journal,* and won a *New York* Magazine Scare Tactic of the Year Award. "On the other hand, I hope people won't take the ad as just tongue in cheek," said a spokesperson for the Skin Cancer Foundation.

"Excuse me, but what's so different about the message in Goldberg's ad and what Joel Mole is saying?" I said, looking at the prancing mole by the door.

Nobody answered. Lunch ended, we went outside, and the sun on the statue of Atlas holding up the world shone very bright.

.   .   .

The thinning of the ozone layer was first predicted around 1973 by University of California scientist Sherry Rowland. He wasn't interested in rain forests. Rowland studied CFCs—man-made chemicals used as coolants in air conditioners and refrigerators, propellants in spray cans, and in foam packaging at fast-food restaurants.

The destructive potential of CFCs, which Michael Prather theorized may be enhanced by rain forest destruction, was unknown at the time. The new chemical was considered safe and nontoxic. It was widely used throughout the developed world. But Sherry Rowland theorized that CFCs grew less benevolent as they rose into the atmosphere. High in the stratosphere, he guessed, CFCs broke into chlorine atoms, which ate away the ozone layer. A single atom of chlorine could destroy up to one hundred thousand ozone atoms.

Sherry Rowland's wife asked him how his work was going one day. "It's really going very well, but it looks like we may see the end of the world," he said.

In 1982, British researchers in the Antarctic confirmed Rowland's fears. They found an ozone hole with lots of CFCs inside it. "The hole is growing faster than we can figure," Prather said. "In Australia, during peak sunbathing months of January and February, ozone levels are down as much as five percent over Melbourne's beaches. New York lies as far away from the North Pole as Melbourne does from the South. If a hole appears over the North Pole, we could see the same effect here."

What each one percent decrease in the ozone layer would mean, said a U.S. National Academy of Science report, would be a rise in cancer rates over the American population of two to five percent. And not only would the rates go up, said Dr. Perry Robbins, surgeon and president of the Skin Cancer Foundation, but victims would be afflicted with several cancers simultaneously. Robbins believed the rise of skin cancer in the late 1980s and early 1990s was due to life-style, not ozone depletion. But he warned if the layer thinned, "patients will get up to ten cancers at the same time." There would be a general weakening of resistance under the constant bombardment of the sun's ultraviolet rays (UVAs), he said. "It will be like leaving a rusty chain out in the sun."

In 1991 the Environmental Protection Agency announced that ozone depletion over the United States was twice the rate that scientists had expected. The agency calculated that by 2040, 12 million Americans will develop skin cancer and more than two hundred thousand would die from it—in addition to the eight thousand deaths a year already caused by skin cancer in the early 1990s.

"It's stunning information," said EPA head William Reilly. "And it possesses implications we have not yet had time to explore."

.   .   .

But the public wasn't waiting for EPA approval before it rushed to protect itself from the sun. As the predictions and findings grew more dire, industries changed to accommodate them. At the Conde Nast building on Madison Avenue, *Glamour* magazine's offices were decorated in white. White desks, chairs, partitions. Health and fitness editor Stephanie Young ate a fruit salad of strawberries and melon balls while we talked about ways that atmospheric change might be affecting the drug and cosmetics industries.

"We hear a lot more about UVAs reaching the earth and holes being ripped in the ozone layer," said the perky, joke-cracking thirty-two-year-old just back from a lunch break workout. She wrote the health and fitness column, reviewed new products in the field, and was deluged with samples and press releases on developments, which covered her desk.

"In the short term, our readers are more concerned about the aging effects of the sun. In the long, they're worried about what kind of cancer they're going to get. There's a big push among companies for more sun protection."

That was an understatement. "It's become a free-for-all," said Deborah Caldwell, marketing director at Westwood Pharmaceuticals. Westwood had introduced Sunblock 29. Max Factor, Chanel, and Giorgio included sunblock in their cosmetics. Estée Lauder advertised "biotan," a compound in makeup to lessen sun exposure by "speeding the tanning process." Coppertone was working on a tanning pill.

Stephanie rummaged through piles of press releases and came up with one announcing a genetically engineered pigment to give tan. "But artificial tanners are a transition," she said. "Tan is going out of style. Take the Bain de Soleil model. She used to be more tan. But she was concerned about what the sun was doing to her skin."

Sunscreens and sunblocks suddenly represented thirty-five percent of the $350 million market for sun care products, according to published reports. Just in the first half of 1987, companies introduced 101 such products, up from 55 in all of 1986. Market analysts predicted the number would rise.

"For the first time *Glamour*'s doing a piece, for our August issue, a hard-hitting article on melanoma and sun exposure," Stephanie said. "We've focused on the sun before—you'll get tan but, oooh, you'll get bags under your eyes. That type of thing. But this piece, it's the first time something like this has been okayed. Our job is to get the drumbeat in the distance and deliver it to the people," she said.

Glamour wasn't the only magazine changing the way it regarded tans. *Self* advised, "Once, the darker the tan, the better. It's become cool to take cover." *Self* commissioned a survey of twenty-five- to thirty-five-year old women to monitor changing attitudes toward the sun. Sixty-two percent of the respondents said they got less sun than ten years ago. "The biggest changes can be seen on both coasts, where nearly 3/4 of women cut down on time in the sun," *Self* reported. Twenty-seven percent said they planned vacations to get suntans, down a third from a decade before. Thirty-five percent used sunscreens with an SPF (sun protection factor) of fifteen or higher. Sixty-nine percent cited fear of skin cancer as the reason they'd changed their minds.

Between bites of blueberries, Stephanie said she had been using sunblock since childhood. Her father, a California doctor, had gotten her into the habit. "Now I'm a mother, and I put sunblock on my baby when I take her to the beach," Stephanie said. "People used to make fun of me for that. Now they want to borrow the tube."

.　　.　　.

"Just gimme a minute! Gimme a minute!" cried Irwin Goldberg, rushing into his East Side waiting room. The advertising man looked about fifty-eight, in a blue blazer, trimmed salt-and-pepper beard and reading glasses that gave a professorial impression which would become harried by the end of the day. Other offices in the Architects and Design building included the Hungarian Commercial Attaché, the Spanish Consul, and Entertainment Union Number 84.

How had the new sun scare strategy come into existence? How had the advertising people reversed themselves on tans? There were no rain forest specialists here, no particular passion for helping the environment. Besides Cancer Garde, I. Goldberg & Partners represented Zigzag rolling papers, familiar to smokers of marijuana and roll-your-own cigarettes; Gentleman's Warehouse, a clothing retailer; Paradise Island, a Bahamas resort; and Van Eck Securities Corporation, a group of specialty mutual funds. Climate change came in there somewhere, as normal as the other clients.

Goldberg had no special connection with environmental matters but had worked for CBS radio. He'd worked on Tarrytown cigarettes at the Gumbiner Agency. At Nadler & Larimer, where he worked for twenty-one years, he'd handled Wild Turkey, Bailey's Irish Cream, CBS Toys, Fabergé.

His windowsills were lined with advertising awards. Four Clios for TV excellence: One for "The Effects of Ice on Scotch," a Famous Grouse Scotch ad. Another for "The Fabergé Tigress," for best in women's products. Four medallions from the international film and television festival of New York. Two Efies.

But Goldberg had none of these clients in February 1987 when he heard that Steve Manenti, ex-head of Fabergé, was looking for an agency to advertise Eclipse, which he had bought. Nadler & Larimer had sold out for roughly $8 million a year before, he said. Goldberg had taken his $1 million share and founded I. Goldberg & Partners. "In advertising, it's always back to point zero," he said. "And Manenti represented a real opportunity. Because the account could be worth millions, sure, but also because of his reputation as a success."

Goldberg knew only that Manenti claimed to have some "new miracle product" when the entrepreneur walked into the office with his entourage; a scientist, marketing director, and lawyer. And that Manenti was leaning toward giving the account to someone else.

They went into an interior conference room. No windows for distraction. Or decorations. Manenti, a fit, well-groomed man who favored expensive suits, was so excited his hands flew in the air. It was time to start changing the way Americans viewed the sun.

"The sun is killing people," he said. "People want protection from the sun. They're concerned about ozone level depletion. Skin cancer is rising, but the big players in sunscreens—Plough, Hawaiian Tropic, Johnson & Johnson, have low SPFs." Manenti got more excited. "There's a $450 million a year industry in suncare and eighty percent is tanning, but by next year sixty percent will be sunblock! I want bold positioning!"

"SPF thirty-three?" Goldberg said when he heard what Cancer Garde was. He'd never heard of sunblock that strong. "You mean you got FDA [Food and Drug Administration] approval?"

Manenti nodded. Then a lanky scientist named Victor Pallazar set up an easel and drew diagrams. A sun on top, and "skin," and "heat rays" coming down. The sun produced two types of ultra-violet rays, Pallazar said, A and B. B was more damaging, but without protection both penetrated the skin, lodged in fat below, and festered. After years they could cause wrinkling or skin cancer. When Pallazar got past the scientific stuff, Skin Cancer Garde seemed to Goldberg to be like a million little mirrors, turning back the rays.

"Everybody was looking at me, waiting for me to react," Goldberg said. React to selling tans as unhealthy, which was utterly alien to all their experience. "It was the trickiest part of the meeting, too early to blurt out any idea, but I had to be enthusiastic too."

Goldberg pretended I was Manenti. "Steve," he said, looking deep into my eyes. "I did Brut, didn't I? Fabergé Organics. I did Babe. I invented the goddamn thing, the product, the bottle. You were part of that company. I was creative director for all that stuff."

"Take a week," Manenti finally said. "I may split the account into two parts. Just do Cancer Garde, not Eclipse."

Goldberg figured, I'll try for both.

But it wasn't so easy. Irwin Goldberg had to change his own orientation too. He phoned the Skin Cancer Foundation for information, desperately trying to come up with an ad. He'd done charity work for the foundation when he was at Nadler & Larimer, and still the medical statistics left him shaken. By 1989 twenty thousand Americans a year got malignant melanoma, and malignant melanoma caused three-quarters of skin cancer deaths.

Goldberg paced in his office all that week, trying to think of a Cancer Garde ad. He talked to himself. He flipped through photography books, coffee table books, hoping the photographs might give him ideas. He saw hundreds of pictures of suns. Low suns over icebergs. Romantic tropical setting suns.

Forget it, he thought. Where was the radiation?

He scanned pictures of girls on a beach, boys playing volleyball.

Goldberg stopped pacing.

Label the sun, he thought.

"We'll make it like a cigarette warning label," he told writer Jim Hammon, who had worked on beer and men's wear ads before joining Goldberg. The two men struggled over wording. Should it include "squamous cell cancer," or was that too technical? Goldberg remembered. "Look at the cigarette warning label. Does it say, 'The Surgeon General has said cigarettes can give you lung sarcoma?' Make your tongue fall out?"

Goldberg hit the books again. How about a picture of an eclipse? Sure! Eclipse Laboratories and . . . nah.

"I wanted an image where the viewer could smell the salt, the whole fun appeal of the shore, and then, boom, that label. I wanted it hot. So hot that when you look at the picture, you start to sweat."

Anxious, Goldberg lay in bed evenings, TV on, magazines and photo books around him, doodling, hoping for an idea. Little thumbnail sketches. Circles. But to him they were faces on a beach. In the books he didn't even look at suns anymore. He looked at anything. Joe Montana fading to pass. Street kids in Ireland.

"Other agencies were probably calling Manenti every seven minutes with ideas," Goldberg said.

And then a weird thing happened. Goldberg grew scared of the sun. For years he had walked from his apartment on Sixth Avenue to and from his office each day, along 57th Street. It had always been a pleasant stroll.

"Now I thought, the sun is hitting me," he said.

Not only hitting him, shining on him, and every time he went out, it was still there. "I'd see someone with a tan and think, Schmuck! You absorbed UVAs. I'd read about ozone, but to me it had been like science fiction. And now here comes this account and I'm working on it. If only someone would zip up that ozone layer. A *mitzvah,* that's what it would be, a good deed."

Two nights to go. Suddenly, at 3 A.M., he shot up in bed.

"You know when you have a great idea," he said.

The headline over the mock surgeon general's warning would be THE SUN. A MATTER OF LIFE AND DEATH.

Irwin Goldberg's opening Cancer Garde ad, the burning sun and superimposed box—"The Skin Cancer Foundation's Warning: Repeated overexposure of unprotected skin to the ultraviolet rays of the sun can result in premature aging of the skin and skin cancer, including basal cell and squamous cell carcinomas and malignant melanoma"—won a Rex award, given to ads judged as the most effective in the health and beauty field by *Drug Store News,* a trade magazine. When Goldberg launched Manenti's Child Garde, a sunblock for kids, a few months later, the ad won a Rex too.

Eclipse Laboratory's earnings rose from $2 million in 1986 to $14 million in 1989, Manenti said.

Goldberg's billings rose too. His success helped attract new clients. His earnings went from nothing in 1986 to over $8 million three years later. He took to wearing hats and sunscreens when he mowed the lawn at his weekend home in Pound Ridge, Westchester. He moved the agency to bigger offices on the twenty-fifth floor.

"I didn't celebrate though. I never celebrate," he said. "That's weird, isn't it?"

Steve Manenti had no complaints either.

"We'll be a tanless society by the end of the century," he said.

.   .   .

Back at *Glamour* magazine I visited fashion editor Kim Bunnel, a slim, fair-skinned blonde whose black jeans and blouse contrasted with the white furniture and whose desk lay beyond rack after rack of dresses and jackets, new styles for the magazine to judge. I wondered if the styles were changing to reflect sun fears too.

Kim was disappointed because her idea for an article, "How to Dress for the Greenhouse Effect," had just been killed.

"But if it gets hot, someone will turn out a line and call it Greenhouse Clothes," she predicted. "It'll have the cachet of environmental consciousness, and it will keep you cool. It will be a statement."

Kim said fashions were changing to reflect fears about ozone depletion. She showed me a copy of the *Tobe Report,* a private forecasting service available to retailers "at great cost." *Tobe Reports* were studied by buyers for clothing stores all over the country.

"As we become more concerned about the erosion of the ozone layer and the effects of the sun's ultraviolet rays on skin," the *Tobe Report* said, "many will prefer to cover up their bodies as a precaution as well as a fashion statement. It is already happening before our eyes. Young boys pair tank tops with bicycle shorts in the water (very turn-of-the-century). Young surfers leave on their surfing shirts with inflatable collars, both in and out of the water; fashionable straw hats become the norm rather than the exception . . . all moves point in the direction of covering up."

"Here's a Ralph Lauren model in a long-sleeved swimsuit," Kim said, flipping pages in a fashion magazine. "Here's a model on a beach, wrapped in a blanket. The thinking is revolutionary. That it is acceptable fashion to be covered on a beach."

"Another fad I've noticed is that baseball caps are in," Kim said. "Personally, I've worn one for years because the brim protects me from the sun. Hats in general are becoming more of a thing. It used to be the only person with a real hat was . . ." Kim threw out her arms and smiled like Holly Golightly in Truman Capote's *Breakfast at Tiffany's*. She lifted her hands to touch the imaginary brim of a wide, protective hat. She ran her fingers around the brim.

"Fashionnnnnn," said Kim Bunnel.

The Rubber Tapper

Josepha slipped rubber shoes over her bare feet, hefted her machete, and called for the boy to come with her into the jungle. "I take him so he doesn't grow up afraid," she said, "so he gets used to it." The fifty-year-old mother and her five-year-old son marched across the grassy clearing, scattering piglets, passed the fenced-in garden and manioc hut, and entered the forest. From somewhere nearby a man's voice screamed in the jungle, "*Get away from me. Stupid chickens.*" It was 7 A.M.

Josepha moved with an easy stride, which had me sweating even in the cool shadows. She crossed a stream by balancing on a log, stopped before an oaklike tree, and jammed the machete into the ground so the handle swayed on the blade. Five feet up, the tree showed an odd series of human-made slashes carved in the bark, like tribal scars on the face of an African. A vertical gouge two feet long. And a series of feeder lines or tributaries running into the main one.

It looked like this:

"Watch out for snakes!" she warned the boy. "Stay on the path, get out of the jungle!" With an ease that showed she had done this many times before, Josepha wedged a tin cup into the bark beneath the main incision, reached up with a razor on a wooden handle, and drew the rusty blade along the top cut. White latex welled up like blood, oozed along the track, and dripped into the can. I put my finger in the cup. The "milk" felt like water at first, but when I rolled some between my fingers, it grew grainier, harder. It became a small ball the color of a rubber band.

"Rubber," Josepha grinned.

"I hate my life!" the man's voice screamed behind us, out of the immense silence of the jungle. "Get away from me, chickens!"

"My brother-in-law," Josepha said. "He's lonely."

From as far away as Washington I had heard about the rubber tappers. They were a hot political controversy. Ranchers wanted to burn down trees on land they used. "They're worse than Indians," one rancher had told me in Acre. "They're filthy." Ecologists called them "extractivists" and claimed their practices could save the rain forest. "They live in harmony with nature, making a profit from the forest without destroying it," a scientist had told me in Manaus. Foreign politicians threatened to halt multimillion-dollar loans to Brazil if tappers weren't protected. Even citizens groups in Brooklyn, where I lived, circulated petitions to help rubber tappers.

Scattered through the jungle, half a million tappers lived in the Amazon, according to the last census, two hundred thousand of them in Acre. They provided one-fifth of the state's annual income, government officials said. But due to the closeness of BR-364, it was colonists, ironically, poor people seeking a better life, who threatened Josepha.

I was thirty kilometers west of Extrema, near New California, and about eight kilometers from the last paved section of 364. The town baker had push-started his old Chevrolet Vega station wagon and driven me to the trail—through the dirt main street of the settlement, up an embankment to the road, by a truck stop restaurant, and finally onto a barely wide enough forest road. We'd passed tappers bringing blocks of rubber to town on mules, parked near a small lake, and walked the rest of the way.

"Josepha's more than just a tapper," the baker had said. "She's an artist. She's the woman who makes the shoes."

Today, all the skills rubber tappers had developed over a hundred years, gathering and processing rubber, would go into making shoes. The family needed shoes to protect them from snakes, thorns, poisonous insects. The shoes were folk art that to the rest of the country symbolized tappers. In the "Rubber Museum" in Rio Branco I'd seen handmade shoes displayed beside turn-of-the-century photos of tappers floating blocks of rubber down a river. Blocks so big they could support men on water. In airports and tourist shops visitors could buy samples to bring home. They resembled the rubber shoe protectors every New York schoolboy hates to wear on rainy days. Every picture I had ever seen of rubber tappers included these shoes. Even at my ecology-minded hotel in Rio Branco, decorated with Amazon crafts—arrows and baskets—a large painting of a rubber tapper dominated the stairs I climbed to reach my room at night. I would stop and look over the pastel blues and forest greens, at the tapper in torn shirt and trousers drawing a razor like Josepha's across a cut in a tree. At the design the gouges made in the bark, identical to Josepha's. At the hat on the man's head against the sun, the way Josepha wore a scarf. At the black rubber shoes on his feet.

The painting could have been made in Acre or Pará or Amazonas, Rondônia, Moto Grosso. The system was the same.

"You can take rubber from a tree for a hundred years without killing it," Josepha said, "if you know how to make the cuts. I make two cuts in this tree, then come back three hours later to collect the 'milk.' I leave the tree alone for three or four days after that. I work my way down the cuts, never using the same two times in a row."

She was beautiful. I couldn't believe she was fifty. Women I had met in the interior often seemed ten years older than their real age, but I had guessed Josepha was thirty-seven. Her face was all soft moon angles. Her frizzy hair was tied in a scarf so I had to look hard to see it was gray. Strong slim calves poked from beneath the flower print dress she wore all three days I visited. The Portuguese she spoke was older than the city type, harder to understand.

The third tree Josepha stopped at was narrower, smooth like a red gum eucalyptus, the thicker bark a natural bandage grown over the cuts. The fifth tree seemed to grow out of another trunk at a deep dip in the trail, beside a fallen tree so big its roots rose up almost three times my height. The ninth tree stood near another footpath, or "rubber road," used by another tapper. The fifteenth tree occupied an area beside the biggest spiderweb I've ever seen, the sun glowing along strands of silk.

"The first tapper to mark a tree gets that tree," Josepha said. "But if a tree's not marked, anyone can use it. Tap another person's tree, people have been killed over that. You don't do it." She shook her head. The law of the jungle.

At each tree the little tin cups waited, upended on twigs, their rims pinched to create an edge that would better dig into the bark. Sometimes dried rubber lay in the cuts, lumpy and crusty-looking, the color of rubber bands. I peeled some off a tree, tied two ends together into a band, and shot it with my fingers at a bamboo shoot.

At Josepha's last tree I saw we'd circled back to the clearing. It was much hotter now as we trudged toward the house, a raft on stilts, leaning in on itself, perched in the jungle. I stepped up on rotting bamboo planks that heaved when we walked on them. I balanced on a bench, but it swayed so much I gave up and lay on the floor. There were two open-air rooms devoid of furniture, but hammocks inside had been rolled up and tied between rafters until night. Seven kids' hammocks. Two for adults.

The kitchen occupied the aft deck of the "raft." I saw shelves holding clean, smoky glass plates, drinking glasses scrubbed with stream water, soup spoons in a store-bought cardboard display, a commercial amoebacide and cough medicine, an armadillo tail hanging near a chopping block, for luck.

"My husband saves a piece of the last animal he hunted. We heat water for steam before his next hunt and wave the animal piece in the steam. Otherwise he doesn't get anything," Josepha said. "Believe me. If we don't do it, nothing. If we do, success."

Josepha fed kindling into a homemade clay stove that emitted a thick, pungent, insect-repelling smoke. She hand-rolled a fat cigarette and spat over the side of the raft. She stood on the aft deck, swishing rice around in a battered tin basin, picking out bad kernels, and flicking them to the ground where chickens fought over them. Through gaps in the slats I saw animals snorting under the raft. A three-legged dog named Pele, after an ex-soccer star, and a couple of goats, a pig, chickens, guinea fowl, a cat. Josepha swept the porch with a homemade broom.

The husband and sons had left at 4:30 this morning to walk an hour and a half to the far trees. They were due back at 11, and after lunch they would walk off again to collect the sap. There was no rushing rubber. Josepha's clock was the dripping of latex in little tin cans.

"When I go into town, the colonists make fun of my shoes," she said. "I don't wear them anymore when I go. I bought sandals."

The voice in the forest got really loud. "I hate my life," the brother-in-law screamed.

.   .   .

South American Indians had probably been using rubber for centuries when Christopher Columbus saw Haitians playing with rubber balls on his second trip to the New World, in 1497, wrote John Hemming, tracing rubber's history in his book, *Amazon Frontier: The Defeat of the Brazilian Indians.* Two hundred and fifty years later French scientist Charles-Marie de la Condamine reported Indians using rubber bottles and boots along the Amazon River. By 1770, London shoppers could buy rubber erasers for pencil marks. Waterproof urine bags followed. Garters. Mackintoshes. Police in Belém wore rubber raincoats during Amazon downpours.

But it was Charles Goodyear who launched rubber into the mainstream of world commerce when he accidentally touched a mixture of rubber gum and sulfur to a hot stove in 1839, and the mix hardened, Hemming wrote. It wouldn't freeze in cold or melt in heat. "Vulcanization" enabled manufacturers to coat wooden wheels with rubber, and when an Irish veterinarian named Dunlop, seeking a way of helping his son win a tricycle race, invented a detachable air-filled rubber tire in 1888, the boom was on, Hemming wrote.

Back in 1827 only 1,000 pounds of natural rubber had been sent from Brazil to Europe. By 1840, after Goodyear, rubber constituted seventeen percent of all Brazilian exports. By the turn of the century, after Dunlop, 34,500 tons of Amazon rubber was sold to Europe each year. Two hundred thousand *seringueiros,* or rubber tappers, worked in the forest. Many had been tricked into coming, told rubber grew on trees in easy-to-pick big balls, told they would get rich harvesting rubber. Meanwhile, millionaire rubber barons lived in mansions in Manaus, sent their laundry to Portugal to be washed, filled city fountains with champagne. They imported marble from Italy and built a $2 million opera house.

These "patrons" controlled vast areas of jungle called *seringals*. They were the kings of all commerce in their areas, sometimes enforcing their whims brutally. Some patrons dismembered *seringueiros* who didn't sell all their rubber to them. *Seringueiros* had to buy all food and tools from their patrons at a high markup. They labored in a debt system likened to slavery. All expenses in the rubber process—initial transportation to the interior, shipment of the rubber to Belém, even processing costs—were passed on to the *seringueiros*. *Seringueiros* died in droves from malaria and other diseases. A U.S. diplomat wrote, "The rubber trade is a hierarchy feeding on the body of the *seringueiro*."

But a fatal flaw was about to wreck the system. Rubber trees had always been susceptible to a deadly fungus. The only protection the species had was the way the trees spaced themselves far apart in the forest. *Seringueiros* never found two rubber trees together. Rubber plantations were out of the question in a place where disease could spread so fast. Only the less efficient, more costly *seringueiro* system guaranteed a constant supply.

As long as Brazil was the only place in the world you could get rubber, the system worked. But then British agents smuggled rubber seeds out of Belém, transported them to Malaysia, and planted them. No fungus threatened the trees in Asia. The first rubber plantations began operating. By 1915 over 107,000 tons of cheaper Asian rubber sold on the world market. By 1923, Malaysia sold 370,000 tons. By 1932, Brazil's share was down to a paltry 5,000 tons. The mansions closed. The champagne stopped flowing. The opera house fell into disrepair. The rich patrons moved east, to more comfortable urban centers like Rio.

The *seringueiros* had nowhere to go. They lived as they always had, on nuts, rubber, manioc, hunting, and fish.

There was one grand effort to recapture the market. American car magnate Henry Ford dreamed of owning his own supply of rubber and acquired a 2.5-million-acre tract in the Amazon state of Pará. The Brazilian government offered him wonderful incentives. Duty-free import of equipment, no taxes for twelve years, and then a small duty of seven percent of profits after that. The top Detroit engineers built "Fordlandia," a city in the jungle with American-style homes, electricity, and running water. Fordlandia absorbed $20 million of Ford's money, but then the fungus struck. Fordlandia became one of those fabulously famous Amazon failures. Ford sold out in 1941 for $250,000.

The British theft still galls Brazilians. Foreign Ministry Secretary General Pauló Flecha Tarso de Lima told me when I met him in Brasília that in the 1990s Brazil would consider trying to market plants with medicinal value on the world market. But he added, half smiling, "As long as nobody steals them, like the rubber!"

When Josepha was born in 1939, near a town called Abuná, close to the eventual route of BR-364, the heyday of rubber was over, but the Japanese were about to overrun Malaysia and set the second boom off. "My father taught me how to tap the trees," she said. Two of her brothers died of disease as boys. "They just got fevers." A sister would die later of illness too. "She ate some oranges and died. It was rainy season, too far to take her to the hospital."

The family fled Abuná during a land dispute with a patron, but Josepha returned to live with an uncle when her father died. She met her husband near Abuná and moved to New California in the 1950s, a period during which rubber was falling in price again, with Malaysia free of the Japanese. The patrons left again. The tappers became more independent. They even started a union and fought for freedom from the debt system in one part of Acre, near the city of Xapuri. They were staring cooperatives. Selling nuts and rubber directly to buyers in Brazil and abroad. Even fighting with ranching crews to stop them from illegally burning the forest. The murder of a rubber tapper union leader named Chico Mendes, farther down the road and south, in Acre, had made international news. Later in my trip I would spend four days with a rancher whom many thought had helped plot the murder. But in New California, the union was distant news. "I heard something about a union, but I'm not sure what," Josepha said when I asked her.

Still in New California daily rhythms were changing. "In the old days we didn't need money," she said. "We exchanged the rubber for goods. A cowboy would come once a month on a horse, leading a string of mules. He would ask what we needed. Coffee. Sugar. Milk. Tobacco. Tools. He always carried a notebook. He'd take the rubber, and the next time he would come he'd say, 'Here are the things you want, and here's what I owe you. Let's see if there's anything left over for you.' "

Our conversation was interrupted as Josepha's sons, nineteen-year-old Raimundo and fourteen-year-old José, came home for lunch, trudging into the clearing from the east, shotgun over Raimundo's shoulder. They lounged on the porch and smoked or chewed grass. They were shy and didn't speak much. Forty-five-year-old Raimundo, Sr., appeared from the other direction, barefoot, carrying an insecticide sprayer. He was a thin, grizzled man in soiled, tattered work clothes. He'd been helping a neighbor. The men wolfed lunch and left.

Then Josepha continued. "One day the cowboy stopped coming. He never came again. The patron must have left, and his sons didn't want to stay here. We knew we'd have to sell the rubber ourselves. We loaded it on the mule and took the mule to the river, a day's walk. Sometimes there were boats on the river, traders called *regetao*. We made a deal with one of the traders. On the third day of every month he met us at the river. Like the cowboy. We'd exchange the rubber for what we needed.

"These days we sell the rubber in town, but we can't get credit. The shop owners know us, but if we have no money, they won't let us have what we need. Or they charge interest!"

Josepha rolled another fat cigarette. She puffed on it out of the side of her mouth. She was getting more agitated. "Now INCRA has brought colonists here. Given them one hundred hectares of land. Us, too, one hundred hectares. The kids grow fruit on it. But one hundred hectares isn't enough to tap rubber, there aren't enough trees. Some of the colonists won't let us tap the trees we've always tapped on their land. We tapped those trees for twenty years. Now we have to go farther away to find trees. It was better before 364. But you make do."

"Worms" was what tappers called colonists, Josepha said. "Be-

204 THE ROAD TO EXTREMA

cause they dig in the soil and we care only about the trees." It was noon now, and the baker returned to visit. He offered to take the heavy rubber blocks into town because Josepha's mule was sick. He strolled around the compound with me. There was a pigsty and a stream below for bathing. The forest as a bathroom. A shed where Josepha pounded manioc into edible flour, called *farinha*. The voice in the forest started up again. "Stupid chickens!"

The baker assured me that colonists and *seringueiros* got along terrifically. There were aberrations like Josepha's unfriendly neighbor, but many colonists allowed tappers to keep working trees on their land. "I do," he said. And besides, he added, tappers had better lives now. "I found an old cemetery near the river, on land I bought. I think it was a murderer's graveyard. In the old days the patron would pay the tapper, then have him murdered so he could get the money back." The baker was full of grim tales of the old days, but I couldn't tell if they were hearsay or not.

"Josepha will probably move to town soon," the baker predicted. "The children are getting used to town. She and her husband are getting old and won't be able to work much longer. *Seringueiros* want their own land. They want cows and a piece of land.

"We try to teach the *seringueiros* how to act," the baker said.

.   .   .

The patrons probably never dreamed that one day *seringueiros* would affect international policies, would become a rallying cry for global ecologists. Flying into Rio Branco, I'd sat near Raimundo da Silva, a rubber tapper syndicate leader being flown to Italy to speak to ecologists. He wrote down names of other tappers I must meet. "They have many interesting facts for journalists," Raimundo told me, squeezing my arm.

In a restaurant in town I spotted the union president eating with two German church representatives. "We gave the *seringueiros* money for seminars, and we're here to see how it's spent," one German said.

"What kind of seminars?"

"I don't know yet."

"You mean you gave money, and you didn't know what for?"

The German went back to his plate of the day.

Strolling in Rio Branco, in a park near the governor's palace, I noticed a group of agitated, ragged men in a circle, involved in some kind of demonstration. But when I started over, my impression changed. I saw a man with a film camera and a girl with a clipboard giving directions. They were shooting a documentary.

Josepha had never met any University of Florida researchers, but one night I sat between one and a Montana magazine writer in a Middle East restaurant. The two Americans started arguing about the rubber tappers. The anthropologist was leading a seminar on extractivism at the Federal University. "The challenge facing Acre is shared by other tropical regions of the world," read her proposal, which had won a Ford Foundation grant. "There is an urgent need to modify current patterns of development in favor of development that benefits rather than excludes local population, strengthens the regional economy, and is based on ecologically sustainable practices for managing natural resources. . . . The objective of our research will be to explore means to increase the income of local small producers while maximizing protection of natural diversity."

The Montana writer had just returned in his private plane from a visit to *seringueiros* in the neighboring state of Amazonas. He was one of four U.S. writers in town, including myself, researching *seringueiros*.

"The political atmosphere you find in Acre is utterly absent in Amazonas," the journalist said, smearing humus on pita bread. "The system is falling apart. There are no Brazil nut trees, and with the price of rubber dropping, the tappers are making no money. They're leaving."

"But they're happy," insisted the anthropologist, a small, intense woman eating lamb shish kebab and drinking iced beer.

"Not the ones I saw."

"Well, you put colonists in and the *seringueiros* are happier," argued the anthropologist. It was important to her that they were happy. The happy *seringueiros*.

"Oh, I don't know," said the journalist, trying the potato salad and liking it. "The *seringueiros* making the most money were growing crops, like the colonists."

"It won't work," the anthropologist snapped. "It'll go the way of the colonists. What are they growing anyway?"

"Manioc."

Reluctant shrug from the anthropologist. "Well, hmm, well . . ."

The anthropologist told me she wanted to help the *seringueiros* socially. She didn't believe they could save the forest. There were too few of them even if their way of life was protected. But she believed that with better schools and a stronger union they could enjoy a good standard of living.

The next morning I ate breakfast at my hotel with another American anthropologist, Steve Schwartzmann of the Washington-based Environmental Defense Fund. Schwartzmann was more hopeful that extractivism might one day halt much forest destruction. I knew that in published scientific papers, many researchers endorsed extractivism. After conducting a project in Peru, one group claimed that in the long run better profit could be made from diversified forest extraction than from pasture or farming. Another group in Costa Rica had convinced local people to start iguana farms, selling the meat, which tasted like chicken, and breeding the animals in the forest instead of cutting it down.

Schwartzmann had been a principal mover in getting the Inter-American Development Bank to suspend a loan for paving BR-364 until Brazil promised to better protect the forest, and the tappers along the way. The loan suspension had just been lifted, and ecologists were nervously watching to see if the new environmental provisions would be instituted or ignored.

"My new project is to study why the *seringueiros* move around so much," he said.

Clearly the ex-*seringueiros* I met in the markets of Rio Branco missed the old way of life. But Josepha told me two of her brothers had become colonists. "One broke both his legs in the forest when a tree fell on him while he was tapping. When he recovered he became a colonist. The other one just chose to stop."

"They say they're happier," she said.

. . .

The sun sank to two o'clock. The heat seemed to coalesce in the bright clearing, to be hemmed in by the jagged line of trees. Josepha hefted an axe, swung a homemade fiber basket up to her head, securing it with a strap around her forehead, and padded back onto the rubber road, the trail. Chico trailed behind, screaming that he wanted fruit and smashing his own machete into every tree we passed. I was starting to suspect that he was more than spirited. He was hyperactive.

At a dip in the trail Josepha swung the basket to the ground, planted her feet wide apart for better power, and lifted the ax. A tree had already been chopped down here, its fall cleverly planned. Rather than lying on the ground, it tilted diagonally upright, supported by a bank of vegetation. The roots had been cut away. With quick, strong strokes, Josepha struck near the bottom of the tree. Chips flew. The trunk got shorter and slid lower, always giving Josepha a target. The tree was a natural assembly line of usable wood for the ax.

Nearby a tree crashed to the ground. Chico had actually chopped it down with his machete. "Fruit!" Ignoring him, Josepha piled her wood into the basket, thirty or forty pounds' worth, hefted it with a grunt, neck muscles straining, and started back toward the house. The boy tried to drag her back. She didn't speak, concentrating on the weight of the load.

By the time we reached the clearing, I saw three girls arriving too. Josepha's oldest, twenty-three-year-old Zeneide, a pretty girl with long glossy hair, carried the same first-grade reader as her youngest, nine-year-old Maria José, *This Is a Dog*. The state government school had only opened this year, and all Josepha's children were in the same grade. The boys had played hooky today to work. They appeared ten minutes later, lugging heavy gallon cans filled with rubber.

Day after day the system never changes. On cold days there's more rubber. In February, rainy season, there's less, and tappers collect and sell Brazil nuts. Right now the family stooped and squeezed into a small thatch-roofed rubber shed by the edge of the clearing, near a path disappearing into the trees.

Raimundo poured the bulk of the rubber, which was to be marketed, into a wooden box with edges stopped by mud to prevent leakage. The rubber would dry into blocks and be brought to town by mule in two weeks. It would be sold for 1.20 cruzados a kilo, thirty-three cents on the black market, about ninety-five cents on the world market.

The rest of the rubber, for the shoes, went into a battered tin washbasin, still looking like milk. Colonists could buy shoes from Josepha for 3.50 cruzados. "Not a big profit," she said, meaning she did it to maintain friendship with the colonists, whose best wishes she sought. "You have to be everybody's friend here," she said, "or you can get hurt."

Who ever thought of getting shoes from a tree? What happened a few thousand years ago to give someone the idea? Was there a fire? Did the trees burn? Did the rubber congeal around an object, a rock maybe, taking on the shape beneath? Is that how the notion began?

All I knew was that Raimundo started the fire, shoving wood pieces into the top of a volcano-shaped mud oven, two feet high. Gray smoke bubbled so thick it looked like liquid. The gritty burning smell of wood filled the hut. A breeze I hadn't even noticed outside the shed seemed to pick up, shifting and driving smoke into everyone's faces. Only I left the hut. I peered back in from outside.

As the fire heated up Josepha went back to the house and returned with a wooden mold of a foot on a stick, and a rag of red cloth. She folded the rag a few times and soaked the whole thing in the white latex. She used an empty rum bottle as a rolling pin to flatten the soaked red rag. She placed the bottom of the mold on the rag, and using long shears, carefully cut a piece of rag corresponding in shape to the bottom of the foot.

"The heel," she said. "The sole."

She carried the mold to the smoking cone as an old man walked into the clearing from the trail near the hut. He was the brother-in-law who had been screaming insanely all morning. He looked pretty ill: an emaciated body with jutting knees, ribs, and collarbone; a head seemingly oversized above the starved frame; mud-streaked bare feet and calves; wide black eyes red with malaria. I asked him how he liked living here.

"It's very nice," he smiled politely.

Josepha bent to the cone. To me, the shoe seemed to take shape more by conjuring than by manufacturing. Holding the wooden mold by the stick, she ladled latex onto its surface, slowly, evenly.

The rubber congealed instantly on the mold, and little heat ripples spread across the glossy surface like waves on a pond. Josepha poured on the second layer, the third.

"I'll need eighteen layers," she said.

Magical transformation. I wasn't looking at a mold anymore but a mass of white vaguely resembling a heavy orthotic nurse's shoe, the kind that zips up the middle. "There are three molds, three sizes," Josepha said. "I bought this one in exchange for a chicken." She pressed the rag to the bottom of the shoe. It stuck, and she kept pouring layers of cool rubber over the whole thing.

The family lounged inside the smoky lean-to, joking. One of the neighbors was crazy, Zeneide said. Not crazy, Raimundo said, legs out, sucking on grass. She just knows a lot of prayers. Crazy, Zeneide said.

"Get away from the rubber, Chico! You'll smell!"

"I did four trees today," the old man said.

"I got stung by a bee!" Chico screamed.

Nobody paid the brother-in-law any attention. "I saw the KEEP OUT sign today," he said. The mood dropped almost imperceptibly, the briefest lull. "Her own son-in-law told her she can't take rubber on his land," he said. "Who am I to say anything about it? It's her son-in-law."

There was a sense of the world squeezing in, pushing against Josepha. There weren't enough trees for everyone anymore, she'd said. Her son-in-law was taking her trees. "We won't fight about it," Josepha said. "I won't fight my son-in-law. But maybe we'll have to move."

I asked the kids if they liked being *seringueiros,* if they wanted to remain *seringueiros.* "Not me," said Raimundo. "No," said fourteen-year-old José, although neither of them had thought of an alternative. Not me, said Maria. Not me, they all said.

The shoe, dazzling white, resembled a high-top sneaker on a stick. But Josepha wasn't finished yet. On the porch, she reached for her decorating tools. A glass dinner plate, a two-inch star-shaped twig. And a spoon.

She ran the fluted rim of the plate around the "sneaker's" sole, giving it a gentle undulating border. She used the spoon handle to press regular wave-shaped indentations up and down the sole, for traction. She grasped the twig and, concentrating, began drawing. A wing shape rose along both sides of the shoe. A meteor shower of star bursts formed a stream above the sole. A track of perfectly parallel circles dropped down the ridge of the ankle. I drew in breath in admiration. She was making a rubber prototype of a stylish sneaker, complete with a latticework of "laces," lines running between the "holes." It was like some Andy Warhol reproduction. I ran my finger lightly along the side. It had been in all that smoky heat, but it generated a cool and pleasant sensation, as if creating its own temperature.

In a week the rubber would start to turn amber. In two weeks it would be black. Josepha would slice away the high top to free the shoe from the mold, and stuff leaves inside to keep it from shrinking. This would be Raimundo's shoe. He wore the largest of the three makable sizes.

I asked Josepha if there was anything she wanted to ask me. I'd already explained my purpose in coming, but she wanted to know why I had so many questions about her life. "Once a man came here and asked questions like you," she said. "He told us we had a bad life. A few days later another man came. He asked us if the first man had been here. He said the first man had been evil. The first man had been a communist. The first man would come back with a truckload of money, and the money would be evil too."

Josepha was looking at me strangely, staring into my eyes. I told her I wasn't a communist, and I didn't have a truckload of money. She seemed relieved.

"He said the man who would come back would be the beast," she said.

I walked to the shed where her children were talking. Raimundo lounged outside, one hip on the grass. I asked him if he liked the idea of the shoes being finished. In his shy way he nodded and blushed. His worn pair of rubber shoes, insteps thin, lay overturned nearby.

If I glanced down I could see my own Italian hiking boots, which I had bought in Manhattan in a store called Banana Republic. I'd sprayed them with silicon spray to keep out the jungle rain. I'd put specially made orthotics inside to help cushion my feet. I asked

Raimundo why he was excited about something he had seen so many times before.

He glanced up sideways, too polite to make fun of the obvious, his amusement a glint in black eyes.

"What do you mean?" he said. "New shoes!"

.   .   .

It was dusk, and the baker drove me back toward New California. The evening would be clear. The sky was going purple and the white full moon was up. Macaws flew in the gaps where the jungle had been cut down. Mercedes trucks were parked in front of the truck stop, and their drivers wolfed down the plate-of-the-day. Only one meal available: More steak. More eggs. More rice. Beans. Potatoes. After their break they would continue driving where there had only been forest a few years before.

The main street, a frontierish dirt road, was fronted by one-story buildings. The bakery. The drugstore. Men in cowboy hats trickled into an open-air bar and picked pool cues off a wall. Housewives hung out of windows. Cocks crowed. A little blond girl spun a half-broken record in the air like a Frisbee. Front yards were all swept clean, and every house I visited was immaculate. Colonists generally took off their shoes when entering homes.

Chuckling at my fear of malaria, the baker drove me to a "safe" house. His own house was extremely unsafe, he said. His family had been infecting and reinfecting each other for two years. He himself had been sick for eight months. Then he had become more religious and had been cured. Hardly anyone took precautions against malaria in New California, although any nurse or pharmacist kept quinine to treat it. New Californians caught malaria almost as frequently as New Yorkers got the flu. The only way to restrict the disease was to completely change your way of life.

The safe house had screens on the windows and belonged to the baker's brother-in-law, the Rondônian administrator, Sergio dos Vas. Sergio pulled his young son and daughter inside and closed his doors at dusk when the mosquitos came out in force. He kept the house shut up all night like a villager in a Dracula movie. As a result of these precautions, he had been infected only three times.

We liked each other immediately. He was a friendly and intellectually curious man, a graduate in psychology from the Catholic University at Curitiba. He taught history in the primary school in town and, like the other colonists, had been given one hundred hectares by INCRA. I did magic tricks for his children, then we watched soccer on color TV. I tried to explain American football to him in crippled Portuguese. "Eleven men, each side!"

"I was sick of the city," Sergio said. "There's no crime here. My kids don't know what robbery is. But I'll tell you something. Land reform is the answer to saving the Amazon. Ninety percent of the people here never would have come if they could have had ten hectares in the South. The Amazon? Forget it."

After dinner Sergio unrolled one of those blueprint maps that divide the jungle into little rectangular ownable tracts. "There are 650 houses in New California, and we hope for 900 more," he said proudly, while the kids played dominoes on the floor and their mother, Bernadette, read them fairy tales. "Even if people don't have land, there will be jobs here, especially when 364 is paved all the way to Rio Branco. We'll be able to get people to the doctor. We'll be able to ship our goods."

Bernadette turned out to be the baker's sister and also the sister of Roberto, the cafe owner in Extrema, thirty miles down the road. "My father had fifteen children and twenty hectares," she said. She showed me a newspaper the land reform movement published which recommended areas colonists could invade. I asked her if she thought birth control might be another way of saving the Amazon. "The priests," she said stiffly, "tell us to make up our own minds."

That night I lay in bed listening to truck noises from 364 and watching mosquitos battering themselves against the screen, although unfortunately many of them seemed to be trying to get out of the house, not in. And in the morning Sergio wanted to show me the colonists' new fields, hewed from the jungle. In a Toyota Land-cruiser, which more and more colonists climbed into as we progressed, we drove to an intersection in the main street marked by an immense severed stump, like a war monument, which I suppose it was. We proceeded through a gap in the trees in an area of fields bordered by jungle. At 7 A.M. colonists were swarming over the land, hewing, tilling, planting, weeding. A little rural city in the forest.

Sergio and Bernadette linked hands lovingly, showing me their field. "Here I'll grow flowers—not for sale, just for beauty. I only want to work on a few hectares. The rest I'll leave as forest. Here I want to try avocados. Here manioc. It protects the ground."

They were learning from the mistakes of the first colonists. This time, Sergio told me, it was going to work.

I was starting to recognize some of the crops, and I looked at two coffee saplings near a small cocoa plant and another newly planted tree. I didn't recognize the last tree, and I asked Sergio what it was. I was thinking that Josepha used to tap this field, that many *seringueiros* used to come here. That all the rubber roads which had wound through this beehive of colonists and fields were gone.

Sergio smiled at me and fingered the green leaves on the new sapling. There was real love in his voice. The colonists reminded me of young Israeli immigrants on kibbutzim in the Mideast. "Why, it's a rubber tree," Sergio said. "The cocoa trees will keep it alive, and in a few years I can tap rubber here. But you have to protect it from a fungus. If you don't protect rubber trees, they die."

The Refugee and the Rain Forest

To predict global effects of Amazon destruction, ecologists and social scientists make educated guesses. They look at other stripped rain forests and have identified a whole new class of refugees straining social services inside their own countries or moving to developed countries as the forests go down. "Environmental refugees" are people fleeing famine or war that erupts when damaged land can no longer support human population.

For instance, the two most deforested countries in the Western Hemisphere are Haiti and El Salvador. They both absorb millions in aid and send huge numbers of illegal immigrants to the United States. In coming years environmentalists warn, they will add millions to the developed world's hidden costs of tropical deforestation in aid, loans for environmental damage, and military assistance. "Environmental dangers threaten to be as destabilizing as arms imbalances," wrote Michael Oppenheimer, a scientist with the Environmental Defense Fund.

Still, of all the connections between rain forest destruction and the developed world, refugee problems seemed the least real to me at first. Surely environmental damage couldn't be causing *wars*, I thought. Talking with refugees or scientists in New York, I often felt silly listening to questions coming out of my mouth. I'd be sitting with someone who'd been tortured, who'd had their fingernails pulled out, and instead of asking about human rights, I'd hear myself saying, "Do you think environmental damage had anything to do with the war?"

But every time they said yes.

"World governments have a choice," said the ex-deputy head of the United Nations environment program. "Trees now or tanks later."

"In many countries," read a World Resource Institute report, "the response to poverty and environmental decline has been civil war and migration to the United States."

"Less food. Less land. No place to stay," said Cecilia Moran, head of the Salvadorean refugee organization CARECEN on Long Island, herself a victim of torture. "If there was no war, one day there would *be* a war because of deforestation."

Brazil, with eighty-five percent of its massive forest still standing, did not yet have the refugee problem more damaged places did. But inside the country people were starting to move, leaving the drought-stricken, deforested Northeast for wetter places or cities. Expanding into the rain forest as they tried to find land on which to grow food. Land wars have grown increasingly violent in Brazil since 1980, Worldwatch reported. Amnesty International chronicled 298 deaths in Brazil just from land disputes in 1986 and "several hundred more in 1987." Already the World Bank and the Inter-American Development Bank were being asked for loans to repair environmental damage caused by new arrivals along BR-364.

What will happen in thirty years if the damage continues, the population keeps growing, and the jungle that has been used until now as a surrogate for political reform gets filled up or destroyed? Will there be riots? Refugees?

"Throughout the Third World, land degradation has been the major factor in the migration of subsistence farmers into the slums of major cities," wrote Jodi Jacobson of Worldwatch. "They produce desperate populations vulnerable to disease, natural disasters and prone to civil strife."

Mark Plotkin, vice president of Conservation International, added, "You ask how tropical rain forest destruction can affect the day-to-day lives of average Americans? Well, if it isn't stopped, one day U.S. troops may be fighting in wars that break out when the forests are gone."

Nigerian ambassador to Brazil, Patrick Delle Cole, put it equally bluntly. He himself came from a land suffering deforestation, and when I asked him what he thought would happen in countries like Brazil and Nigeria if the environment continues to decline, he said, "Refugees move to the forest, and when it is gone, they move somewhere else. The Vietnamese boat people captured world attention, but they were very few in number. In Brazil and Nigeria there are millions of people. When that many people start to move, before long you have a major unstable condition that cannot be contained in the continent."

Delle Cole seemed to think of something that amused him.

"Who knows where we'll go. Maybe the United States," he said.

.   .   .

"I was walking on the highway when a truck full of soldiers stopped," Julio Carrera said. "They made me get on the truck. They told me I was in the army. They took me to a barracks."

Julio was a shy, round-faced twenty-two-year-old with a scraggly boyish mustache, a wiry beard, and the remnants of acne still on his cheeks. He was a diligent gardener, talking only when I prompted him, as we spread fertilizer and raked leaves. We'd finished eighteen houses by 4 P.M.

In Oyster Bay, Long Island, passersby paid little attention. Salvadorean gardeners were common here, and perhaps harbingers of refugees from other countries, including Brazil. Now an Oldsmobile pulled into the driveway and a housewife got out, didn't look at us, and walked inside. A day maid passed on her way to the railroad station, going home. Two high school girls in letter jackets glanced at Julio when he wasn't looking, whispered, and giggled. When they turned away, he looked back.

In Salvador he'd been an economics major. As rain forests go down all over Latin America, thousands more Julios will be heading north.

"I was at the barracks for three days," he said. "Then my mother came, talked to one of the officers. She gave him money."

Eighty thousand Salvadoreans have fled to Hempstead, Long Island, to get away from a war. Over a hundred thousand more live in New York City, with up to 850,000 undocumented Salvadoreans in the U.S. By 1990 the United States Immigration and Naturalization Service reported Salvadoreans as the second biggest group of undocumented aliens entering the United States—and that from a tiny country the size of Massachusetts. The cost of this influx to federal and local governments is astronomical. Even conservative estimates top millions to pay for immigration officers, deportation proceedings, detainment camps, time spent by legislators, not to mention $1.4 million in foreign aid each day to Salvador.

"The soldiers let me go when my mother paid," Julio said, raking leaves. "But I knew they would take me again. So I left. I had about $200. I walked north and took buses. In Mexico I had to spend half the money to pay police. They kept stopping the buses and asking for papers. I didn't have papers.

"Everywhere I went I asked Salvadoreans if they knew how to get into the United States. Finally, at the border, near Baja, there were Mexicans who could take me across. I didn't like them. They were" Julio said, casting around for the right word in English, "rough. Doing drugs and drinking. Smoking all the time."

Today, Salvadoreans. Tomorrow, from Brazil. "I paid $2,000, which I borrowed from a Salvadorean. I'm still paying it back."

With sixty other men, women, and children, Julio followed the guide across hills one night into California. "It was cold. The children were sick from the temperature. When we got to the border, police saw us. Everyone was running, screaming," Julio said as we loaded leaves into a lawn bag. "I hid," he said. His partner Alfonso loaded the lawnmower into their van. "I saw some women get arrested. But I got away, found the car that took us to San Diego. My sister sent the plane fare to New York."

In the van we gulped water from a plastic bottle. The work was heavy and my muscles ached. I asked why there were so many Salvadorean gardeners here, and Alfonso said, "You don't need papers to work." Their salary was $40 a day, under the table.

"You know how many people live in that house?" Julio said, pointing to a big two-story white Colonial where a French poodle yapped in the driveway. "Only two."

"I call that lawn 'the airfield' because it's so big," Alfonso joked.

"Good thing we didn't have to do 'the racetrack' today," Julio said. Both men laughed.

Julio started the van, and a cloud of blue smoke erupted inside, swirling between the ripped seats, the Charlie's Angels sticker on the windshield, and the Taco Bell sauce packs on the dashboard.

Julio didn't even want to be in the United States. He was afraid of being deported, afraid to go back, afraid to visit doctors when he got sick because he had no Social Security card.

We drove through golden falling leaves and early rush hour traffic.

"At the airfield I fly like a plane," Alfonso said wistfully, sitting among the garbage bags. "At the racetrack I work like a horse."

. . .

Nobody blames deforestation for single-handedly causing the war in Salvador or unrest in Haiti, but conservationists consider it an important factor and speculate that variations on the process will one day occur in Brazil.

"Wrong utilization of tropical forests leads to poverty and social unrest," wrote Marc Dourojeanni when he was head of the Inter-American Development Bank's environment program. "The situation in Haiti and El Salvador, with its impact on U.S. security, could have been avoided if assistance had been given to ensure sustainable development."

The way the whole system works is pretty straightforward. International demand for cheap beef, bananas, coffee, or sugar results in better land in tropical countries being bought up or seized by the small wealthy class. Poor people are pushed into less productive land like rain forests, as in Brazil. When the deforested areas produce no food because the soil is bad, the poor crowd into cities. And violence erupts.

"It's Yankee imperialism, goddamn it," Peter Thacher said. The ex-deputy head of the U.N. environment program was now a distinguished fellow at the World Resources Institute. Staffers there study environment, population, natural resources, and how they are connected to sustainable development.

Thacher, a Canadian, looked the maverick in his wide-brimmed Indiana Jones–style hat, long green overcoat, and bears on his tie when I met him at the institute.

"We as a society have been funding the destruction of forest cover for over one hundred years," he said as he packed to give a speech in Denver. "Dole Pineapple. United Fruit. The driving force has been capital looking for something to do.

"The New York banks? They've been boasting about recycling petro dollars in the mid-1970s? All they've been doing is pumping in money to destroy forest cover in order to grow cheap beef for American consumers, which is to say, we don't want to destroy *our* grasslands, we'll destroy someone else's."

In a speech Thacher gave to the House Subcommittee on Western Hemisphere Affairs, he said, "The expansion of commercial agriculture puts the burden of growing basic food on peasant cultivators. But it deprives them of lands that are good for crops. This forces them into higher, steeper areas, and they are driven by poverty to clear forests and plant on erosion-prone lands.

"This is the start of the *real* falling dominoes. Deforestation leads to downhill soil erosion, loss of watersheds, siltation, floods, and all the attendant social and economic hardships which lead to instabilities that invite foreign intervention of all sorts."

Arranging papers in a briefcase, Thacher seemed angry about it. His political leanings were reflected in the art outside his office, a glassed-in montage of newspaper clippings with headlines like TREE FARMING COULD STEM FOREST DECLINE.

"U.S. domestic economic policy has far more impact on prospects for economic and social progress in Latin America than any benefit in foreign aid Congress is likely to provide," Thacher said.

.   .   .

And what is life like here for the refugees themselves and the thousands more who may come?

"Refugee influx expected," read a newsletter at CARECEN, a storefront refugee help group where Julio and Alfonso worked as volunteers two days a week. Alfonso operated the mimeograph machine. Julio picked up donations of food, medicine or clothing. Both men collected toys for children at Christmas.

Life of exiles. For women they went to prostitutes. For every ten Salvadorean males arriving in Hempstead, there's one Salvadorean woman. For medicine they relied on CARECEN's free clinic once a month. For housing Alfonso lived in a rooming house. And Julio slept in a studio apartment with his brother and sister, undocumented aliens too.

Still, three to a room was better than others had. One day Alfonso and I drove into a Hempstead shopping center. He pointed out a small burned-out store near a bank, department store, and supermarket. Shoppers were going in and out of the stores.

"Salvadoreans live there," he said.

"There?" The building seemed so ruined, I couldn't imagine anyone inside. The roof had collapsed. The brick was charred.

"I have to make sure there are no police around before I go in," said Alfonso, who was more outgoing than Julio. He lit a Salvadorean brand Rex cigarette, and sauntered toward the building. He was a slight, frail-looking man with thick lensed glasses and a biting sense of humor. I'd visited poor countries where the destitute lived next door to the rich . . . Ethiopia . . . Peru . . . and that's where this kind of juxtaposition was supposed to be. For an instant we were in Salvador, not New York. Or Pôrto Velho.

Alfonso paused by the door, pushed inside. I followed him by gripping the bars and inching over a concrete ledge above a crater filled with debris. The building had been a furniture store. Blackened velvet loveseats lay in the pit with rainwater, half burned kitchen stools, planks, empty vodka bottles.

"I lived here for a month," Alfonso said.

The building was a way station, a sleeping place for new arrivals. Pigeons cooed on rusting girders. Wind creaked tin siding half nailed to a wall. In the shadowy cave beneath what remained of the ceiling, I made out a tarp spread like a tent. Alfonso ducked underneath. His match flared, and I saw mattresses, bunched covers. Empty now and smelling of cold.

"It's too depressing for them to stay here during the day," Alfonso said.

But even *this* was better than going back before the war was over. Forty-eight thousand Salvadoreans applied for asylum in the United States between 1983 and 1988, according the Congressional Information Service. In 1988, after the Immigration and Reform Act passed Congress, 145,000 more asked for legal status. By 1988 only 667 of the applicants had been granted asylum.

Twenty-three thousand had been turned down. By 1990 over 200,000, including Julio, were pending. Is this what will one day happen with refugees from other countries, such as Brazil?

Salvadoreans who got turned down for asylum had to leave the United States.

"My friends who get deported are back in Hempstead within a month," Alfonso said.

"If I get turned down, I'll move to another house, but I won't go back," said Julio.

Meanwhile, they worked and learned English. One night I sat in the back of a junior high school classroom in Freeport, Long Island, with Julio and five other refugees, four from Salvador.

"Orlando? Take the next exercise," said instructor Sal Rizza, a forty-two-year-old substitute teacher in the Freeport system. "Say the sentence as it's written. Then make it into a question."

A baby-faced man wearing a black peaked hat turned backward stared at his paper. He said softly, "You . . . had . . . a . . . head-ache. *Did* you had a headache?"

"Have," the teacher corrected. "Did you *have* a headache?"

"Deeed you *have* a headache?"

"You guys," said Sal Rizza. "How many times have I heard people ask a question the wrong way? If you say it the wrong way, people know you can't speak English. It's harder for you."

Julio had put in eight hours on the lawns today. Class lasted from seven to nine-thirty. Then dinner. Bed. Eighteen lawns tomorrow.

"What does 'a good ending' mean?" Sal Rizza said. A student had just repeated the sentence, "The movie had a good ending."

"Who knows what 'a good ending' is?" repeated Rizza. "You go to a movie. Juan meets Maria. They go bowling. They become lovers. He meets Maria's family. But then Maria drowns in the ocean. Is that a good ending?"

The men shook their heads.

"You come out of that movie, you say, 'That stank!' " Sal Rizza said.

Nobody laughed.

The junior high was filled with adult language students. Over a thousand of them three nights a week, most of them from Salvador. One day from Brazil? The federally funded course was free. Nobody asked students for passports. Or immigration cards. No one asked students how they'd gotten to the United States.

Sal Rizza was saying, "Christmas is coming up. Let's make a list of what it means to have Christmas in the United States. Anyone?"

Nobody spoke.

"Come on," Sal said. "Remember we did this at Thanksgiving? You said good food. Dimitrius?"

Dimitrius, who came from Greece, looked confused.

"Orlando?"

"Good . . . food."

"Good! What else?"

"Stores . . . have . . . sales," somebody said.

"Sales," Sal wrote on the blackboard. "How about the weather?"

"It's terrible," Julio said.

"Snow," someone said.

"Ugh." The men shuddered.

Everyone laughed. "And families?" Sal said. "Maybe Christmas is a time you feel sad. Maybe you miss your families at Christmas." The men nodded. There was quiet in the room.

"Put that down," Julio said.

"Families," came the whisper from Orlando who liked to repeat things. "Miss . . . our . . . families."

.   .   .

In Washington, Peter Thacher gave me a copy of a speech he had given to the House Subcommittee on Western Hemisphere Affairs, in which he called for "major departures from traditional approaches to foreign aid," to stop supporting deforestation.

To help curb the downward spiral of poverty, overpopulation, and environmental decline, Thacher suggested new international lending policies. He cited studies showing that properly funded small farms could earn more profit per hectare than large ranches. The United States, Thacher told the congressmen, should lend money to small cooperatives, not large agricultural projects that sustain the status quo. The United States should take the lead in establishing regional organizations to "integrate land distribution with resource planning," he said. Developed countries should set up a series of trust funds administered "without regard to short-term political pressures" by a professional staff of local people.

"Agrarian reform and effective management of natural resources are *the* questions that must be addressed in Central America," he said. The same is true in vast stretches of Latin America. "We are not suggesting that other issues—industrial expansion, unemployment, health care, and human development—are unimportant. But until the underlying problems of land utilization and resource planning are resolved, such issues will remain intractable."

I went back to do more lawn work with Julio and Alfonso. In late fall most of the job involved collecting leaves. There were so many leaves the men only had to finish four houses a day. It took eight hours.

Leaves fell in a steady blizzard. Leaves piled up in chainlink fences, hedgerows, behind ladders, under porches, on driveways, in flower beds. Dogshit smeared the leaves. Leaves stuck to toy cars left in the backyard.

"In Salvador, leaves are green all the time," Alfonso said wistfully.

We knocked leaves out of hedgerows with rakes. We ducked under bushes to drag out leaves. We stood anchoring garbage bags with our feet, and stuffed leaves inside. I was starting to hate leaves.

As we worked, a cream-colored Cadillac pulled up and the boss got out, a tan and fit-looking high school teacher who owned the business on the side. Julio whispered that the boss had a Mercedes and a house in the Hamptons.

"Julio tells me you're a writer," the boss said, shaking hands. "My kid wants to be a writer. He tells me he wants to write about the human condition. I told him that's fine, whatever you want to do, fine. You pay the bills."

The boss smiled. "My kid calls me a capitalist," he said. "Well, speaking of capitalism, I have to go make money."

After he drove off, Alfonso said, "I think his son is a better person than he is. Writing about the human condition."

Alfonso told me, as we kept talking, that next year he and Julio were thinking of starting their own gardening business. "I was saving to go back to college, but I think we can make money faster this way. You can get an old van for $600. I have a cousin who can fix it up. I'm going to run off flyers, business cards. There will be a picture of a house on the cards and a big lawn with many shades of green."

Alfonso eyed the piles of leaves. "We'll call the business 'Forever Green,' " he laughed.

"What else will the card say?"

Alfonso rested on his rake, turned his face upward, and said like a hawker on a television commercial, "The best work for the lowest price." He laughed. "Well, at least for the first year. And the card will say, 'Call Ralph.' "

"Who's Ralph?"

"Me."

We started laughing. The leaves were gusting around us. "Why Ralph?"

"People will think there's less problems," Alphonso said, meaning people will think he's not Hispanic.

"Ah ha!" I said. "*You'll* be the capitalist then."

"No," Alfonso said. "We'll be a cooperative. We'll share the money. And whatever we make, we'll give ten percent to Salvadoreans for food or medicine. Or to send home. You call that capitalism?"

"Benevolent capitalism," I said. "Anyway, I personally like capitalism. And besides, this is what you say now. Next year you'll be a power-hungry manager complaining about the workers."

"They're lazy," Alfonso grinned.

"They goof off all day," I said.

"They're always complaining."

"You have to watch them every minute."

We were laughing when Julio came around the side of the house with the blower. He shut it and began shoving leaves in a bag. His jeans were torn at the knees. He wore a hooded sweatshirt in tropical blues that said LONG ISLAND. "I heard you guys might be starting your own business," I said.

Julio smiled shyly and kept working.

It was growing colder, a thick mist covered the neighborhood, and our breath was frosting at 4 P.M. Across the street another truck of Salvadoreans glided by, finished for the day or going to another house. Maybe the brick Colonial with the cardboard pumpkin in front, left over from Halloween. Or the lemon-colored house with the curtains over the breakfast nook. Or the pint-sized Tudor with the huge lawn covered with oak leaves.

"Are you starting your own business?" I asked Julio again.

There was something in the question he didn't want to answer. Maybe it was a private matter. Maybe to open a business meant he was putting down roots in a new country. Maybe it meant he wouldn't go back. He was always saying he wanted to go back, he *would* go back.

"There are no statistics on undocumented immigrants, even though in recent years they may have outnumbered the documented ones," a sign says in the great hall of the Museum of Immigration at Ellis Island, New York.

I looked at Julio as we worked, and the mist made everything slick and wet. "Come on," I said. "How come you don't want to answer the question? Alfonso's hot to start the business."

"Because it's a dream," Julio said softly, raking, stuffing. He tied the black garbage bag by knotting the plastic ends. He carried the load to the curb and leaned against a dozen other bags. He rested on the rake. "A dream," he said sadly, going back to work.

Kilometer 480

The Accused

"Look into my eyes and you will know the truth," said João Branco. "I did not kill Chico Mendes. You will write it. Other people will write it. And after a while everyone will know. I had nothing to do with the murder."

I had not come to visit João Branco to talk about Chico Mendes. The rubber tapper leader had been killed months ago. Suspects were in prison, a trial scheduled, a witness in protective custody, shielded by fearful police.

I had come to Rio Branco to write about ranching, not murder. Deforestation. Not trials. At the Santa Carmen Ranch I'd spent time with a government-funded rancher, but now I wanted to visit private ones, ones who risked their own money when they went into the forest. To get their side. And what better spokesman than João Branco, rancher, newspaper owner, lawyer, former regional head of the UDR (União Democrática Rural), the ranchers' political organization.

But a dead man kept getting in the way.

For instance, two days earlier we'd ridden to a ranch outside of town. The taxi driver had joked with João Branco the whole way. The second João had gotten out of the cab, the driver had whispered to me, "He was in on the murder."

On another ranch the owner had joked in front of João Branco, "Pretty brave guy, hanging out with the man who killed Chico Mendes." Both of them had started laughing.

And every evening when I strolled through Rio Branco, around the plaza, past the governor's palace and the war monuments, I saw graffiti. Huge black letters scrawled for yards: THE DEATH OF CHICO MENDES WILL NOT BE WHITEWASHED. The Portuguese word for white, BRANCO, was underlined.

Now João Branco and I were relaxing at the airport bar, watching girls go by at dusk, sipping Antarctica beer. In Rio Branco the ranchers hang out at the airport, stop for an express coffee before breakfast, meet for steak and beans at lunch, drive by for more coffee five times a day.

João Branco poured fresh beer. "You're the only journalist who's even asked me about this," he said. "People think I was involved, but no one ever asks."

"Why not?"

João Branco laughed. "Maybe they're afraid of me," he said.

·   ·   ·

If the Amazon is rich in rubber, Acre is the bonanza. Rubber is why thousands of Brazilians came here in the first place, in the 1800s, when Acre belonged to Bolivia. Rubber is why the Bolivians tried to tax these newcomers, causing them to rebel. Rubber is why Brazil annexed the state. Rubber is why Chico Mendes was murdered.

For a hundred years rubber ran on the patron system, which I had learned about when I met Josepha and her family near Extrema. Rich landowners reigned over vast tracts of jungle called *seringals*. Tappers living in the *seringals* sold all their rubber to the owners and bought all their tools, food, and medicines from him. During rubber booms the landowners lived in Acre and took a closer interest in their land. During busts in the cycle they moved away, and the *seringueiros* lived in the forest on their own.

The system worked until the 1970s when Brazil began encouraging colonization in the Amazon. All over the region, which is fifty-eight percent of the country, governors tried to attract settlers. In Acre that meant cattle, a perfect business for opening up a frontier. Cattle didn't need roads to get to market. They could walk. And land was cheap. New owners like João Branco moved west.

But in order to establish ranches they had to cut down forest. In Brazil "cattle ranching is the leading cause of deforestation," a 1988 World Bank report said. In just 1985, according to Landsat satellite information, five percent of Acre was burned.

For thousands of *seringueiros* this was the end. They moved to towns or across the border to Bolivia. They became gold miners at camps along the rivers to the east. Some made deals with the new owners, selling their meager rights for cash or a small piece of property. Others were driven away by hired *pistoleiros*. Either way, they couldn't tap rubber anymore.

Then, in one part of Acre, Chico Mendes changed all that. Mendes was a rubber tapper who created successful strategies against ranchers. When ranchers sent workers into the forest to cut trees, hundreds of rubber tappers and their families would materialize out of the forest, women and children in front. They would ask the workers not to cut the trees, sometimes even wrecking the camps. After the outnumbered workers left, *seringueiros* would continue the fight in court. Sometimes the land title was unclear. The ranchers lost.

Another new plan electrified ecological organizations around the world. Environmentalists had been looking for ways to prove that rain forests, left standing, could provide more income than pasture. Could provide profit and be preserved at the same time. Mendes came up with a solution. Zone the forest. Set up areas called "extractive reserves." Inside these areas deforestation would be prohibited. Tappers could live as they always had, harvesting rubber and nuts in the off-season. Even in the short run, the land would be more profitable.

In 1988 the governor of Acre established the first extractive reserves in the world.

Two months later Chico Mendes was ambushed as he left his house one night, going out back to take a shower.

To João Branco's assertions of uninvolvement, the citizens of Acre had lots of questions. Like how come two weeks before the murder a columnist on João Branco's newspaper predicted that "a bomb of two hundred megatons would explode in Acre? How come reporters from the paper were on the scene of the murder within an hour of its being reported when it takes four hours to reach Xapuri from Rio Branco? How come João Branco left town after the killing, flying off in his private plane? But like many ranchers in Rio Branco, João Branco said he didn't understand what the big fuss was about. The murder, he said, was a personal dispute. A rancher named Darli hated Chico Mendes. Part of Darli's ranch had been turned into an extractive reserve. And Chico Mendes had been trying to get Darli arrested. Chico Mendes had found out that Darli was wanted for murder in another part of Brazil. Darli's son had confessed to the murder of Chico Mendes. "All the outcry about a plan to kill him, lies," João Branco said.

"Chico Mendes wasn't a real ecologist," João Branco said. "He was a political leader, a syndicate leader." João Branco shrugged. "On the day he became a false ecologist, he was killed."

. . .

João Branco is a rich man. His two ranches have thirteen thousand acres and fourteen hundred cows. He owns one of Rio Branco's two newspapers, *O Jornal*. He's a partner in the biggest concrete company in the state. He's a broker for ranchers whose land has been seized by the government. He's a lawyer by training who travels all over Brazil.

Like many ranchers he lives in town, in a walled one-story house fronted by flowers, five minutes by foot from the governor's palace, across the street from the former mayor, down the block from the military police. Last year João Branco took a trip to the United States to help a friend buy a horse for $50,000. This year he's considering sending his daughter to school in Paris where his sister lives.

"I want to show you the three most important things to me about being a rancher," João Branco said. "If you don't understand these things, you'll never be able to understand what I do."

We were in the back of a maroon Volkswagen taxicab, pitching our way east along BR-364.

On satellite maps this part of the highway forms one of those deforestation pictures that strike terror into the hearts of ecologists. A long, meandering strip of deforested blue resembling a series of gigantic connected crystals, ranches, hugging both sides of a thin line that pushes its way through the massive Amazon green. But from the road the view was peaceful. Rolling pasture. Contented-looking Nelore cows. The tops of high Brazil nut trees floated above the Georgia red haze thrown up from dust on the rutted road. Mercedes trucks materialized out of the distance, their wooden sides swaying like accordions. The air filled with a horrible blood stink. We were passing the brand-new slaughterhouse.

"Love of land," João Branco said, leaning toward me. He was not a physically large man, but there was something in his manner, the dark flowing hair, black mustache, billowy shirts, that seemed to accentuate power. Sometimes he wore reading glasses, the kind that make math teachers look wimpy and judges appear stern.

João Branco told his history. He had grown up part of the time on his grandfather's ranch. Had gone on to become the first Branco to graduate law school in the three-hundred-year history of the family in Brazil. "I was a broker in Rio. I lived in Ipanema on the beach. I had girls. Cars. Everything a young man would want. But something was missing."

Land. Land was missing. At Christmas in Minas Gerais, the family used to sit around eating beef and telling ranching stories. The story of João Branco's grandfather's wooing of his bride. The story of how Grandfather was never the same after selling the ranch. The story about João Branco's father, a truck driver, marrying into a ranching family and going to work with an ax.

As João Branco spoke I couldn't help be reminded of a haunting beginning of the top-running Brazilian soap opera, an odd, mystical scene showing a man, poor and in rags, walking resolutely across a field, then a farm, then a futuristic city. As the music continued, the man kept walking, getting smaller, stepping into space until he was gone.

"The further away you go from the land," the words to the music went, "the further you go from God."

I also realized that the rubber tappers had used exactly the same words to explain *their* life. "If you want to understand us, understand love of land."

"In 1973 I was invited to Rio Branco by a real estate company here, asked if I wanted to be their lawyer," João Branco said. "I fell in love with Acre. I quit my job and moved here within a month.

I worked for eight years to buy my land. I didn't borrow money from the government. In Rondônia the government took bad land and gave it to people who didn't know what to do with it. Of course they failed. I had my land tested before I bought it. Acre land is the filet mignon of the Amazon. That's why people fight over it. Would you fight over an ugly woman? No. You fight over a beautiful woman."

The taxi turned up a red dirt driveway, past lush pasture, toward a cookhouse on a beautiful ranch. Cattle grazed on gently rolling slopes. A finger-shaped lake filled a long depression. There was no evidence of burning or cutting or forest destruction. No blackened stumps. No cut brush. The presence of high, wide-canopied Brazil nut trees accentuated the sense of naturalness. Had I been magically transported to this place and not known its history, I would have had no idea it had ever been jungle.

"How do you like our desert?" João Branco bragged. "Go ahead. Write it's a desert."

On quarterhorses, we toured the grounds. The ranch belonged to Alemaó, a friend who ran a farm machinery company in town and another thirty thousand-acre ranch in the South. Alemaó had owned this ranch for sixteen years, João Branco said. He was attacking the notion that ranches always failed because the land was bad. Alemaó made a good profit, João Branco said. Alemaó wasn't a land speculator, or he would have sold out long ago. All the ranchers around here worked to make their places as beautiful as Alemaó's.

João Branco kneeled down and put his hand on the earth. He ran his hand along the grass. He stood up and struck himself, once, over his chest.

"Land," he said.

.   .   .

The bishop of Acre, Dom Moacyr Grecchi, was a quiet-looking man in a short-sleeved cotton shirt and horn-rimmed glasses. An accountant, you might guess, or a social worker. A small electric fan hummed on his desk. A squarish Byzantine icon of colored tiles showed Jesus Christ. The bishop smiled gently and gestured at an empty chair.

"The ranchers are assholes," he said.

In an hour the bishop was scheduled to say a memorial Mass for Chico Mendes. Chico Mendes had been dead for six months, and over a thousand people would crowd into the church. Printed prayer sheets in the chapel, piled and waiting for use, included lines like, "The hands of the tyrants. To take land. To have profit. Killing. These are their plans."

By "tyrants" the prayer meant "ranchers."

"When I arrived here in 1972 there were thirty-two thousand people in Rio Branco," he said. "Now we have two hundred thousand. Most of them came from the forest. They left because they were threatened. They couldn't exist there anymore. Sometimes they were so frightened they left pigs, hens, chickens."

Downstairs, in an office where church workers met with *seringueiros,* I'd seen a poster that said, WITHOUT AGRARIAN RE-FORM YOU DON'T HAVE DEMOCRACY. That one showed a peasant climbing over a barbed-wire fence. Another poster was a photograph of Chico Mendes on the floor of his house, eating a simple meal, looking with joy at his son.

"João Branco is right when he says there was no strife between ranchers and *seringueiros* until seven years ago. The *seringueiros* would run away until seven years ago. Nowadays it happens less. There's organization."

The bishop looked at his watch because it was almost time for the Mass. He explained that Chico Mendes had devised his ecological strategies in conjunction with the left-wing Workers Party and the Church. He told a story about a rancher who had altered the deed to his land, enlarged the number of acres so the document stated he owned a thousand times more land than he really did. Then he sold the land he didn't own and kept the money. "The ranchers," Bishop Grecchi said, "get land in illegal ways."

I knew there were many in Brazil who said deforestation would never stop until land reform was instituted. In the early 1980s thousands of the peasants who crowded into the region had lost their small farms in the South when large agricultural concerns had taken over the land.

"Brazil has 12 million families without land," the bishop said.

"And I'm talking about people who live on the land but don't own it. That's 50 million people."

The bishop said that the day Chico Mendes was killed, he was the eighty-third union leader to be murdered in the country in 1988. I thought of how the rubber tappers had joked that UDR stands for Usamos Dinero e Revolvers: "We use money and revolvers."

The bishop's office was a five-minute walk from João Branco's house. All I had to do was walk outside, down a hill, across the main square, past the war memorial, and onto João Branco's block.

I asked the bishop if he had ever met João Branco.

"No," the bishop said.

. . .

The phone woke me ringing at 3 A.M. and I heard drunken laughter in the background. João Branco's hoarse and familiar voice said, "Want to go to a party tomorrow, fellow? It's the second thing I want to show you. Good friends."

The next morning João Branco picked me up at the hotel in a new Ford pickup, and we set off south on the road to Xapuri, where Chico Mendes had lived. It was a paved road, but João Branco preferred driving on the rough dirt shoulder. "It's more fun," he said.

We passed cocoa farms and rubber farms. And, as always, ranches. The road ran parallel to and a few miles away from the Bolivian border. After a while it started drizzling, and João Branco pulled the truck over to help three hitchhiking women. They carried a baby and were grateful to get the ride. Two of them got out ten miles later, and the third went on a while more. When she got out, near a small thatched farmhouse, she leaned back into the cab and gave a huge smile. She wanted to thank João Branco properly so she asked his name.

"João Branco," he said.

At once the smile dropped. The woman turned, staggering, and tottered away. She never looked back.

"Funny people," João Branco said. "They don't even say thanks."

Soon we reached the Santa Lucia Ranch, which belonged to one of João Branco's best friends. Arisbeu Medeiros was a tall, lean man in Ralph Lauren jeans and a peaked cap that said Diesel Power. Aragao Silva, the other friend, was shorter, stockier, and famous. I'd seen his picture in *Manchete,* Brazil's version of *Life* magazine, only a week before. In the picture Aragao had been instructing forest workers who would clear jungle for pasture. Aragao had gotten a license to clear the land.

The party turned out to be a celebration of castrating steers. We sat in the cab of a Caterpillar bulldozer and drank beer from long-necked bottles. Drunken cowboys wheeled horses in a corral, lassoed steers, and cut their balls off with knives. They dabbed medicine on the wound to keep flies from nesting in them. They were a little too rough with the first steer, and they broke its leg.

"How are you going to write your article?" Arisbeu asked in friendly challenge. "Will you write about this?" he said, meaning the green rolling pastures, the well tended fences, the fat cattle, the achievement of creating a ranch. "Or this?" he said, meaning the drunken cowboys. "Ecology?" he said. "Yes. Ecologists? Shit."

Aragao asked me if I wanted to see some rain forest being cut. His ranch was down the road, and his crews were in the jungle today. In two cars we headed back onto the highway, a lazy Saturday among friends, a stop at a roadside stand for cheese empenadas and soda. When we reached the Tres Marias ranch, lots of activity was going on. Cowboys herded Nelore cattle into new corrals. Bare-chested men with machetes strapped to their waists pounded posts into the earth for fencing. In a jovial mood, the friends accompanied Aragao on a tour of the property. Of the housing he had built for twenty-seven families. Of the school he had constructed too. Arisbeu and João Branco made admiring comments, appraised pasture, tested new doors on the cattle chutes. Then it was time to see the forest cut.

Brazilian law mandates that only fifty percent of a ranch can be deforested, and Aragao had not reached his limit yet. On foot, on a dirt road, we walked into the rain forest. The pasture disappeared, and huge trees rose around us. Strangler vines wrapped buttresses. A macaw flew overhead. We reached an area where the brush had been cut and lay in piles at the foot of the larger trees.

João Branco explained that when you burn rain forest, it is necessary to chop the small plants first and allow them to dry. Otherwise the big trees fall on them, they never get cut, and when you set fire to the forest, it does not burn.

Smoke rose around a bend in the forest. When we got closer, I saw motor oil cans scattered on the ground. And then a migrant worker camp. Two thatch-roofed open air shelters, hammocks hanging inside. Cooking fires going to discourage insects. Men playing dominoes on wooden cartons. A woman breastfeeding a baby. A little girl clutching an empty beer bottle as a doll.

The workers had quit for the day, but in honor of my presence, they would cut a little more. Aragao gave instructions to a shy-looking man with a gap in his front teeth, and the man picked up a chainsaw and waded into the drying brush, deciding which tree to cut. He pulled the starter, and the scream of the gasoline engine filled the forest. I glanced at my watch. I was curious to see how long it would take the man to end the life of the tree. I had heard a tree could be cut down in ten minutes. He selected an average-sized tree, two feet in diameter, and I guessed ten minutes would be about right.

The blade bit into the wood, the tree tilted. Two adjacent trees blocked its fall. Smoothly, the worker swung the chainsaw, and the blade sliced through all three. They fell together. A hole interrupted the forest canopy, gray sky where green leaves had been a moment before.

"How long?" I heard João Branco say beside me. I didn't realize the friends had been timing it too.

"Forty-five seconds," Arisbeu said.

Aragao smiled up at me. "No more forest," he said.

"The Brazilian frontier is a lot like the old American frontier," Kenton Miller, a research fellow at the World Resource Institute in Washington, had once told me. "You had thousands of poor people moving west. The only difference in 1989 is that we have chainsaws, not axes. We have vans, not wagons."

In the cookhouse, Aragao's cook grilled us fresh steaks from the ranch, and beans, rice. The friends drank whiskey and told jokes. "You can fuck my wife," João Branco said, reaching the punchline of a story, "but don't fuck me." Arisbeu was laughing so hard, he had trouble breathing. He gasped, fumbling with his shoelaces, "Did you ever see the way Portuguese people tie their shoes?"

They weren't tyrants or murderers or plotters at that moment. They were just three guys telling jokes. It was pleasant, and dusk was falling in the Amazon. There was a cold mist outside. João Branco said the mist meant the rainy season was over. It was like all the moisture of the jungle was being sucked out of the ground, dissipating in white smoke rising into the sky. João Branco said the mist would last three days, as would the cold. Afterward the dry season would begin.

When I got back to my hotel, I glanced at Rio Branco's other newspaper, the one João Branco did not own. Aragao's name caught my eye. It seemed investigators were looking into his term as mayor. During his term as mayor, Rio Branco's education funds had disappeared.

.   .   .

Judson Valentim bounded out of the Jeep and into the field. He was a short, dark-haired scientist in a black tractor hat. He'd taken me thirty miles south of Rio Branco to show me ways to save the Amazon. He bent low in what looked to me like weeds, but deep satisfaction lit his face.

"I don't want Acre to become like southern Brazil," he said. "Cattle compact the soil and wreck pasture."

All through the region I'd heard proposals to make cattle ranching more profitable, more environmentally acceptable. On an island in the jungle a recluse Hungarian refugee had shown me cows wandering forest trails, eating wild fruits. "You don't have to deforest," he'd said. In an air-conditioned office in Pôrto Velho, the head of the state industrial commission had insisted fertilizer was the answer. And the state of Acre was trying to zone its western regions, sending soil experts into remote forest to test the earth, judge its affinity for settlement. Areas would be designated by the government, said spokesmen. This is for colonies. This is for preservation. This is for ranches. This is for farms.

The bottom line, like it or not, was that people were going to keep coming. "If we continue the way we're going, we will deforest large areas, and those areas will be degraded," Judson said.

But now I was looking at a green miracle. A real before-and-after scene. On one side of a dirt road, degraded cattle pasture. Clumps of weak, lackluster grass poked from compacted earth. On the other, lush, green kudzu. Fat cattle. A riot of growth. "In 1979 we started working in Acre," Judson said. "We knew it was only a matter of time before people started arriving. We tried to prepare. We tested five hundred kinds of grasses to see which would be best. We tested legumes, fertilizers. We didn't expect the big result we're having, but now we'll be able to triple the amount of cattle in the state without having fights with ecologists."

We left the ranch where Judson's kudzu was growing thick on the slopes and drove back to EMBRAPA, the Brazil Corporation for Agricultural Research, where he works. Here, on a fourteen-thousand-acre experimental farm, we drove to a field where workers were growing garlic. "Most garlic in the Amazon is imported," Judson said. "Why can't we grow our own?" We walked through plots where disease-resistant beans were being developed. Judson fingered peanut plants coming up. These could feed cattle, he said. He showed me cheap irrigation pumps that could easily be used by farmers.

In the labs, scientists tested oranges for sugar content. There were projects for pineapples, black pepper, coffee, Brazil nut trees, lemons, rubber trees, cattle, and goats.

"Options, options," Judson kept saying. "I have to assume something will attack the new crops. I have to give farmers options for their arsenals."

Like thousands of other Amazon ranchers, Judson's father had gone broke in Pará when the land he tried to develop was too weak to produce. Judson's father died, and Judson went off to get a Ph.D. in biology at the University of Florida. "Anybody who says anything about what percentage of the Amazon is productive is guessing," he said. "There hasn't been good fieldwork yet. We need more research to develop rationally."

Develop. It all sounded rational, considering the needs of the people here. Judson added, though, that even with technical improvements, cattle ranching is not the best use of the soil. "It's not as productive," he said. When we were finished, we drove to Rio

Branco to have lunch in a good restaurant. Judson glanced at the menu and made his choice. His meal came, and he looked down at it steaming on the plate. He smiled.

"Look at me," he said, "eating a steak."

.   .   .

Colonel Roberto seemed different than I had expected. He was a tall, lean man wearing Ghandi-like round wire-rimmed glasses. He gave me an autographed picture of beautiful Amazon flowers. The inscription read, "You are my friend. This makes me happy." Colonel Roberto was the commander of the Acre military police.

Outside the barracks, platoons of teenage boys in uniform marched in a courtyard flanking the Rio Branco main square. They were Colonel Roberto's urchin corps, delinquent boys he provided jobs to so they could better their lives. Armed guards stood at doorways. Soccer trophies lined the office walls.

I explained to Colonel Roberto that I had not come to Acre to write about Chico Mendes. I added that this must sound odd since I was asking about him. But it seemed impossible to talk to anyone about João Branco without the subject coming up. I had heard that Colonel Roberto had a witness in custody who had linked João Branco to the killing, and Colonel Roberto nodded pleasantly and said this was true.

Colonel Roberto turned more serious when I asked if I could see the witness, a boy named Genesio. Genesio had been held in protective custody in these very barracks the night before, but even with all the guards, he had not been safe and had been moved. He was being moved every day. Genesio didn't want to talk to reporters, Colonel Roberto said. He added that he could not talk about a pending case.

But he agreed to answer yes-no questions, to confirm or deny information I had heard in town.

I said, "Did Genesio work on Darli's ranch? Did he say that Darli was a killer and that the ranch itself had been payment for murders he carried out for ranchers?"

Colonel Roberto considered. "Yes."

"Did Genesio say that eight people had been murdered on the ranch and that their bodies had been burned?"

"Yes."

"That two of these victims were drug smugglers? That one had wanted to marry Darli's daughter? That two of them were *seringueiros*?"

Colonel Roberto nodded.

"Did Genesio tell you that João Branco had been on Darli's ranch for a period of five days, drinking whiskey with Darli? That the murder of Chico Mendes had been discussed by the men present?"

"Yes."

"Did he say Darli said to João Branco, 'What will happen if I kill Chico Mendes?' Did he say that João Branco replied, 'Nothing, like the others. And if something does happen we will help you'?"

"Yes."

"Was Genesio supposed to be in the room when this happened? Or did he hear it from other men on the ranch? Did he say he actually heard it?"

"Yes."

"Are you sure I can't meet with Genesio?"

Colonel Roberto smiled.

"Colonel Roberto," I said, "you're a policeman. You have experience with people telling lies. You've talked with Genesio. Do you believe what he said?"

Colonel Roberto blinked behind his round Ghandi-like glasses. There were more bright pictures of flowers on the wall behind his desk. Even Bishop Grecchi, who hates the ranchers, told me Colonel Roberto was a good man.

Colonel Roberto looked unhappy. "I don't know," he said.

. . . .

This is my problem. I liked João Branco. He was nice to me. He told funny jokes. He seemed to love life. I admired his independence. He talked like ranchers I knew in Montana—the way he hated government interference, the way he couldn't believe people accused him of hating the earth. He was capable of personal kind-nesses. He had lent a favorite worker money so the man could buy a ranch of his own.

I hoped João Branco had nothing to do with the death of Chico Mendes, but the truth was, I had no idea.

By the time João Branco invited me to see the third thing he loved about ranching, production, I began to see something else. Whether or not he was involved, the fact that so many people were ready to believe he was said plenty about Acre. And Brazil. And ranching. And the Amazon.

To some, João Branco was sophisticated evil incarnate. To others, he was the premier spokesman for rational future development of land.

Once again we were on a road in the Amazon and on another ranch that was growing—10,000 hectares, 2,000 cattle, with aspirations to keep 8,000 more. This owner looked like Martin Sheen except he wore short pants with cuffs and backless slippers, even when he rode a horse.

João Branco had bought two hundred head. As we stood on raised platforms overlooking a system of chutes in a corral, one by one bucking livestock were herded and shouted into the chute. The doors swung shut. Holding a red-hot iron with both hands, the owner leaned down, pressed metal to flesh, and smoke rose. The 2J João Branco brand appeared in black on the animal's right rear flank. This was a tradition—the seller applying the buyer's brand to the new cows as if they were a gift.

"You have a good life here," I said to João Branco.

"Ha ha ha," João Branco laughed. "Certainly."

It was mid dry season in July, and all over Acre forest was being cut. In September the big burning would begin, but already in the afternoons I could sometimes see streams of gray smoke rising over trees or along the roads. With a contented, peaceful expression, João Branco explained his vision of the future, what Acre would be like in ten years. There would be no more *seringueiros*. Their way of life was doomed. Not only by ranches. But by simple market logistics. Soon huge rubber plantations in southern Brazil would begin operating, the government would stop price hikes on imported Asian rubber, and the *seringueiros* would lose what little income they had and would have to move away.

There would be more ranches, João Branco said, lots of ranches. More cattle. More roads. More jobs for settlers. "They want work," he said generously. "We have it." Why, in the old days, the butcher had been the most powerful man in Rio Branco. Once a week a plane would fly in with beef from Bolivia, and in the meantime the butcher would get all kinds of favors from hungry citizens. A house even. Was that any way to live, from week to week?

There would be no more labor problems. Or ecologists. "The concern about the Amazon is a fad," João Branco said. "People will realize it isn't in danger. You can fly all the say to Manaus. Forest! All the way to Lima. Forest! People will turn to something else."

In face, João Branco said as we left the ranch and turned back to town, many ranchers were purposely not burning land this year, waiting for world attention to flag, waiting for the press to get bored and move on to Africa, or Beirut or wherever those lightweights would gravitate to next. And then the ranchers would be able to get on with what they were meant to do, produce.

In October big fires would be burning all over Acre. Smoke would be so thick the airport would be closed, staffers at the state environmental institute had told me. People would rush home after work, lock doors and windows, and turn on air conditioners.

"There is no other way, no better way to clear land than to burn it," João Branco said, lighting another cigarette. "If the developed world wants to help us, that is something to discover, a way of clearing forest without burning it. But for the time being, the burning will not stop."

This was not just João Branco's opinion. This was everyone's opinion in Brazil: politicians, environmental policemen, governors, scientists, journalists, farmers. There was simply no better way to clear the earth, to clean old lots, to get rid of residue in fields.

I told João Branco that at home in the United States when people see those fires, sweeping, massive blazes on TV, they see genocide of species, they see death. I asked João Branco what the fires meant to him.

The pickup rocked over the hard red earth. Rio Branco was coming up in the distance. I caught sight of the airport tower toward which I knew we would be heading to drink coffee, joke with other ranchers, to see who was coming in and out of town.

"When I see fires," João Branco said, "I see beauty. I see transformation."

The Activist and the Rain Forest

The last wailing saxophone note died with the spotlight, and the musician plunged into blackness. Saint John the Divine erupted in hoots, screams, laughter, drumbeats. Then the overhead lights flooded the cathedral; the columns thick as sequoias, the arches low as gray clouds. Men wearing cat masks. Women dressed like clowns. Doped-up Grateful Deadheads drifting among the folding chairs in tie-dyed T-shirts.

Harlem, New York, is as far from a rain forest as any spot on Earth, especially with a blizzard blanketing the corners, the coffeehouses, the homeless people, the fenced-in Tudor gardens of the biggest cathedral in the United States.

Boom, a drum went. *Boom! Boom!*

Stiff with fear, a pale-skinned man in a crewneck sweater leaned against a speaker at the bottom of the stage. He mouthed words on a paper held shakily in one hand. It was winter, 1989.

"Speak up for the plants and animals," he said.

Almost three thousand people had paid to attend the fund-raiser, "Carnival for the Rain Forest." And the round-faced twenty-eight-year-old in spectacles and black cowlick, who seemed to be shrinking as his moment on stage approached, was a dream-come-true for conservationists, a nightmare for many rain forest country politicians. Symbol of the groundswell in environmental activism. Average citizen without formal training, suddenly influencing policy far away.

"I've never spoken before so many people before," Dan Katz said.

To make matters worse, he looked up to see the Very Reverend James Park Morton, dean of the Cathedral. New York cool guy, with his scarf thrown over his collar, his locks of thick gray hair, his bearish, commanding presence, his deep authoritative voice. "You have a big gig here," he advised Katz. "Try to be spontaneous."

Dean Morton patted his intestinal area to show the advantages of visceral appeal. Dan Katz looked at his notes, horrified.

"Not read it?" he moaned.

On stage Dean Morton looked bigger, actually quieted the seething mass. "We're talking about great issues here. The Amazon," he said. "Yayyyy," three thousand people screamed. "Dan Katz, president of the Rain Forest Alliance, will tell you how you can involve yourself."

Katz couldn't see anything, only lights burning into his face. Talk about topping the previous act. The evening had opened with Paul Winter playing solos in an alcove above the main floor. The "Forces of Nature Ensemble" had danced down the aisle, men and women in dashikis, shaking gourds. Mickey Hart of the Grateful Dead had played an original tune, smashing a hatchet into a steel skeleton over and over. A dancer named Nassim had gyrated in a sequined body stocking while "Pe De Boi," her group, made the walls tremble with heavy drumbeats.

A giddy orgy of musical anarchy all leading up to Dan Katz from Cincinnati, Ohio.

"Thank you, uh, Dean Morton," he said in a quiet nasal voice.

The man who had been sitting next to Katz in the audience bolted up. Katz looked pretty meek up there.

"*That* guy?" he said.

Dan Katz helped raise $12,000 for rain forest conservation that night.

·   ·   ·

Twelve thousand from a concert. Twenty-five thousand from a grant. Money to pay for brochures, fellowships, research, meetings. Cash turned into influence. By the late 1980s, before the 1990 recession and the war with Iraq, all over the developed world, people who had never seen a rain forest adopted rain forest preservation as their cause. It was still a flush time for rain forest protection. A good time.

Definition by wasn'ts. Dan Katz wasn't a scientist. Wasn't an economist. He had no formal training in banking, anthropology, forestry. He was a rabid Cincinnati Reds fan. A poker player. A Chinese language major. An eternal cracker of bad jokes. For saving rain forests, what kind of qualifications were those?

"When I talk about interdependent ecosystems, it's intimidating," he said.

We sat in his office alcove, near a window overlooking a Soho autobody shop. A white, sunny space built by volunteers, people who had gotten it into their head to "save rain forests." Like the construction company owner who'd remodeled. The lawyer who'd drawn up contracts for promotional T-shirts and shower curtains, for free. The designer who'd come up with the frog-against-the-New-York-skyline logo, which Katz said symbolized interdependence.

"I started reading about rain forests in 1981 at Ohio State," Katz said. "There was no one to speak up for the plants and animals and people of the forest. That sounds mushy, but it's true. I became obsessed. In English class I wrote a paper on the state of the rain forest. In physical science, on what rain forests were.

"I tried to join a group working on conservation of rain forest ecosystems, but there weren't any. I didn't want to just send money."

Still, after graduation he got a job in his chosen field, becoming "China Coordinator" at Shearman & Sterling law firm. He took visiting dignitaries to New York restaurants and answered questions like, "Is it safe to walk around here?"

One day he attended a conference on deforestation, and listening to the grim statistics, was overcome by the old passion. He turned to the stranger next to him. "Are you ready to do something?" he said.

Pretty funny. Two guys deciding to save the rain forests. A toxicologist and a China program coordinator. Next scene: a living room on the upper East Side. Dan, and Ivan Ussach, the toxicologist. A masseuse. A retired publishing executive. An actress. Christening themselves The Rain Forest Alliance over fried vegetables and beer and carrot juice. Deciding to "educate the public."

Outside, as they debated about medicinal plants and climate connections, homeless people wandered New York streets. AIDS clinics needed volunteers. Libraries were desperate for literacy workers. Help was needed to clean parks, walk crime patrols, gather money to fight cancer.

What was it about a place so far away that pulled at people, got them involved?

"I was drawn into the void," said one Alliance founder, Monica Whalen. "My theory is, when a tremendous amount of life is destroyed, it creates a physical void. The power of that vacuum drew me in."

"I've been in the Amazon," said Anna Pindar, a Brazilian and Soho art gallery owner who threw a benefit for the Alliance. "My uncle showed me the devastation."

"It's the most important issue we have in front of us these days. The future of the planet. Will we make it?" said rock singer Bob Weir of the Grateful Dead, a frequent spokesman on rain forest issues.

"Many people give money because it is fashionable," said Sonia Riquiera, a Brazilian heading Conservation International's Brazil program. "For some it is a matter of conscience. They've done bad things, and they want to do good."

"We Germans are romantic, romantic about trees," said Michael Gagern, a Munich economics professor I met in western Brazil. He was traveling the region on a three-week tour, trying to figure out how to donate $2 million that wealthy friends had decided to spend on rain forest preservation. None of them had been to a rain forest.

"We thought of ourselves as an education and public awareness group," Katz said. "At the time very few people knew about rain forests. We weren't sure what we could do, but there were things that needed to be done. We wanted to find things to spark people's interest, *good* things people could buy, not just boycott bad ones. We saw that rain forests were far away from New York, and people might not see a direct impact from their destruction, but they were in our backyards."

Back in Manhattan, Katz suggested the newly formed Alliance sponsor a conference on rain forests. The other people thought it a bad idea, but he pushed it through. He even quit his job to make phone calls organizing it.

No one had ever heard of Katz. At the crumbling old Victorian group house in Brooklyn where he lived with his girlfriend and seven other people, housemates joked about Katz's huge long-distance phone bills. He ran out of money and got a job selling books. Late at night he and Ivan took long walks, looking out at the Verrazano Bridge, talking about the beautiful rain forests where Katz had never been.

But the conference turned out to be one of those watershed events in the life of an idea. Katz got then New York Botanical Garden Senior Vice President Gillian Prance to speak. Prance helped bring in Tom Lovejoy from the Smithsonian Institution and Peter Raven from the Missouri Botanical Garden. Suddenly environmentalists and congressmen started calling Katz, *asking* to be included.

A foundation Katz had never heard of donated $25,000 because they "heard we were doing good work. That became my salary." The three-day conference featured fifty-seven speakers addressing issues like, "Are Bankers Responsible?" "Debt-for-Nature Swaps." "Indigenous People." There was Indonesian and Brazilian music at night and a trip to the Bronx Zoo's "Jungle World." A woman walked up to the podium as Katz prepared to speak and said, "I think I have an office for your organization." An heiress called after the conference, took him to lunch, and asked if $10,000 would help.

"Ten thousand would be good," Dan said. "But twenty would be better."

"Okay," the heiress said.

By 1987 money was pouring into environmental coffers everywhere for rain forest protection. Katz was on $25,000 salary, and the Alliance budget was $80,000. Small but growing. It doubled the next year. Alliance speakers appeared at colleges, churches, community groups. They started a newsletter to update five thousand paying members on the status of forests around the world. As they grew they specialized. Instead of everybody doing everything, Ivan Ussach concentrated on coming up with a program to certify tropical hardwoods as sustainably grown and acceptable for purchase. Sarah Laird took over the "Periwinkle Project" designed to alert the medical field to links between loss of potential medicines as forests were destroyed. Katz signed on with a speakers bureau. Tom Lovejoy became a member of the board of directors. So did Leonard Schwartz, an ex-president of Brentano's and executive vice president of Times Books. The Alliance hired a professional office manager and fund-raiser. Salaries remained low.

"Everyone's hand is on the chainsaw," Katz told audiences. "The cabdriver who needs a rubber fan belt. The mayor of New York who has input on building material specifications. Everyone."

He still hadn't been to the jungle. But finally he got a chance. He went to French Guiana with Gillian Prance on a research trip, then stayed for a week in a village.

"I was nervous," he said. "I thought, what if I hate it? I'd lived in Wuhan, China. They have humongous mosquitos there. I swelled up from them.

"When I got to the rain forest, I spent days just walking. One time I was walking and I heard this thump. I saw the end of a mammoth snake. I yelled "holy shit" and jumped back. But that snake was more scared of me. I crept up on it. I pulled out my camera. I almost had a heart attack. I thought, get lost here, it's good-bye baseball." Katz grinned. "But it was peaceful. I loved it."

"Would you want to live in the jungle?" I asked, remembering a story I'd heard in Pôrto Velho. A Brazilian environmentalist had gone to that city to fight for preservation. But one day her host found a note from her on his table, reading, "It's too hot here. I can't stand it. I'm going back east. I'll work from there."

Phones rang around us in the office, and a police siren wailed outside.

Katz laughed. "In bits and pieces. Nature is more like my God. I wouldn't want to live in a temple," he said, "but I want to know it's there."

.   .   .

Whispers shot through the Beverly Hills crowd: "Elke Sommer. Elke Sommer."

Dan Katz swiveled and tried to glimpse the famous actress, but it was impossible through the wall of bodies. Women in fur coats. Men in ponytails and $800 suits. This time the fund-raiser was at the Hermès of Paris boutique, on Rodeo Drive. For its "Year of the Outdoors," the French-based company had decided to send Dan Katz to cities around the United States.

"Funds raised from this event will promote research into how tropical rain forests can be utilized without endangering the peoples, plants, or animals that live within them," read an invitation emblazoned with smiling jungle animals.

Waiters in silk sashes, billowy shirts, and gaucho hats offered rattan trays of *crème brulée à la rain forest*. Film people and favored guests sipped champagne. A gigantic rose-colored bottle of Amazone perfume centered the boutique on a glass pedestal. On the second floor, a Brazilian duo played samba music near the Chinese bathrobes.

"I was relieved to find out I didn't have to give a speech," Katz said.

All over the boutique, people bent to kiss each other, pulled back before actually touching, and cried, "Mah!"

Katz caught up with Elke in the hallway. The star of *A Shot in the Dark* was talking German with the caterer. She looked stunning in a long black dress with see-through sleeves, a bow on her crimped hair, only her hands showing age. Her dazzling blue eyes turned on Dan.

"Vat is being done about the rain forest!" she demanded.

"Uh, more and more," Katz said. "We're trying to work with govern—"

"Excuse me! Hello! Mah! *How* much is being destroyed?" she said, whirling back.

"A hundred acres a minute."

"Oh Gott! They're nuts! They're nuts! I wished always to go to the rain for— Excuse me. Mah!"

"We'll take you there," Dan said.

"Yah?" Elke wanted a cigarette. Two gauchos ran toward her holding fistfuls. A third stood by with an ashtray.

"El-ke! El-ke!" they cried.

Elke asked questions about rain forests. "I lost my trees in a hurricane," she said. "A hurricane?" Dan said. "Not a hurricane hurricane," she said. "Vind! Who's gonna stop it! Who's gonna do it! Not until the big, fat, rich people are taken care of! Give him my number!" she commanded her escort, a tall, smiling Lufthansa executive who'd driven her here in a Mercedes sports car.

Pretty funny. Customers paid for Hermès "Equateur" scarves with platinum American Express cards. Salesgirls had French accents, but none seemed to be from France. A gaucho offered "stuffed mango bread with rain forest fruit filling."

The Hermès campaign raised $95,000 for the Rain Forest Alliance.

At 9:30 we strolled to a nearby restaurant. Beverly Hills eateries seemed to have New York names. Tribeca. Carnegie Deli. The Brooklyn Bar. Dan ordered scotch while we waited for a table, and we went back over the day's events. His judging of a graphic design contest at the Fashion Institute of Design and Merchandising, cosponsor of the Hermès party. His meeting at Universal TV with the senior vice president for dramatic and long-term programming, where Katz wanted to know if there were any rain forest movies coming up.

But the Universal meeting had been strained. Katz's plain folks delivery worked with people predisposed to help, but Charmaine Balian hadn't seemed that way. In an office of dark woods and English jockey prints, Balian had sat legs crossed, black velvet high heels half-buried in beige pile. She said the lawyerlike decor, unchanged since the time of founder Jules Stein, was a perfect example of how hard it was to change big corporations.

"Social messages don't sell," she said, explaining the limits of what a concerned person could do. "The way we're going about it in TV is good. Subliminal. Like there won't be any Styrofoam cups in our shows. There'll be paper cups. You have to find ways."

The sense of distance sharpened when Katz mentioned an upcoming radiothon to raise money for parkland in Costa Rica.

Charmaine gasped. "You want to *buy* a rain forest?"

Not buy, Dan said, his quiet voice dropping into a void. We want to work with local groups.

"*We're* producing more of the greenhouse effect than they are," she said. "We should be focused here. Why are we taking people's means of support without giving them other ones? Who's going to prevent them from cutting trees anyway? It sounds very elitist to me.

"I never hear the other side," Charmaine said. "I never hear people say, 'We have to come up with an alternative.' " It wasn't a corporate brush-off. There was genuine concern and confusion in her voice.

Dan tried to tell her he worried about misplaced altruism, too, but the meeting was over. And now in the restaurant I asked, "What do you tell people who say, 'You live in a city? Who are you to tell people in rain forests what to do?' "

"I'm not telling anyone. We're trying to find ways of utilizing forest without destroying it," Dan said, unfazed.

"What about people who say you're fighting over something you have no understanding of?"

"Well, I don't have an understanding of living in rain forests, but I do have an understanding of how they work. I know I'm part of the problem. I should be part of the solution. Look at Costa Rica. It was because of our demand for beef that they altered their economy. Just to boycott Costa Rican beef isn't a fair alternative. We need to work with them. The same with tropical timber. We want to work with countries. To help find ways to promote sustainable logging. Maybe to come up with a labeling program."

"What about the greenhouse effect?" I echoed Charmaine. "Ten percent of it is from deforestation, but twenty percent comes from the United States."

The waitress brought ravioli and wine. Dan's schedule was grueling this week. Parties in Houston, Chicago, Los Angeles. TV interviews in San Francisco tomorrow.

"More and more I have to talk about North America when I talk about the tropics," he said. "But because we have problems doesn't mean we should ignore other people's."

Katz sighed and continued. "I told you. I don't tell anyone what to do. I studied rain forests on my own for years. I'm self-trained. I still feel inadequate when I talk about science issues, economic issues. I'm a generalist. I'm Jack. I think that's one reason why people relate to me. I'm Joe Schmo, and I'm talking from my heart."

.   .   .

Rain forests were in. Tendrils of ivy dangled from models' clothing in Paris fashion shows. Producers including Robert Redford battled over film rights to the Chico Mendes story. Foundations including the Threshold, Pew, Packard, and Ford earmarked grants for protection or research. Publishers Simon & Schuster, Little, Brown, and Houghton Mifflin commissioned books.

A Virginia power company planted trees to replace carbon its plants pumped into the air. Ticonderoga pencils stopped buying a rare tropical softwood. The Arizona legislature banned tropical timber in building projects.

In New York, Mayor Ed Koch proclaimed Rain Forest Awareness Week. "New York, the financial, media, and cultural capital of the world, is in the unique position of using its resources to promote the cause of global rain forest conservation," Koch said.

These were small efforts against the tide of deforestation, but to Dan Katz, a hoped-for beginning of real change.

"Last year foreign debt was chic, this year it's the rain forest," Brazilian Ambassador to the United States Marcilio Marques Moreira remarked wryly. "So I'm chic."

The groundswell of interest was welcomed in some rain forest countries, like Costa Rica, which was trying to raise capital for conservation. But it was regarded as interference in countries like Brazil.

"Nongovernment organizations have too much power, too much influence with the World Bank," lamented Foreign Ministry Secretary General Paulo Flecha Tarso de Lima when I met him in Brasília, right after the bank had stopped disbursements of a loan for an Amazon highway, on environmental grounds.

"We are worried by a universal trend of dealing with ecology as a worldwide problem without frontiers," he said over hot coffee.

"The pope in Madagascar said there should not be borders for the ecology problem. Very imprudent."

De Lima had seemed more sad than angry, leaning back on his leather couch. "It's a worldwide fetish," he said. "Part of it is due to a relaxation of cold war tensions. People of the Northern Hemisphere can devote themselves to more humanitarian issues, to fight the common enemy, the destruction of the planet. But the more pedestrian explanation is politics. Politicians feel the pressure of young 'green' electros, and they cater to them."

I asked Ambassador Moreira if he felt pressure over environmental issues. "I feel like a smoker in a New York restaurant," he said.

Never mind conservationist talk about "working with local groups." *Which* local groups? Traitorous ones, the Brazilian military charged. And to de Lima and many Brazilians at best the Dan Katzes of the world were well-intentioned dilettantes trying to force rain forest countries to follow the conservationist line. At worst they were puppets in an orchestrated campaign to stifle development in the Third World so profits could eventually be stolen by the North. To block the construction of BR-364 so American soybeans, not Brazilian ones, got shipped to Japan. Many places I went in Brazil, people asked me, suspiciously, "Who paid for you to be here?"

"You want to know Brazil's image?" hissed one Brazilian economist at a lunch at a U.N. diplomat's Manhattan apartment. "*This,*" she said in disgust, tossing a paperback book on a table. The cover showed two naked Amazon Indians wrestling. "That's our image," she snapped. She added indignantly that a friend of hers in Nevada had sent her a Reno newspaper clipping critical of Brazil's treatment of Indians. "Nevada," she snorted, as if anyone so far away could understand the situation in Brazil. Brazilian politicians warned there could be a backlash against environmentalism if the pressure didn't let up.

"I never even saw an Indian," remarked the host, an ex-São Paulo lawyer turned diplomat.

"We might as well attack capitalism," said his wife, a U.N. Brazilian deputy consul.

"Of course there are problems," said the economist, mollified by her outburst. "Brazil is addressing them."

"It's so hard throwing all these lunches for friends of Brazil," the deputy consul said.

. . .

"Mr. Almost" was a figure out of Chinese folklore, Dan Katz said. Send him to market for onions, he'd come back with scallions. "They're almost the same," he'd say. Mr. Almost got sick and went to a veterinarian instead of a doctor. "They're almost the same," he said.

"He died because he didn't go the extra mile to find out what was necessary," said Katz. "I never want to be Mr. Almost."

The radio in his Plymouth Horizon broadcast K-ROCK, New York. "*Lots* of music. *Lots* of guests. *Lots* of opportunities to save the rain forest."

Katz parked on Madison Avenue, and we rode the elevator five stories to Infinity Radio's station. It was Radiothon Sunday. There were only three or four people inside at 9 A.M., but by tonight, with Washington, Boston, Philadelphia, and San Jose stations hooking in, the radiothon would reach an estimated 5 million listeners.

WHO'LL SAVE THE RAIN FOREST? read the headline in the *Daily News*. For only $60, callers could preserve an acre of Costa Rican forest. "It will be owned by Costa Ricans, in whose hands it will remain," the article said.

Dan Katz had become a conduit, a conductor for ecology. *Mr. Smith Goes to Washington*. A little guy talking to other little guys. A voice saying you didn't have to feel stupid because you weren't an expert.

"You think he's shy at first, but he's not shy," said Elysabeth Kleinhans who funded a two-year $30,000 Alliance fellowship on how to use rain forests for profit without destroying them.

K-ROCK producer Kathryn Lauren, who had thought up the radiothon idea, could have called any one of a dozen groups to offer them sponsorship. Why Katz? "I did some research. I liked that they wanted to work with people down there. I called him up." It's what Paul Winter had said. And the Hermès people: "I researched groups. I called him up."

In showers and cars and bedrooms and weekend houses, people were turning their radio dials, tuning in to listen. "Take a deep breath when you consider today's guests," the *Daily News* continued. It listed a few. The Grateful Dead. Keith Richards. Phil Collins. Aerosmith. Alice Cooper. Michael Douglas. Tony Bennett. John Sebastian. Kris Kristofferson.

Dan Katz.

"Hey, Mo!" a Three Stooges voice cried over the radio. "They're burning the rain forest!"

"Attention! This is Sergeant Slaughter! Send Money!"

A day-long orgy of nonstop promotion. "This is what the Rain Forest Alliance is about," Katz said proudly. "Individuals giving money they don't have a lot of because they care."

"Hey, man, the witch doctors in the rain forest, they used the drugs from the forest before *we* did," said Rick the bass player.

One hour into the radiothon, pledges totaled $24,000. By 1:15, $64,000. By two, after the other stations had hooked in, $81,163. Then $148,000.

Dan Katz walked between Kathryn's office for the hourly totals, to the lounge, where volunteers brought food and beverages all day, to the control booth, where he listened to guests. He took the mike himself during the late afternoon. "Great to be here. Greaaaat day," Katz said to DJ Meg Griffin, except he didn't sound like Katz, at least the nervous one I'd been listening to for months. He was glib. "I bet anybody listening that you already used at least five products that originated or were synthesized from tropical forests just today," he said.

"You sound different," I said when he finished and Meg put music on.

"Yeah. I did a lot of TV on the Hermès tour. I don't feel nervous."

By 8 P.M. the radiothon had raised $218,000. At $60 a caller, that represented thousands of contributions.

"How come a Marin County lady like yourself is doing these chic causes?" DJ and Turtles member Mark Vollman asked Grace Slick over the phone.

"You can't ask someone who's starving to death to contribute $25," she said. "They're trying to keep their stuff together. It sounds like a celebrity fad. Celebrities are the ones who should be doing this. They've got the money. They've got the power to make the situation known. I don't care if it's a fad."

In the end, seven thousand people pledged $500,000 to help the Costa Rican forest.

A few days later Katz went to a wedding and sat at a table where he didn't particularly like the guests. The men kept making cracks about women in the ceremony. But during the meal they asked him what he did for a living, and when he mentioned the radiothon, one of them said, "I heard that in Philadelphia. Pretty good."

"You did?" Katz said.

"Me, too. It was good. I heard it in California. I bought an acre," someone else at the table said.

"You did?" Katz explained that a pledge didn't really buy an acre, it just preserved it. That was fine.

The guys at the table kept talking about the radiothon. Almost all of them had heard it.

Katz looked down at his plate.

"It got me," he said.

.   .   .

We were up after dawn, on Indian horses. Trotting across Chilean pampas toward snow-dusted volcanoes ahead. When did he change, I wondered. When did he add the new layer? He was still quiet, soft spoken, self effacing. But when did he stop being the shy speaker who got slides upside down?

In 1990 the Rain Forest Alliance had raised over a million dollars. They had eighteen people on full- or part-time staff. And over fifteen thousand supporters and members. They were about to start a research fellowship in Brazil to study medicinal plants. They were initiating a conservation program to help save the Amazon river, with Brazilian conservation groups. They were doing a debt-for-nature swap in Costa Rica with Randy Curtis at the Nature Conservancy and Lamond Godwin at American Express Bank, with the money they'd raised in the radiothon.

The Rain Forest Alliance was starting a labeling program for tropical hardwoods, a rain forest seal of approval to be stamped on woods harvested sustainably. It was about to go on-line in Indonesia, and Ivan Ussach was on his way to Honduras to consider offering the seal to a timber company there.

The Alliance had found its niche in the movement. It was one of the moderate groups, the groups that tried to work with businesses, with governments. "Dan Katz has been effective in setting up the Rain Forest Alliance, giving it membership, giving it long-term viability. Whether he's been effective in changing the tropical timber industry, I have to say no," said Randy Hayes, head of the Rain Forest Action Network, which has called for boycotts of tropical timber products. "But in fairness, it's too early to tell. We're more of a lean, mean, fighting machine, confronting corporations, saying if it's bad, shut it down. They're more into constructive engagement. I'd rather go to the bargaining table with more punch."

Either way, with a recession hitting, banks failing, and U.S. troops gathering in Saudi Arabia to attack Iraq, the chic days were waning for the rain forest movement. Fund-raisers reported feeling the pinch. Direct-mail solicitations were down. "By the end of the decade there will be a major conflict between short-term financial woes and long-term environmental impact," said Peter Seligmann of Conservation International. "It will take place in the pocketbooks and minds and the consciousness of the American consumer. We're just beginning to touch that point."

Even an Alliance fund-raiser produced less than Katz would have hoped for.

But the Rain Forest Alliance was thinking about widening its focus.

"Rain forests are still more mainstream as an issue now than they were," Katz said. "Besides, they're really endangered, and there's only a certain amount of time left before we reach the point of no return. We're not going to shrink. Our programs are going to keep us growing. We're going full steam ahead."

That's one reason we were in Chile. The Alliance was considering including temperate rain forests—rain forests in colder climates—in their conservation attempts. Katz had come to Chile as part of a Kellogg Foundation seminar but had stayed on to gather facts about the forests. Over half of Chile was forest, some of it rare alerce, the protected southern sequoia. Chilean temperate rain forests are the most genetically diverse in the Southern Hemisphere. Chile has actively promoted tree plantings in the last twenty years and operates one of the better forestry services in Latin America. But debates rage over ultimate effects of the forestry industry, which provides ten percent of Chile's exports, worth $800 million in 1990.

Chilean forests were in danger. They were well preserved. They were being bought up by Japan. They were managed by experts. Those were the claims. "I wanted to find out the truth," Katz said in the Lan Chile jet flying south from Santiago toward Temuco, capital of the southern region, looking down at green valleys and towering cliffs and escarpments, sipping free wine. "And to find out if I could help."

To find out we'd squeezed into a four-wheel-drive Diatsu Jeep and headed south on the Pan-American Highway through spring hailstorms and lush Oregon-like valleys. We'd climbed into mountains as a blizzard started. It felt like Switzerland. Guards in greatcoats came out of checkpoints to raise barriers and wave us through. We bumped through a railroad tunnel, on the tracks, passed through by another trooper, a man standing beside a broken light designed to show whether the tunnel was clear. Southern Chile was a remote alpine wilderness, a mountain traveler's dream. "Beautiful, beautiful," Katz kept saying.

Dan had interviewed forestry experts, ranchers, furniture makers, exporters. Last night he listened to a midnight plea. We'd been on a ten thousand acre horse ranch belonging to Edmundo Fahrenkrog, who was leading the riders today. A ranch he'd grown up on, which he'd mortgaged to start a sustainable silvaculture (treegrowing) business. A ranch in trouble because of a recession. A ranch in hock to the bank.

Edmundo was going to have to sell a mountain, half his ranch, to pay off the bank. "I don't want to see it cut," he said. "I'm wondering if you know a conservation group in the United States that could buy it and preserve it." The cost would be $300,000.

Katz had leaned against the blackened timber making up the fireplace mantel. We sipped warm red wine and smelled sausages frying in the main house. All around us were horse mementos. Stirrups on the wall. Engravings. Statuettes.

Dan had looked concerned but had not actually addressed the request. It was clear he was thinking about it. But he'd stirred at the world *banks*. "Banks," he'd repeated, heating up. "This is a problem with banks around the world. Not only international banks but local ones. Banks strap people."

In fact, the Rain Forest Alliance was considering involving itself in creating "community banks" in rain forest countries, he said. Local lending institutions geared toward working on small environmentally beneficial projects, with no interest rates. "Keeping the big boys out."

Now, as the others pulled off, Katz reined close and said he'd been thinking about Edmundo's mountain. But he didn't want to get Edmundo's hopes up. He didn't know whether the mountain was important enough to save. "It's beautiful, but being beautiful isn't enough anymore," he said. Then he said his work on the Alliance had helped him land a seat on the World Parks Endowment, a Washington-based group formed to raise funds to help parklands around the world. Not just rain forests. Parks. "I don't know if Edmundo's mountain would apply, but it might."

Dan would be in Chile one more week. We'd visit the temperate rain forest at Puyeuhue, farther south beyond alpine valleys and glacier-carved lakes. We'd walk miles through downpours to get a view of the alerces. We'd hack through bamboo forest with a machete, trapped halfway up a mountain, dusk falling, as Katz joked all the way.

Now, as we turned back toward the scrub pampa and lake below, Dan said, "I've been remembering that first rain forest conference." Edmundo rode ahead, trying to find a clear way down. "And the walks with Ivan," he said.

Edmundo called that there was no open way toward the lake. He pointed to what seemed to be an impassable thicket, a four-hundred-yard stretch of high bushes we would have to plunge through. It was Dan's first time on a horse.

Dan headed for the thicket, riding slightly ahead. The funny man who'd decided to "save the forest," the man who'd convinced other novices to join him and call themselves an "alliance." The man who had started with nothing more than passion and built a million-dollar environmental organization in New York.

"It seems a long time ago," Dan said.

He tugged on the rope around the mare's neck, and she was nervous and didn't want to go into the thicket. But Dan Katz persisted. The horse moved ahead, and soon only the tops of branches moved where he had passed.

Kilometer 500

The Flower Man

Looking for cancer cures, Doug Daly wandered off again. Walked away from the scientists loading animal traps. A hundred yards up the sun-splashed trail, he marched through bamboo forest. A lean, compact man loaded with a laboratory's worth of supplies. Australian bush hat on his head, side flap up, against the sun. Wicked looking machete of Colombian steel, tied with leather thongs at his belt. Long aluminum pole with tongs for snipping samples. Homemade plant collector's press over his shoulder, latticed wood sides squeezing six inches of Rio Branco newspapers. Pictures of this week's exotic dancer. Editorials wishing foreigners would stay away.

Back in New York, Darlene Huertas had been saved because of an anticancer drug that came from the rain forests. Andrew Von Bassion had died because no new drug existed to combat his form of the disease.

Daly halted now and brought binoculars to his eyes. He stood absolutely still, craning toward the canopy. Dozens of sweat bees crawled on the wet streaks on the back of his khaki shirt.

"See it?" he said. "There!" But to me one tree seemed to merge into another. In bamboo forest the big trunks seem to grow out of bamboo bunches. Magnified, branches loomed. Vines. Leaves. Epiphytes.

Finally, in focus, the tiny fruit, sixty feet up.

Daly had the knapsack on the ground and he pulled out his climbing irons, barbed steel mandibles he strapped to his boots. The barbs would dig into the bark as he rose. He buckled on a

waist harness and looped a rope around the trunk, the ends knot-
ted to the harness. He started to climb. The sweat bees were on his
neck, face, and hands now. They didn't sting him. They ate sweat.
"Lung cancer!" I called. The old bad joke after three days in the
forest. What I meant was that the fruit would contain what he
searched for. A miracle chemical compound. A lifesaver for a few
million people. A symbol to make the Amazon worth saving.

He was so high already that his boots stuck out of the branches.
Daly emerged into an open spot, the irons wrapping the trunk. He
leaned back, swinging free, fifty feet up. He reached for the fruit.
Too far. He'd need the aluminum snipper. His voice floated down
in the forest, quiet, contained.

"Lung cancer?" Daly said. "Well, that would be nice."

.   .   .

Doug Daly is an economic botanist. He studies the relationships
between man and plants, and between plants and world econo-
mies. For three months a year he works in Amazon countries,
walking trails, riding rivers, climbing trees. He interviews Indian
shamans in their villages and woodsmen on their trails. He tracks
hints of rumors of cures. The mysterious cancer-killing vine of
Iquitos. The alleged blood-cleansing seed of Peru.

He's caught hepatitis in Eastern Amazonia, roundworms and
hookworms in Colombia, watched as people on expeditions with
him erupted with botflies; flies that lay eggs in human skin so that
the larvae erupt and leave inch-wide holes. For two days running in
Pará he narrowly missed being bitten by fer-de-lance, the deadliest
snake in the world. "They travel in pairs," he said. Eighty feet up
in a wild rubber tree he was attacked by wasps while trying to
retrieve a flowering branch. "It was the fastest descent known to
man." Another time hundreds of biting ants rained down on him,
into his hair, shirt, pants, when he disturbed a nest high in the
canopy. "Very uncomfortable." He's driven Jeeps across bridges
that looked like they'd collapse any minute, two slats above rivers,
quivering from the weight.

"There's something I love about the tropics," Daly said.

He's also dined on monkey meat in the field. "It's weird. It looks like a child. Little hands floating in the stew." On paca. "The most delicious meat in the world." On fresh grubs. "Buttery." On Indian manioc beer fermented with spit. "Sort of like grainy Pepto-Bismol, but it tasted different." In Peru, to test the hallucinogenic effect of a woody vine with alleged curative properties, he ate some and watched a wall of water shoot around the hut he was in for hours. There wasn't any water near the hut.

A long journey for a California boy who became interested in plants at Harvard. "I was sitting in a class watching slides taken by my professor, Richard Schultes. He'd spent fourteen years in the Amazon. I was listening to his voice, really sonorous, and looking at the Indians, the jaguar. Something started to creep into me.

"After I got down here, I knew this was it."

Daly got a Ph.D. from the City University of New York and went to work for the New York Botanical Garden collecting samples in the tropics for the herbarium. In 1986 he became one of the principal researchers in the United States working on a $5 million National Cancer Institute search to locate tropical plants that might fight cancers and AIDS.

Researchers from the New York Botanical Garden, the Missouri Botanical Garden, and the University of Illinois spread out from Indonesia to Madagascar, from Hawaii to Peru, combing native markets, learning dialects, sending back forest cures.

"It's a race against time," said Dr. Michael Balick, co-head of the New York team. "Species are being destroyed faster than we can identify them. We collect fifteen hundred a year in a hemisphere that has over one hundred thousand species. That does not bode well for the future."

He wasn't talking about only plant extinction either. In the Amazon alone, it is estimated that one Indian tribe a year has gone extinct since 1900. Each time a tribe disappeared, so did its knowledge of the forest.

Even in cases where shamans were sharing information with scientists, sometimes it was too late. "Some species are very rare," Daly said. "In one study the World Wildlife Fund looked at three adjacent hectares of forest, near Manaus, at all trees over 10 centimeters in diameter. They found only six species in common out of

170. They expanded the study to fifty hectares. They found many species represented by only one tree. Some organisms are so rare that one lost tree can affect the survival of the species.

In other cases, traditional cures were falling out of favor with the Indians, who preferred modern pills to ground-up plants. "The young people don't want to learn about the forest anymore," Daly said. Dr. Mark Plotkin, who heads Conservation International's plant program, put it another way:

"Each time a shaman dies, its like a library burning down."

.   .   .

Doug Daly had two purposes in the Acre forest: He was teaching part of a course on how to study jungle plants and animals, sponsored jointly by the New York Botanical Garden, the University of Acre, and the University of Florida, and he was scouting unofficially for the National Cancer Institute, memorizing potential plants to include in the program. Brazil had not yet allowed NCI researchers in the country, but an agreement was being negotiated. Under it, Brazil would share in development and profit from any discovery. Daly wouldn't touch anything until the agreement went through. "That's fair," Daly said, "but they've been talking for months."

He bent right on the trail, gazing with admiration at a foot-and-a-half-high plant the size of poison ivy. In the forest Daly tended to be quiet, concentrated. "This is a cycad, a living fossil," he said. The waxy green leaves hung opposite each other along slender stems. "They're really interesting chemically. People have been poisoned by 'em. I'd collect them if I could."

Ten feet later he stopped again. "Burseraceae." He pointed to a bush with leathery dark green leaves. "Indians and *caboclos* (acculturated Indians) used it against blood problems. I could find it in Peru or Colombia, but species are different in different places. I'd collect this too."

"Acre is a frontier in botany," Daly said. "We know almost nothing about the plants here."

The Acre forest was slightly drier than the Amazon to the northeast. Fewer epiphytes hung from the canopy, and since epiphytes can bring trees down from sheer weight, fewer trunks lay on the ground. In wet forest, moss covers trees. Here, more bark was visible. "In wet forest you feel like you've taken a bath by the time you've climbed a tree," Daly said. The bamboo forest gave way to a more open variety. More light reached the understory. Butterflies flitted in bright shafts, and rays seemed to glow out of fan-shaped leaves.

"The end of the wet season is better for flowers," Daly said. "But even in the dry, trails give you opportunities you wouldn't otherwise have. They're artificial breaks in the forest, so they let more light and moisture in. Flowers flourish out of season. I can find rarer understory plants."

Daly fingered a woody vine that undulated into the canopy in ravioli-shaped sections. The vine draped itself over a high bough and disappeared, swallowed up above.

"Tortoise ladder," Daly said. "I've collected some in Peru. The genus is used all over the New World tropics as a cancer remedy. It's very highly regarded."

"By doctors?"

"No, by forest people. They make tea from the leaves. In Iquitos it's called 'cat's claw.'" He had his machete ready to cut samples and his newspaper ready to pack them. He'd flown four thousand miles from New York to reach this vine. But he didn't take any.

Daly got the emotionless look on his face that meant he was frustrated. "It's worth testing, all right," he said.

"What happens if no agreement is ever signed?" I asked.

"Well," he said, "even if I can't test it, somebody could."

.   .   .

Outside Brazil, when Doug Daly decides he's found a plant that might cure cancer, he clips the fruit and stores it between newspapers in his homemade press. He sends a sample for identification to New York and a bulk sample to Washington, D.C. NCI workers pick up the samples at airports and drive them north, into rural Maryland, past farms, suburbs, and government contractors like Comsat and Fairchild Industries. They leave Highway 270 in Frederick, bypass an Army fort containing the cancer labs, and pull up before a warehouse with AUTHORIZED PERSONNEL ONLY signs on doors. Inside, over one hundred thousand samples await testing in ten-foot-high freezers lining two stories of steel decks.

Dr. Michael Boyd, who headed the program when I visited it, opened a freezer.

"Some of these will have to wait ten years," he said. "Tens of thousands of samples keep arriving, not only from our people but from companies and universities."

The freezer smelled like plants and dead sea life. Icy smoke roiled off the shelves. The temperature was four below zero. The samples lay in sacks, the gooey extracts in gallon plastic jars. Boyd had already showed me the giant Mercator map in the conference room by his office, where colored arrows marked the position of NCI teams around the world like invading armies. Green, for the New York Botanical Garden, in Colombia and West Africa. Blue, for the University of Illinois, in Australia and the Philippines. That team hunted potentially valuable marine organisms. Red, for the Missouri Botanical Garden, in Madagascar and Zaire.

"We fractionate the plants in the labs to try to break them down into anticancer constituents," Boyd said. He was a trim, soft-spoken forty-two-year-old whose squarish horn-rimmed glasses gave him a slight resemblance to the comic strip character Funky Winkerbean. "Then we needed a simple biological test or screen to test the samples. And we needed cancers to test them against.

"For the cancers, tumors were removed from human patients. The cells were established in long-term cultures. They'll grow for years. They'll give us a representation of that kind of cancer. Lung. Colon. Renal. Doctors are desperate for better drugs to treat breast cancer, melanomas, prostate, brain. Cancer is not just cancer. It is a complex set of diseases with some common features. The term cancer is almost as global a term as 'infectious diseases.' Lung cancer is completely different from renal cancer. We needed a screen to test many different forms."

An NCI van took Boyd back to Fort Detrick, past the guard at the gate, the United States Army Biomedical Research and Development Laboratory, the Naval Material Support Command. Building 560 was the nerve center for the project. In the "extraction lab," workers wearing face masks and gloves carved up samples of

Indonesian bark, using saws to cut the pieces and hammers to smash the samples to dust. They poured the dust and water into two-foot-high glass cylinders. They waited while the mixture percolated into extract. The extract went back to the freezers to await testing later on.

In the "preparation lab," workers stored cancer cell lines in more freezers labeled BIOHAZARD. A million vials of extract were stored too.

In the "cancer screening lab," scientists conducted Boyd's simple and elegant test. They started with small glass dishes the size of tape cassette holders. Each dish was lined with rows of tiny wells, each row for one kind of extract, each well containing extracts diluted to different strengths. Scientists added living cancer cells to the wells, and a purple stain. They incubated the dishes for forty-eight hours.

"Live cells absorb the stain. Dead ones don't," Boyd said. "If there's no stain at the end of forty-eight hours, the cancer is dead. Then we can graduate to preclinical tests. A few extracts have already shown activity against AIDS and cancers." Boyd showed off potential cures in his office. A small cardboard package labeled TAXOL held what Boyd hoped would be a miracle drug of the future. It came from the bark of the Pacific yew tree. "It's turning out to have some interesting activity against ovarian cancer."

Ipomeanol, a toxin from moldy sweet potatoes, was being evaluated in clinical trials against lung tumors. A sample box on a shelf beside Boyd's sign, "To Be Average Scares the Hell Out of Me" was labeled CAUTION. NEW DRUG.

Boyd was excited about the expansion of the program, but he had a nightmare too. Even though the new screens would test samples against 150 kinds of cancer, Boyd worried that 150 wasn't enough. What if a potential wonder drug was bypassed because the type of cancer it cured wasn't in the screen? It had happened before.

It had happened, in fact, with the most successful drug to come out of the tropics in the twentieth century; vinblastine, which had helped cure Darlene Huertas's Hodgkin's disease. Back in the 1950s an extract from the rosy periwinkle plant, which would later be developed into vincristine, had been been run through the old

NCI screen. But at that time the screen included only seven kinds of cancers, and the tumors had been from mice, not humans. The extracts had no effect, and NCI dropped the plant from the program.

Later, corporate and university researchers discovered the plant's potential.

Now Boyd said that while NCI waits for results from the new trials and the clinical trials that follow successful initial tests, terminal cancer patients and their doctors regularly phone his office, begging to be used in any tests.

"What do you tell them?"

Boyd looked emotionless. All around him in the conference room were the photographs and trophies of the program's successes. The huge charts explaining to visitors the progression of tests on a new drug. The map. The pictures of the bearded researcher in a white baseball cap in the jungle being handed plants by an Indian. Or of a scientist in blue shorts clipping bark off a jungle tree with an ax. Or of a Suriname shaman squatting in the forest, wearing red armbands and loincloth, hair down to his chest, eyes red from the flash of the camera. In another photo a scientist gently folded three spruce-shaped leaves into the pages of an Oriental newspaper.

"I tell them it's too early," Boyd said.

.   .   .

Doug Daly was at the Acre market, looking for medicinal plants.

At 6:50 A.M., men in shorts and ragged shirts hammered wood together, erecting stands. They draped black plastic sheeting over the rickety walls for roofs. They hauled wire cages heavy with chickens, hung mesh bags of onions on nails, laid out succulent-looking carrots, limes, and apples in crates along sidewalks. Fishing boats were in from the Acre River with fish, and the smell clogged the piazza of the *seringueiros*.

"Taste this," Daly said. It was a dark green leaf resembling spearmint. It was bitter. My tongue started tingling. Then it lost all feeling.

"That's jambu. It has some effect. It's used for flavor here, but it might be worth sending." Daly walked to the next stand, scanned the products. "What I'm always looking for is a potential chemo-therapeutic agent. Something that's extremely toxic for the patient as well. Once I found this spiny plant, in the potato family. A weed in manioc fields. People told me if you get cut by its thorns, the wound never heals. I started to think. What are chemotherapeutic agents? They're for impeding cell growth, cell division. I mean, let's hope that someday in the near future chemotherapy as it is now will be obsolete because what we're looking for is a poison that will get to the cancer but not hurt the patient too. You're always dealing with two things that are extremely toxic. Anyway, that thorn was the most exciting thing I'd heard about, and then I heard the people use the fruit from the weed against tumors."

"Did you collect it?"

Daly scowled. "We didn't have the agreement."

"Could you just smuggle it out?"

Daly laughed. "It's a big country. But tropical botany is a very small world."

In the market now, in his pale-gray-and-purple rugby shirt and black Reeboks, he kept searching. "Sometimes in markets you get a lead. You have to dig up the woodsman somewhere else. But it's hard. He makes his living holding on to knowledge, not sharing it."

Daly twisted past shoppers, fish for sale with their heads cut off, gigantic purple vegetables that seemed to be expanding out of crates.

"Excuse me, is there anyone at the market who sells plants used for medicine?" he asked a boy in a black Fiorucci cap, in fluent Portuguese.

Sure, the boy said. An old man sold medicinal plants. The boy conferred with a friend. The old man might be in the main part of the market, inside a roofed-in area.

Daly squeezed his way into the main market, past rows of hawkers. The fish smell was overpowering. Only one old man was disappointing, but you never knew what plants he might have.

"Iquitos has a whole street devoted to medicinal plants," Daly said. "We have a project inventorying them, with a Spanish doctor and a woodsman. The doctor and woodsman administer a verbal questionnaire to the vendors. What's the common name of the plant? Where was it found? What does it do? One vendor will say, 'This cures cancer.' The next, 'Nothing, it's for decoration.' "

Daly got more excited. "How do you find what something cures anyway? Someone will say, 'This is for blood problems.' What does that mean, blood problems? Or this is for bad air. But what the hell is bad air?"

"Now we're trying to get western definitions. The Spanish doctor works in a clinic. When patients come in, she gets a list of symptoms. That way we find the range of maladies covered by a term. Then we go into the forest and track down the plants. Lots of researchers sweep through the Iquitos market, but nobody is tracing the plants back to their sources."

No old man was selling medicine at the market, but a vendor told Daly there was another market. "People sell plants there, definitely."

Daly hailed a cab and sped off.

.   .   .

Doug Daly hoped his students would become a new generation of forest protectors. They were already an esteemed bunch: graduate students from the University of Minais Gerais, in Brazil's first graduate degree program in environmental studies; the Brazilian representative for Conservation International; anthropologists working for the governments of Acre and Rondônia, with Indians and rubber tappers. There was even a German philanthropist's representative along for a day, an economics professor from Munich looking to donate $2 million for environmental work, traveling the country to decide how to allocate it.

Trekking through the jungle most days, Daly showed them how to climb trees and how to identify plants without having to climb trees—by noticing the number and location of the seeds and by looking at the pattern of scars on the fruit when it falls from the vine. Daly peeled skin off fruits and sucked the pulp for taste. He leaned toward trunks like a perfumer, sniffing. He turned over leaves to check the pattern of veins underneath.

"Never let sources know answers you want to hear," he said. "Don't phrase questions so people think you're from the government, especially if you're interviewing them about hunting, which is often illegal. Asking questions is tricky. I knew a researcher who lived with Indians for a year. After that much time he figured it was okay to ask about contraceptive plants. They threw him out when he did. In that tribe, women things were off-limits."

Daly told his students about the "doctrine of signatures." "It comes from the Middle Ages. People take a plant that resembles part of the body, and they use it to treat that part. A vine with a red latex is used for blood disease. A fruit shaped like a kidney might be used for the ear."

Daly was full of funny stories. "We have some plants with interesting names in the herbarium in New York. A collector who couldn't speak Spanish was in Mexico. 'What's this called?' he asked a woodsman. 'Gringo asshole,' the guy said. The plant was tagged and shipped, and that's what it's called today."

Once, walking in the forest, I spotted a beautiful red-and-black caterpillar crawling on Daly's collar. "Knock it off," he said, "and don't use your finger, or you might be in bed for two days. They're poison."

Poison to the layman meant a possible cure to Daly. "Once I heard about rubber tappers who died from just touching a caterpillar. I dismissed it as another Amazon fantasy, but later I came across a bunch of really mean-looking hairy caterpillars in Brazil, and I took their picture. A year later I read an article about a caterpillar that causes fatal hemorrhages in people who come in contact with it. There was a picture of the same caterpillar.

"So I started thinking. I talked with a friend at the University of SUNY-Stony Brook in New York who works on heart disease, on plasminogen activators. They're substances that prevent blood clotting and break up existing clots. Scientists have been trying to develop them against heart attacks. I asked my friend if there was any chance the caterpillar could have a plasminogen activator. A good chance, he said. We got a Lindbergh Foundation grant, and in October we'll go to Bolivia looking for the caterpillar."

Now Daly's cab pulled up to the smaller Rio Branco market. Looking out the window, he frowned. "Doesn't look good," he said. Only a few stands were up, and the market strung out along an area less than half a block long. There was an old amusement park nearby, a few rides, closed in the early morning. Daly asked around, and his suspicions were confirmed. Nobody sold medicinal plants at the market.

"There is a homeopathic pharmacy in town, though," said a man selling onions. "They sell medicinal plants."

Daly brightened. "Homeopathic pharmacies are always good," he said.

At 7:30, Rio Branco was starting the work day. Across from the market of *seringueiros*, open-air stalls were selling cheap knapsacks, sunglasses, slippers, skirts. Blue buses rolled by stuffed with commuters from the suburbs, which in the Amazon means slums. White Volkswagen taxis cruised, honking. The Banco do Brasil wasn't open yet. The mini malls downtown, filled with clothes for sale, would open at eight.

The sky was blue, but in a few weeks it would start to cloud over from fires.

"Do you really think that what you do could help the rain forest?" I said.

"God, yes," Daly said. "I do this for two reasons. I'd like to find a superstar to knock out one form of cancer. And if I find it, that's an argument to save the forest. It's something concrete. It means you really have to study an area before you burn it."

Daly got into another cab. Time to head back for the seminar. "I'll try the pharmacy later."

"I have a good feeling about this," I said. "Herpes. AIDS."

Daly smiled. "Yeah," he said.

.   .   .

When pineapple breeders in Hawaii needed to strengthen the roots of their crops recently, they interbred their pineapples with wild varieties from Brazil, reported Dr. Mark Plotkin of Conservation International. California barley farmers protected their $160 million-a-year crop from the deadly yellow dwarf virus with genes from a wild relative from Ethiopia. Chemists looking for biodegradable pesticides found them with Amazon Indians who had been using a plant called *lonchocarpus* for centuries to stun fish.

"The value of tropical plants to the developed world goes far beyond medicines," said Dr. Michael Balick. "Tropical plants strengthen domestic crops and may someday serve as valuable cash crops themselves."

Scientists have estimated that wild genetic input has increased the value of U.S.–grown and imported crops by as much as $6 billion a year.

"Ninety-eight percent of U.S. crop products are based on species that grow outside the country," wrote Plotkin. "Among our common foodstuffs, corn, rice, bananas, sugarcane, pineapples, sweet potatoes and coconuts all had their origin in the tropics. A typical American breakfast is based almost entirely on tropical products."

Plotkin and other botanists hope new foods for export and local sale will be found in tropical forests and will help save these forests.

"In the old days, a farmer would come to the jungle, burn it for crops or pasture, and move on in three years when the land failed. The nutrients would be gone. The soils would be leached. The watershed would be damaged. And the man would keep going deeper and deeper into the jungle, destroying more of it," Balick said. "Imagine if he could make the plot productive. He wouldn't have to move. He'd stay put."

Balick hoped for a compromise between conservationists and developers. "Most conservationists have come around to the view that it's impossible to keep people out of the forests. There's too much population, economic, and social pressure. But if these people could make a decent profit using the forest, growing crops compatible with the forest, sort of domesticating the primary forest, the other areas would be preserved. And the nutrients wouldn't be gone. The watershed would be preserved."

Scientists like Balick and Plotkin have suggested crops they think might one day be profitable from the jungles:

• The *lulo tree* from Colombia and Ecuador is a shrub about three feet high. It produces a fuzzy yellow-orange fruit already sold as concentrate in Central America and Italy.

• The *guanabana tree,* a medium-sized tree from South America, produces a greenish fruit slightly resembling a bunch of grapes pushed together. "It's an absolutely delightful dessert fruit," Balick said. "You make a custard or a pie out of it." Guanabana fruit is already made into yogurt and a fruit drink in Australia, China, and Africa.

• The *buriti palm*, which can thrive in swampy areas poorly suited for other crops, grows a deep-brown fruit that looks a little like a hand grenade with scales, but the flesh inside is rich in vitamin A. The oil can be used for cooking.

• The *uvilla tree* is in the fig family and grows in the lowlands of the western Amazon. Indians already eat its purple grapelike fruit. Harvard professor Richard Shultes has predicted the fruit will become a multimillion-dollar crop.

• The *pataua palm* is a wild tree from the lowlands of South America. Its fruit is dark purple, the size of a large California black olive. Its oil is identical to olive oil. "It can be marketed as an olive oil substitute. Olive oil costs three or four times as much as other oils," Balick said, "so it's potentially quite profitable."

• The *babassu palm* can produce up to half a ton of fruit in one year. The seed can be used as charcoal. The fruit oil can be refined into edible oil or used to make plastics, detergents, soap, margarine, and edible oil, according to Plotkin. After you squeeze the oil out, you get a twenty-seven percent residue that is made into animal feed, Balic adds.

• The *sorva tree*, already being grown in plantations near Manaus, produces edible fruit and a latex used in chewing gum.

Plotkin has theorized that in the future, wild species of coffee, fifty of which grow in the rain forests of Madagascar alone, might be used to combat fungus in cultivated crops. That two wild species of tropical potatoes, which have leaves that trap insects, might eliminate some need for pesticides on potato crops. That a near-extinct tree in Ecuador related to the avocado might help fight rot with root grafts. That guarana, which is grown on plantations in Brazil and processed into a soft drink, might turn out to kill mosquitos too. Guarana has three times as much caffeine as coffee, and tests at Harvard have shown that caffeine can kill insects.

"Should further tests reveal that caffeine will be an effective insecticide, guarana could turn into a major crop throughout the tropics," wrote Plotkin.

For people who believe the notion of turning little-known trees in the jungle into major export crops is farfetched, Plotkin likes to use the example of the kiwi fruit. Almost unknown in the United States twenty years ago, millions of these fruits were sold in 1989. "All of the South American species were discovered by indigenous people," Plotkin said.

. . .

The homeopathic pharmacy occupied a small square shop across from the main plaza and beside the Hotel Rio Branco and a women's clothing store. Behind a wooden counter, "remedies" lined shelves, in labeled plastic bags or commercially manufactured cardboard boxes. More showy examples included a box with a pink-and-white sketch of an American Indian, headdress included: INDIAN FORMULA OF THE AMAZON it said. "Purifies the blood. Cures nerve problems, syphilis, alcoholism." Another box was labeled ELIXIR OF NATURAL SPECIES: "For anti-obesity." There was ELIXIR 914 in a plastic bag: "For digestion, sickness of the bladder, anemia, liver disease." Chocolate-covered candies made of jelly from the capu-acu tree filled glass jars. Shampoos were sold in boxes of rainbow colors. Behind a curtain of bright beads, in a back room, small labeled bottles lined shelves.

Daly joked with the owner of the shop, a young woman in a peasant dress. He explained he was looking for local medicines.

"Sorry," the woman said. "Most of our medicines come from São Paulo, but there's a *mateiro* in Acre who collects the plants and sends them to the company there. Would you like to meet him?"

Daly took the woman's number. He kept turning the packages over, reading labels, sniffing, joking and chatting all the while. The owner thought it funny that Acre plants had to go all the way to São Paulo, two thousand miles east, to come back in a package.

After a while she asked Daly to wait, disappeared through the beads into the back room, and returned to put an unmarked bottle on the counter.

"An old Indian came in last week," she said. "He said this cures cancer. He said it contains oil from the andiroba tree [a member of the mahogany family] and three drops of snake venom. He sold it to us for fifty cruzados." Daly blinked at the enormous sum. Fifty cruzados was twenty-five percent of an average month's wages in Acre.

"I haven't sold any of it to anyone," the owner said. "I'd be afraid to, unless a patient had tried everything else. Unless he was terminal."

They stared at the bottle. A superstitious respect coalesced in the little shop. The fact that the seller had been a shaman seemed to give the claims of potency weight. Nobody was laughing, but nobody knew what to do with it either.

"Would you test it?" I asked Daly.

"Of course. Actually, the andiroba tree is prized medicinally all through the Amazon."

Hours later Daly was drinking with his students. It had been a very hot day, dusty, and the Cerpa beer went down icy and delicious. They were sitting in an outdoor restaurant called Cashuara that offered live Brazilian music on Monday nights. The tables were packed. Teenagers danced in the aisles. The students were getting drunker, laughing, and when they danced, all their body parts seemed to jiggle in different directions at the same time. Rio Branco's lone mime, a kid in a black body suit and white face paint, did his Marcel Marceau imitation, weaving around tables. He pretended to run into walls. He pretended to be attached to a string. He was pretty bad, and since he showed up at all Rio Branco public functions, the students were moaning. Oh no. Not the mime.

"I had eleven different parasites once," boasted a graduate student from the University of Florida.

"Oh yeah?" said a Brazilian who worked with Indians. "How do you know it was eleven?"

"I had botflies in my head," said the Brazilian representative of Conservation International. "Doctors had to cut them out."

Could anybody top that one? "I had a new parasite," said another student. "They told me, 'Leave it alone. We want to learn the life cycle.'"

Laughter. In the bright light from overhead bulbs, Daly seemed relaxed. He didn't dance, but he was always talking with the students. Some of the crispness eased in him. He hadn't been bothered by the fact that there had been no local plants in the homeopathic pharmacy. That was part of his job. He'd been to Brazil at least twenty times in the last few years. He'd spent a few thousand hours in jungles, and within a few years he'd spend a few thousand more.

He was a junglephile, a lover of the Amazon. Of the heat and the insects. Of the rain. Of the flowers. To Doug Daly the jungle was a series of questions and possibilities.

"You could spend your life studying ten square yards of Amazon and never know all that's going on there," Daly said.

When I rose from the table, Daly got up too. He lowered his voice when he came over, but despite the loud music, he came through quite clearly.

"I didn't tell you all the reasons . . . when you asked me before why I do it," he said. "When I started the NCI program, my mother got cancer. She was fine, and a year later she was gone." The music got louder. Daly said, "If I can find something that really knocks out one form of cancer, well, it's something I want to do." Daly thought a moment. The music grew louder, and the students were laughing at a joke. "You know what the Italians say," he said. "Revenge is a dish best eaten cold."

What event likely to occur in the 1980s will our descendants most regret, even those living a thousand years from now? My opinion is not conventional, although I wish it were. The worst thing that can happen—will happen—is not energy depletion, economic collapse, limited nuclear war, or conquest by a totalitarian government. As terrible as these catastrophes would be for us, they can be repaired within a few generations. The one process ongoing in the 1980s that will take millions of years to correct is the loss of genetic and species diversity by the destruction of natural habitats. This is the folly our descendants are least likely to forgive us.

—Dr. E. O. Wilson
Harvard University entomologist and sociobiologist

The Last Mile

I've always loved travel books, the kind where a writer journeys far from home, has adventures, and comes back. At the end, safe with his family, he contemplates the gap separating the place he visited and the place where he lives. London and Tibet. San Francisco and the Andes. They seem so far apart, it's almost as if he never went.

In my own case the opposite happened. When I returned from the Amazon I felt closer to it. I bought coffee and cocoa in a Brooklyn grocery and wondered which forest they came from. I ate a sundae at the ice-cream store, and the nut topping and bananas came from the far south. My wife went to the hospital for an operation. She needed anesthesia, which came from the Amazon. I visited the beach at Rockaway. The boardwalk timbers were stamped BRAZIL. Banks were in trouble throughout the United States. The bank where I kept my money, Manufacturers Hanover, merged with Chemical Bank. Some news reports attributed Manufacturers Hanover's troubles to faulty Third World loans that hadn't worked out.

Over three thousand miles separate Acre and Rondônia from New York, but they are close too. If I boarded a jet at Kennedy Airport, I could be in Pôrto Velho faster than I could reach Denver if I drove.

That was the first lesson. To preserve rain forests, we must destroy their illusions: that they are protected by magical distance. That they are unconnected to life thousands of miles away.

One day after I got home I took the number-two train to the

Bronx Zoo and "Jungle World," the $9.5 million re-created rain forest. Indoors, I strolled past waterfalls plunging from cliffs. Gibbons on vines, otters playing in mangrove roots.

Jungle World's epoxy and concrete forest skillfully evoked the real thing. It was hot, steamy, and filled with bird cries. The "lichens" on the trees were dabbed-on paint. The "vines" the monkeys swung from were made of rubber. Jungle World was consciously designed to be an intersection point between the jungle and the developed world. There were signs and charts everywhere relating jungle products to life in New York. Signs that said, "Jungles are growing renewable resources. If cared for, they can help stabilize climate, serve as storehouses and laboratories for agriculture and pharmaceutical products and discoveries—fruits, nuts, flowers, livestock fodder, and countless medicines."

And, "Jungles enrich our lives. They are important to us all."

But Jungle World was a purist vision of nature too. It did not include the people of the jungle. No zoo in the world exhibited Indians, farmers, colonists, squatters, *caboclos,* ranchers.

Yet programs to stop deforestation must take these people into account. I didn't meet many villains along BR-364 but mostly good-hearted migrants who wanted a better life. What they'd gotten, due to poor planning, mismanagement, and graft, was bad land, malaria, and poverty.

Developed countries funding rain forest projects must push for forest zoning and better monitoring of loans. The zoning should be conducted by scientists, teams that will determine which areas to develop and which to save. The scientists should be dropped into areas before plans are finalized.

By guiding development and conserving areas of high diversity, zoning will help the poor, encourage profit, and protect the biologic heritage of the forest. Brazil has started some zoning. And Brazilian Congressman Fabio Feldmann has even called for a ten-year moratorium on big projects while scientists research what is there.

And by monitoring loans *after* zoning has taken place, lenders can make sure projects are finished, maintained, and don't rot within a few years of completion.

Banks and lending governments should hire inspectors—in the

Amazon, Brazilian inspectors—to check the books and construction sites. Provisions for regular, compulsory inspections should be written into loans. The cost would be far less than the money wasted on bad loans. Some Brazilian officials will call this interference, but if U.S. taxpayer dollars build projects, taxpayers ought to know how the money is being spent.

That is a concept that up until now has been laughed at by many in the World Bank.

"Look," retorted one bank loan analyst to me when I suggested the bank ought to know more about how its money is spent, "the way it works is, the government of Peru or Brazil says, 'We're gonna spend $100 million on a road.' It gets construction companies or the army to build it. All the World Bank gets back is a statement. Maybe a copy of general bills. A, B, C, D contractors. It says the work was done. The World Bank doesn't have aaaaaany idea of whether it really was. Despite the fact that the bank has a lot of employees," sneered the man, "it doesn't know if somebody *did* or *did not* put a *drain* under a *road*."

But look what happens because of that. A year after visiting scientist Rosa Lemos at the Samuel dam, I went back to see her again. The previous July, when I'd left Pôrto Velho, the workers had lived in comfortable special housing. The dam complex had been new and sparkling. Samuel had been due to go on line in two weeks. But when I stopped at the power company's little town in Pôrto Velho before going to the dam, on my return, the shock began. I felt like I'd walked into Gabriel Garcia Marquez's novel, *Autumn of the Patriarch*.

From a California subdivision lookalike, Electronorte town had deteriorated into a slum. Houses sat dark and empty. Garbage bins overflowed because refuse pickup was late. Weeds four to five feet high grew on lawns, curbs, commons. At the oddly empty pool a fat man drank beer by the filthy bar area. "I . . . am . . . the . . . doctor," he slurred.

I drove to the dam. The private road linking BR-364 to Samuel was crumbling. Flakes of rust marred the "Samuel" signs. Weeds tangled the formerly mowed median strip. Workers had abandoned the little town at the site, and a lone cat bolted under the empty school.

"The companies just ran out of money," said engineers in the skeleton crew operating two working turbines, not enough to supply all of Pôrto Velho's power, let alone the state's. The other turbines had never been turned on.

Rosa was at the scientist's barracks, but she and her husband Paulo were the only researchers of the dozens here a year before who had come back. "And I'm only here because I got grants from the World Wildlife Fund, Conservation International, and Chicago's Lincoln Park Zoological Society," she said. "The other projects are down the drain."

Rosa had bought a used car with her grant money, paid for her own food and hired a woman from town to cook and do laundry.

I took a walk to the dam at dusk, past the abandoned Shell gas station and the power lines that had not been hooked up. I noticed more mosquitos out. No money to pay for spraying.

Afterward, I visited the Electronorte Power Company's headquarters in Pôrto Velho and met Heli Marcos Ferreira, regional manager, highest company official in the state. He was a trim, fit looking man whose jaw muscles seemed clenched and whose engineering training was evident in the way he kept drawing lines while we spoke.

"There is no construction work now at Samuel," he said sadly. "Our job is maintenance, keeping everything okay. There's no provision for completion any more. Electronorte just ran out of money. The other dams won't be going into construction. The workers here normally would have moved to another site, but they were fired. The plans we had for tourism at Samuel, the nautical club, fishing, the marina, no more. The nature reserve is in danger of being invaded. We have no guards there. Already hunters are in the area."

Ferreira stubbed out a half-smoked cigarette by smothering it in an ashtray with his index finger. He lit another. His face shone with a red tinge associated more with high blood pressure than the sun. He seemed genuinely distressed by the news he conveyed.

I told him sometimes my job included asking unpleasant questions. Ferreira nodded, and when he said, "Go ahead," I said, "*Why* did Electronorte run out of money?"

"The plan was good," he said. "We had money, but they spent

it on other things . . . things they shouldn't . . . social facilities . . . cars. They built roads just to spend the money, roads they didn't need." Ferreira looked down, drew hard, quick lines with a pencil. He wasn't doodling exactly. He was letting out energy.

"Every worker at the dam had a car," he said.

And twenty-seven-cent lunches, I remembered. And a pool club that management joined for fifty cents a year.

"You seem like a committed man," I said. "Did that make you angry?"

Ferreira stubbed out his second half-smoked butt. He looked miserable. "Of course."

"That nature reserve, so big, and everyone was proud of rescuing the animals," I said.

"Very sad," Ferreira said. "The plan could have been effective if Electronorte wanted to do it." Ferreira lit another cigarette. A color photo of Samuel decorated the wall over his desk. The new concrete towers. The beautiful blue water.

Rosa Lemos's barracks would be just out of the picture, on the right.

Ferreira said something else, but he spoke so low I had to ask him to repeat it.

Bitterly he said, "That's what always happens in Brazil. That's the way it always is."

When I left he looked unhappy, sitting with nothing to do. An engineer in charge of an incomplete dam. He seemed to regret speaking frankly. He looked like he wanted to call me back and retract what he'd said. I felt him wanting to say that. I felt how miserable he was.

But Ferreira didn't say it. He nodded, and stubbed out his third cigarette, and went back to drawing useless lines.

And that's why the World Bank ought to know if a contractor thousands of miles away puts a *drain* under a *road*.

Still there was possible good news for Brazil's forests. In 1991, President Collor said he was committed to environmental reform. He appointed José Lutzenberger, Brazil's most prominent environmentalist, as his minister of the environment. The new head of IBAMA fined a mining company $1 million and a timber company $1.9 million—the biggest environmental fines ever issued in Brazil.

Two accused killers of Chico Mendes, the Alveses, were convicted. In Acre the "Chico Mendes Extractive Reserve" was demarcated, guaranteeing three thousand rubber tapper families a traditional living on that land.

Banker Lamond Godwin and the Nature Conservancy announced they were closer to closing the first debt-for-nature swap with Brazil, with the Brazilian group SOS Mata Atlantica. Proceeds would help Brazil's Atlantic forest. And the Rain Forest Alliance initiated joint research programs along the Amazon River, with Brazilians.

Brazil stopped subsidies for ranchers in rain forests. Satellite surveys showed only 5,334 square miles burned in 1990, the lowest level in recent years, down from 7,273 in 1989.

But it was too early to tell if these developments were a trend, public relations, or lucky circumstance. Ranching subsidies had been stopped before and restarted. Cynics cautioned that the decreased burnings could be caused by Brazil's economic turndown or its longer rainy seasons. José Lutzenberger said he was having trouble getting his own workers to accept his vision of what needed to be done in the Amazon, and kept threatening to resign if big projects went through. President Collor ordered illegal gold miners' runways on Indian land blown up in Roraima, but only fourteen were dynamited, and miners built more. It remained to be seen whether the penalized mining and timber companies would pay the fines. As we went to press with this book the debt swap had still not been announced. And death threats against rubber tapper and union leaders continued on the frontier.

In the Amazon, any appraisal of environmental progress must cover years, not months.

.   .   .

In Jungle World I saw displays of spices, furniture, and medicines from rain forests. Charts linked world population rise to shrinking forests. ENDANGERED SPECIES signs announced the white-cheeked gibbons, Malayan tapirs, and gharials.

"How can I help? I'm just one person," said one mother as we watched a video of burning forests. Her five-year-old son, holding her hand, seemed transfixed.

I'd heard the question often since returning home. There are many things concerned people can do. You can write congressmen and senators to tell them how you feel about loans to rain forest countries. You can change your buying habits and purchase sustainably produced products. You can support organizations fighting to save forests: The Nature Conservancy, Conservation International, and World Wildlife Fund manage reserves, pay for research, and do debt-for-nature swaps, among other programs. The Rain Forest Alliance and Rain Forest Action Network have tropical timber programs. The New York Botanical Garden, Missouri Botanical Garden, and National Cancer Institute conduct medicinal plant research. The Environmental Defense Fund and National Wildlife Federation monitor loans from big banks. That is only a partial list of activities and organizations. And most rain forest countries have conservation groups desperately in need of funds.

If you are influential in a corporation or government, even a local government, you can examine policies. Ticonderoga pencil recently stopped buying one kind of endangered tropical softwood. The Arizona state legislature banned tropical woods in state construction projects. Burger King halted the purchase of beef from Central America. A Virginia power company started planting trees in the tropics to replace carbon their factories spew into the air.

You can visit tropical forests. Ecotourism—sensitive travel to jungles—helps preserve them by showing that, standing, they can provide more income than when they are cut down. Even Acre and Rondônia are easily reachable to any tourist. Pôrto Velho has a five-star Villa Rica Hotel. The hotel just started a fledgling tourist program. You can sleep in a treetop hotel on the Madeira River, take air-conditioned boat rides, visit the mining camps.

Or you can rough it, take buses, get off at the colonies, and get by if you speak Portuguese, Spanish, or have a Portuguese translator.

Varig Airlines' $440 Brazilpass makes a journey to the frontier easier. It gives the holder five trips anywhere in Brazil.

"If we have a large contingent of people visiting the Amazon, ideas will change," said Silvio Magalhaes Barros, president of Emamtur, Amazonas's state tourist agency.

.   .   .

Thousands of small acts have helped destroy rain forests, and thousands of small acts can help save them. If we don't act personally and as a country then someday artificial trees like those in Jungle World might be our only reminders of forests that still cover six percent of the Earth.

I started thinking that in 1984 when I'd begun research on forests, the United States was in a boom period. Banks expanded. People had cash to spare. Rain forests were shrinking.

By 1991 rain forests had become chic and were already fading in the public mind, replaced by other news stories. Conservation groups reported contributions dropping. War loomed with Iraq. A recession threatened to worsen into a depression. Banks closed. Businesses failed. But rain forests were still shrinking.

Rain forests will keep shrinking whether they are in the headlines or not. There are thousands of roads to Extrema in the world—roads pushing into Java, Zaire, Honduras, Peru, Brazil, Australia, Madagascar, Hawaii. When they are finished and paved, and the people start moving down them, will they enable the world to meet its needs in harmony with nature, or will they be highways of plunder, extinction, death?

As I left the zoo, I remembered the flight back over the Amazon. The green endlessness, the dark hollows where trees had fallen, the lazy, slow S curves on brown rivers, the huts like islands, the rainbows in mist. A landscape so primal and mighty and baffling, it made me believe an Indian story about the Earth. That the trees hold the sky up, that if we cut down the trees, the sky will fall.

Index

About the Author

Bob Reiss writes for many national magazines including *Rolling Stone, Smithsonian, Washington Post Magazine, Parade,* and *Outside,* where he is a correspondent. Parts of this book were nominated for a National Magazine Award. Reiss lives in New York with his wife, author Ann Hood.